Political Foundations
for Becoming
a Teacher

Political Foundations for Becoming a Teacher

Forrest W. Parkay
Washington State University

Boston • New York • San Francisco
Mexico City • Montreal • Toronto • London • Madrid • Munich • Paris
Hong Kong • Singapore • Tokyo • Cape Town • Sydney

Executive Editor and Publisher: Stephen D. Dragin
Editorial Assistant: Meaghan Minnick
Marketing Manager: Tara Kelly
Production Editor: Annette Joseph
Editorial Production Service: Modern Graphics, Inc.
Composition Buyer: Linda Cox
Manufacturing Buyer: Andrew Turso
Electronic Composition: Modern Graphics, Inc.
Interior Design: Glenna Collett
Photo Researcher: Po Yee Oster
Cover Administrator: Kristina Mose-Libon

For related titles and support materials, visit our online catalog at www.ablongman.com.

Between the time website information is gathered and then published, it is not unusual for some sites to have closed. Also, the transcription of URLs can result in typographical errors. The publisher would appreciate notification where these errors occur so that they may be corrected in subsequent editions.

Library of Congress Cataloging-in-Publication Data
Parkay, Forrest W.
　Political foundations for becoming a teacher / Forrest W. Parkay.—1. ed.
　　p. cm.
　Includes bibliographical references and index.
　ISBN 0-205-42424-4
　　1. Education—Political aspects—United States. 2. Education and state—United States.
3. Teaching—United States. 4. Teachers—Professional relationships—United States. I. Title.

LC89.P215 2006
379—dc22

　　　　　　　　　　　　　　　　　　　　　　　　　　　　　　　　2005050907

Printed in the United States of America
10　9　8　7　6　5　4　3　2　1　　RRD-IN　09　08　07　06　05

Brief Contents

Contents

3   Educational Philosophies in Conflict 60

4   Legal Issues in U.S. Education 100

5 Competition for Educational Resources   154

Preface

Teaching is one of the world's most important professions—and one of the most challenging. With continuing calls for higher standards, greater teacher accountability, and legislation such as the No Child Left Behind Act of 2001, becoming a teacher requires more professionalism and expertise than ever. To facilitate your journey toward becoming a successful teacher, *Political Foundations for Becoming a Teacher* explains how political forces have influenced our nation's schools.

Education is not (and never will be) apolitical. Successful teaching, therefore, requires an understanding of the political foundations of education—the political trends, issues, and forces that shape public and private education in the United States. For example, the book will help you understand how high-stakes testing, formal and informal assessments, and standards-based curricula will influence your future as a teacher. In addition, you will develop an understanding of how diverse political interest groups seek to influence what is taught in today's schools.

Several features of the book are designed to give you a realistic picture of how politics influence the teaching profession and how you can take advantage of teachers' expanding leadership roles. A Teachers' Voices feature in each chapter presents a short, first-person article written by a teacher to illustrate how teachers apply chapter content to actual classroom situations. The features will provide you with firsthand insights into real-world challenges teachers face and practical solutions for meeting those challenges.

To help you get the most out of your teacher education program, each chapter of this book includes a feature titled Relevant Standards. This feature illustrates how chapter content relates to standards developed by four professional associations: the Interstate New Teacher Assessment and Support Consortium (INTASC), the National Council for Accreditation of Teacher Education (NCATE), the Praxis Series: Professional Assessments for Beginning Teachers, and the National Board for Professional Teaching Standards (NBPTS).

Each chapter also includes a Case for Reflection designed to give you an opportunity to reflect on the contemporary issues teachers must deal with on a daily basis. The cases focus on controversial trends and issues that have aroused public opinion and have attracted media attention.

A Technology in Teaching feature in each chapter illustrates how educational technology is related to chapter content. This feature also provides current examples of how educational technologies are influencing schools and the profession of teaching.

Political Foundations for Becoming a Teacher also includes many learning aids to help you prepare for a rewarding future in teaching. Guiding Questions at the beginning of each chapter present the questions posed in the main headings within each chapter. Realistic opening scenarios present decision-making or problem-solving situations teachers frequently confront. At the end of each chapter, Reflective Application Activities (Discussion Questions, Professional Journal, Online Assignments, and Observations and Interviews) present further opportunities to apply chapter content.

The book also includes a Professional Portfolio feature that will enable you to document your professional growth over time. These features present guidelines for creating portfolio entries that you can use when you begin teaching, or you may wish to use selected portfolio entries during the process of applying for your first teaching position. As a further study aid, Key Terms and Concepts are bold-faced in the text and listed with page cross-references at the ends of chapters. A Glossary at the end of the book can help you quickly locate the definitions of key terms and concepts and the text pages on which they appear.

Acknowledgments

Many members of the Allyn and Bacon team provided the author with expert guidance and support during the writing of *Political Foundations for Becoming a Teacher*. The author benefited from the consistent encouragement and excellent suggestions provided by Steve Dragin, Executive Editor and Publisher. His extensive understanding of textbook publishing was invaluable in conceptualizing the book. In addition, Meaghan Minnick, Editorial Assistant, provided helpful feedback on the manuscript and steadfast support and encouragement.

The author also appreciates the support of his friends and colleagues while writing this book. In particular, Phyllis Erdman, Chair of the Department of Educational Leadership and Counseling Psychology at Washington State University; Gail Furman, Coordinator of the Educational Leadership Program Area; Len Foster, Coordinator of the Higher Education Program Area; and Eric J. Anctil, Assistant Professor of Educational Leadership, provided invaluable ideas and much-appreciated encouragement and support.

In addition, the author gives a sincere thanks to students (many of them now teachers and school administrators) in the classes he has taught at Washington State University. Conversations with them over the years have been thought provoking and professionally rewarding. And, for demonstrating the power of professional inquiry, he owes a profound debt to a great teacher, mentor, and friend, Herbert A. Thelen, Professor Emeritus, University of Chicago.

Lastly, the author would like to thank Wu Mei for her friendship, spiritual support, and encouragement during the writing of this book. Ni shi diyige, ye shi zuihou yige, wode yiqie.

Forrest W. Parkay

Political Foundations for Becoming a Teacher

1 Politics and U.S. Schools

I have to be very careful about what I say about _____ [a commercial reading program adopted by my school] because it's almost heresy to suggest that something else might work as well or even better. *I don't know why these teachers won't say what they believe.* They are frustrated with it but they won't say anything against it. If they do, it's reported to the principal and he reprimands them for "being against [the reading program]."

—A teacher quoted in Elaine M. Garan,
In Defense of Our Children: When Politics, Profit, and Education Collide,
2004, p. 84 (words emphasized in original).

You have just entered the teachers' lounge on your planning period. At once, you know the four teachers in the lounge are having a heated discussion.

"Look at No Child Left Behind. That shows how the federal government is a pawn of big business," says Alex, a PE teacher. "Big business controls the schools."

"I don't see how you can say that," says Cheng-Yi, a science teacher.

"Well, high-tech industries are worried about international competition," Alex continues. "So, they exert political pressure on the feds. Then, the feds lean on us to teach the skills industry needs to be competitive."

"That sounds far-fetched, almost like a conspiracy," says Cheng-Yi, breaking into smile.

"Yeah, what does No Child Left Behind have to do with big business?" asks Kim, an English teacher, before taking a sip of her diet soda.

"No Child Left Behind mandates testing in math and reading," Alex continues. "It doesn't say art and music, does it? What about literature and history? Those subjects won't make us competitive in the global marketplace."

"Alex's got a point," adds Anita, one of the school's four master teachers and chair of the site-based council. "Big business has a lot of political clout when it comes to schools. Believe me, when a businessperson on the site-based council talks, we listen."

"That's the way it is," says Alex, nodding his head.

"Remember when the president of the chamber of commerce came to our September in-service and talked about how the schools produce a product?" asks Anita. "In her eyes, the 'product' we produce is workers with basic skills."

"Exactly," Alex says with enthusiasm. "Education in this country is really controlled by big business."

"Come on," Kim sighs. "You two have got to politicize everything when it comes to education. Cheng-Yi's right, there's no business-sector agenda that's being played out in the schools."

"Right," Cheng-Yi says. "Remember, No Child Left Behind was developed by politicians, and *we* elected them—that sounds pretty democratic to me. I mean . . . 'we the people' control the schools."

"Wait a minute," Alex says. "No Child Left Behind is really being pushed by big business."

"Yeah, think about the ultimate aim of No Child Left Behind. Is it really to produce citizens for democracy?" Anita interjects. "No, the real aim is to produce good workers, good consumers—people who strengthen the economy."

"Right," Alex says.

"Well, I still think you're stretching things," says Kim. "Why don't we ask the new teacher here. What do you think?"

The four teachers look at you, awaiting your response. What do you say?

Guiding Questions

1. Why do you need to understand educational politics?
2. How do educational politics place teachers "in the line of fire"?
3. What groups are competing for control of schools in the United States?
4. How is restructuring changing how schools are controlled?
5. How is the privatization movement changing school governance?

The history of education in the United States reveals countless examples of how political forces have influenced our schools. Education is not (and never will be) apolitical. The opening scenario for this chapter, for example, illustrates how political interest groups seek to influence what is taught in today's schools. Successful teaching, therefore, requires an understanding of the **political foundations of education**—the political trends, issues, and forces that shape public and private education in the United States. The political foundations of education influence the effectiveness of schools and the learning of children and youth across the country.

Why Do You Need to Understand Educational Politics?

At this point in your teacher education program, you are probably most concerned with meeting the challenges of teaching—ensuring that all students learn; creating a positive classroom climate; and learning to work with teachers, administrators, and parents, for example. Compared to these challenges, understanding educational politics may not seem important.

As a beginning teacher, you know that you must acquire knowledge and skills to survive your first months of teaching. Though you may not realize it now, understanding educational politics is also an important form of professional knowledge. For example, the teacher quoted in this chapter's epigraph provides an illustration of how educational politics can influence teachers. Her principal is acting politically—that is, he is attempting to influence the behavior of teachers, to suppress their criticisms of the school's reading program. Similarly, if this teacher decided to encourage other teachers to express their concerns about the reading program, she would be acting politically as well.

Thus, **politics** refer to how people use *power, influence,* and *authority* within an organization to persuade others to act in desired ways. And **educational politics** refer to how people use power, influence, and authority to affect instructional and curricular practices within a school or school system. The situation highlighted in the epigraph illustrates how a principal might use his *formal authority* as principal to influence the behavior of teachers. On the other hand, the teacher quoted in the epigraph might use her *informal authority* (for example, the degree of respect she has among her colleagues) to influence the behavior of other teachers.

While the preceding example illustrates the "negative" effects of educational politics on teachers, educational politics can have positive results, as the following examples suggest:

- Two teachers, members of the Local School Council (LSC) for a school in a poor urban area, organized a group of parent volunteers that eventually helped reduce student truancy and improve students' attitudes toward school.

- Three high school English teachers received a state grant to develop a humanities program. Their grant application included letters of support from the president of the board of education and the superintendent.

- A group of teachers went door-to-door passing out information about a much-needed remodeling and expansion project at their school. Two months later, voters approved funding for the project.

You may think that politics and teaching should remain separate. However, it is a fact of life that school policies are developed in a political milieu, and "reforming schools is essentially a series of political acts, not technical solutions to problems" (Cuban 2003, 59). Whenever educators act to influence educational policies, they are acting politically. If teachers "desire change in school programs, they must be good politicians" (Nunnary and Kimbrough 1971, 1). As a result, you will have much to gain from becoming politically involved in the teaching profession. To help you achieve this goal, Appendix 1.1 presents "Guidelines for Teachers to Think and Act Politically" and "25 Ways to Become Involved."

Five Dimensions of Educational Politics

To facilitate your journey toward becoming a successful teacher, Chapters 2 through 6 of *Political Foundations for Becoming a Teacher* examine five dimensions of educational politics that influence teachers (see Figure 1.1). Chapter 2 explains how political influences at the federal, regional, state, and local levels impact schools and teachers in the United States. From federal legislation such as the No Child Left Behind Act of 2001 to local school bond issues, politics at these four levels will influence your life as a teacher.

Since the political actions of educators and citizens who wish to influence education reflect their beliefs about the purposes of education and the forms of knowledge that are of greatest worth, Chapter 3 examines the philosophical foundations of education. Actually, people use educational politics to influence others

Figure 1.1 Five dimensions of educational politics that influence teachers.

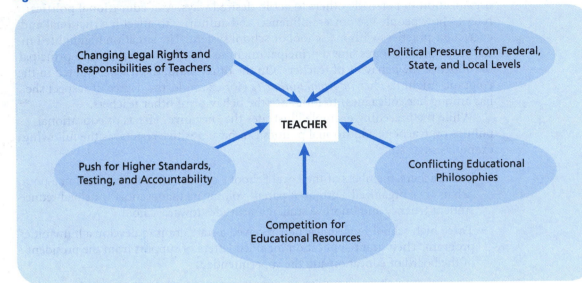

to adopt their educational philosophies. The curricular and instructional decisions you will make as a teacher will be influenced by your educational philosophy. Similarly, the decisions of school officials and policymakers reflect their educational philosophies. And lastly, the efforts of parents, citizens, businesspeople, and others to influence schools reflect their educational philosophies.

Chapter 4 explains how the legal rights and responsibilities of teachers and students are continuously changing, often as a result of conflicting political views about education. As a teacher, you will need to be knowledgeable about such legal issues as the teacher's responsibility for accidents, discriminatory employment practices, freedom of speech, desegregation, student rights, and circumstances related to job termination or dismissal. Without a basic knowledge of education and the law, you will be ill-equipped to protect your rights and the rights of your students.

Chapter 5 examines the competition for educational resources in the United States. As anyone who has voted on a school bond issue knows, the allocation of resources to schools can easily become a political issue in a community. In spite of the many successes of U.S. education, inequities in resource allocation remain. Some schools in the United States are "rich," while others are "poor."

Lastly, Chapter 6 examines three of the "hottest" politically charged issues in education today—(1) the push for higher *standards*, (2) mandated *testing* to ensure that students have mastered those standards, and (3) calls for *accountability* to ensure that schools, teachers, and administrators produce results.

As you read this book, keep in mind that political influences on schools are very complex; no one has yet provided *the* explanation of these influences. As Frederick Wirt and Michael Kirst (1997) point out in *The Political Dynamics of American Education*, "Among the 14,000 school districts of the nation, it seems as if everyone is trying something new in the way of curriculum, organization, finances and so on. But the impression left to the observer is that of disorganized focus on problems and remedies." Nevertheless, as a professional teacher, you will have an obligation—to yourself and to your profession—to ensure that your actions are shaped primarily by the needs of students rather than by the intense, often conflicting, political forces that impact schools.

Professional Standards and Educational Politics

To ensure that teachers understand educational politics, professional standards for teacher performance include knowledge of the political influences on schools and teaching. Most likely, your teacher education program will use one or more of these sets of standards to evaluate your progress toward becoming a professional teacher.

The professional standards that have had the greatest impact on teacher education programs nationally (as well as on teachers' continuing professional development) are those developed by the **Interstate New Teacher Assessment and Support Consortium (INTASC)**, the **National Council for Accreditation of Teacher Education (NCATE)**, the **Praxis Series: Professional Assessments for Beginning Teachers**, and the **National Board for Professional Teaching Standards (NBPTS)**. Figure 1.2 presents an overview of standards developed by each group. Which set of standards has most influenced the teacher education program in which you are enrolled? Does your state have a set of professional standards that also applies to your teacher education program?

To help you develop competencies in professional standards, each chapter of this book includes a feature titled Relevant Standards. The features illustrate how professional standards developed by these four organizations are related to chapter content. For example, this chapter's Relevant Standards feature on page 8 stresses the need for teachers to become politically involved and to serve as advocates for students and the profession of teaching.

How Do Educational Politics Place Teachers "in the Line of Fire"?

Comments by the teacher quoted in this chapter's epigraph illustrate how educational politics can influence what teachers teach and how they teach it. As a result of **within-school politics** at this teacher's school, she must be "very careful" about criticizing the reading program adopted by the school. It is no exaggeration to say that educational politics have placed this teacher "in the line of fire." Using Figure 1.3 on page 10 as a reference, let's examine how educational politics—from the national level to the within-school level—have placed this teacher "in the line of fire."

Relevant Standards

Political Involvement and Advocacy for Students

As the following professional standards indicate, teachers have an obligation to connect with their surrounding communities in ways that support students' growth and development. In addition, teachers must become politically involved and serve as advocates for students and for the profession of teaching.

- "[Teacher candidates] are able to foster relationships with school colleagues, parents and families, and agencies in the larger community to support students' learning and well being." (National Council for Accreditation of Teacher Education [NCATE] 2002, 18. Supporting statement for Standard 1: Candidate Knowledge, Skills, and Dispositions.)

- "There are two broad areas of responsibility [for teachers]. One involves participation in collaborative efforts to improve the effectiveness of the school. The second entails engaging parents and others in the community in the education of young people." (National Board for Professional Teaching Standards [NBPTS] 2002, 18. Supporting statement for Proposition #5: "Teachers are members of learning communities.")

- "The teacher acts as an advocate for students." (Interstate New Teacher Assessment and Support Consortium [INTASC], 1992, 33. Knowledge statement for Principle #10: "The teacher fosters relationships with school colleagues, parents, and agencies in the larger community to support students' learning and well-being.")

- "[The] teacher is highly proactive in serving students, seeking out resources when necessary." (Praxis Series, distinguished level of performance for Domain 4: Professional Responsibilities, Component 4f: Showing Professionalism.) (From Danielson 1996, 114)

The teacher works in a state in which the state board of education allows school districts to select from only two commercially published reading programs. The state has limited the choice of reading programs to two identified by the federal government as "scientifically approved core reading programs." If a school does not use a federally approved reading program, it does not receive federal funding. Though "scientifically approved" might appear to be an objective criterion for selecting a reading program, federal and state officials and publishers also use "politics" to influence decisions about which reading programs will be approved and which ones not approved.

The federally funded reading program the teacher criticizes is a "scripted" program, which means that the teacher must read directly from a teacher's manual as students work through program materials. The publisher of the reading program even encourages school districts to pay for "coaches" who observe teachers to make sure they follow the manual verbatim and don't use other books or teaching materials.

Figure 1.2 Professional standards for teachers.

INTASC Standards

A consortium of more than thirty states that has developed standards and an assessment process for initial teacher certification. INTASC model core standards are based on ten principles evident in effective teaching regardless of subject or grade level. The principles are based on the realization that effective teachers integrate *content knowledge* with *pedagogical understanding* to assure that all students learn (INTASC 1993).

1. Knowledge of Subject Matter
2. Knowledge of Human Development and Learning
3. Adapting Instruction for Individual Needs
4. Multiple Instructional Strategies
5. Classroom Motivation and Management
6. Communication Skills
7. Instructional Planning Skills
8. Assessment of Student Learning
9. Professional Commitment and Responsibility
10. Partnerships

NCATE Standards

Standards for the accreditation of colleges and universities with teacher preparation programs. Currently, fewer than half of the 1,300 institutions that prepare teachers are accredited by NCATE. Although NCATE standards primarily apply to teacher education programs, not to teacher education students per se, NCATE believes that "the new professional teacher who graduates from a professional accredited school, college, or department of education should be able to" do the following (NCATE 2002):

- Help all prekindergarten through twelfth grade (P–12) students learn
- Teach to P–12 student standards set by specialized professional associations and the states
- Explain instructional choices based on research-derived knowledge and best practice
- Apply effective methods of teaching students who are at different developmental stages, have different learning styles, and come from diverse backgrounds
- Reflect on practice, act on feedback, and integrate technology into instruction effectively

What knowledge, skills, and dispositions does society expect teachers to possess?

NBPTS Standards

A board that issues professional certificates to teachers who possess extensive professional knowledge and the ability to perform at a high level. Certification candidates submit a portfolio including videotapes of classroom interactions and samples of student work plus the teacher's reflective comments. Trained NBPTS evaluators who teach in the same field as the candidate judge all elements of the assessments. NBPTS has developed five "core propositions" on which voluntary national teacher certification is based (NBPTS 1994):

1. Teachers are committed to students and their learning.
2. Teachers know the subjects they teach and how to teach those subjects to students.
3. Teachers are responsible for managing and monitoring student learning.
4. Teachers think systematically about their practice and learn from experience.
5. Teachers are members of learning communities.

Praxis Series

Based on knowledge and skills states commonly require of beginning teachers, the Praxis Series assesses individual development as it corresponds to three steps in becoming a teacher. These three areas of assessment are Academic Skills Assessments: entering a teacher education program (Praxis I); Subject Assessments: licensure for entering the profession (Praxis II); and Classroom Performance Assessments: the first year of teaching (Praxis III). Praxis III involves the assessment of actual teaching skills in four areas (Danielson 1996):

1. *Planning and Preparation*
- Demonstrating knowledge of content and pedagogy
- Demonstrating knowledge of students
- Selecting instructional goals
- Demonstrating knowledge of resources
- Designing coherent instruction

2. *The Classroom Environment*
- Creating an environment of respect and rapport
- Establishing a culture for learning
- Managing classroom procedures
- Managing student behavior
- Organizing physical space

3. *Instruction*
- Communicating clearly and accurately
- Using questioning and discussion techniques
- Engaging students in learning
- Providing feedback to students
- Demonstrating flexibility and responsiveness

4. *Professional Responsibilities*
- Reflecting on teaching
- Maintaining accurate records
- Communicating with families
- Contributing to the school and district
- Growing and developing professionally

Figure 1.3 Levels of educational politics: teachers "in the line of fire."

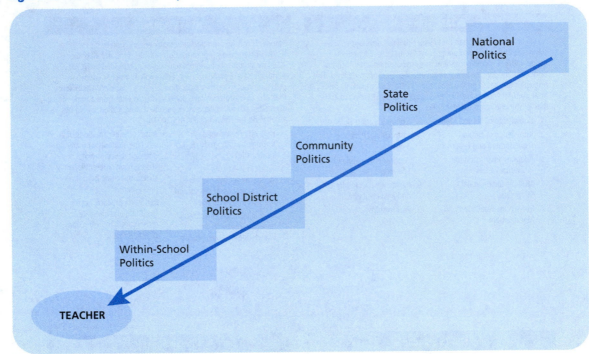

While the federal government has identified the reading program as "scientifically approved," the consensus of most experts on teaching reading is that "there is no research—government or otherwise—that supports the use of any commercial [reading] program" (Garan 2004, 86). In spite of the lack of rigorous research to support its effectiveness, a reading program identified by the federal government as "scientifically approved" can bring its publisher huge profits from sales of the program throughout the country.

School districts and individual teachers such as the one quoted in the epigraph can experience enormous political pressure from the federal, state, and local levels to use certain curriculum materials. For example, when New York City schools decided to adopt a much less expensive reading program—one that was not "scientifically approved" by the federal government—President George W. Bush's reading advisor criticized the decision in a letter to the *New York Times* (Garan 2004). In addition, three members of the federally sponsored National Reading Panel signed another letter critical of the New York City schools' decision. The letter stated that schools are "not likely to qualify for federal funding" if they do not use an approved program. Moreover, the letter pointed out that "some of us [the letter's authors] are serving on committees at the federal level involving the No Child Left Behind legislation" (Garan 2004, 82). In commenting on this letter, the author of

Teachers' Voices

Thrown to the Wolves

John Flickinger

January 6, 2003. I was excited to get back to my students after the Christmas break, and especially happy to be starting my yearly exploration of the mind of Henry David Thoreau. We began with *Civil Disobedience*.

Soon, my students' hatred for Thoreau's verbose nineteenth-century style gave way to amazement at his brilliant intellect and his wonderful ideas. By the end of the week, fine young minds were interpreting the transcendental concepts of Henry David Thoreau, showing me things I had never thought of in all my years of teaching.

Then along came A-B block scheduling. We were told that instead of seeing our students every day for 50 minutes, we would see them every other day for 90. Two teachers surveyed the faculty: 149 against, 13 for. We took the results and a stack of research showing the folly of block scheduling to the school board. Their reaction was a "so what" shrug. "We are placing you on block scheduling. End of discussion."

The next day, the teachers wore black ribbons mourning the death of site-based management. It was decisions made by people in the trenches that made Montwood a national Blue Ribbon school. And site-based management is mandated by our state education department. But A-B scheduling was a done deal.

My students asked, "What should we do?" Being a teacher, I answered their question with a question. "What does Thoreau say?"

They dug into *Civil Disobedience*. "It's not only our right but our responsibility to make our feelings known," they said. I was so proud of them.

Students and parents organized to express their opinions. Two meetings were called by the district and abruptly canceled. Then, I heard rumors of a student walkout. I wrote on my board, "No Walkout."

The next morning, one thousand students left class and gathered in front of the school. They chanted and waved placards, peacefully expressing their dissatisfaction.

Panic stricken, the district called the police. A hundred riot gear-clad, helmet-wearing officers turned a peaceful protest into a riot. The smell of mace hung in the clear January air. Afterwards, the superintendent told us this riot was "entirely the teachers' fault."

The next morning, I sent an e-mail praising the actions of 99.9 percent of our students. I blamed the incident on arrogant district officials.

Security showed up at my door. I was told to report to the principal's office. I was suspended for improper use of district e-mail.

National attention was now focused on our school. A sacrifice was needed. One other teacher who stood up for our students and I were chosen.

That night, I was ambushed on my porch by a local TV station with ties to the district. I refused to speak. On the 10 o'clock news, there I was peeking out of my front door. "The teacher rumored to have incited the riot refused to speak to us." My e-mail was read, edited to sound like support for the riot and an appeal for more violence.

Then e-mails began to arrive from places like Stanford, MIT, Columbia, and Notre Dame, from my former students. "Emerson and Thoreau and their life-changing philosophy are the reason I am here today," they said.

At the next board meeting, a parent delivered a stack of letters testifying to the influence of my teaching. Parents and students held signs: "Give us back our teacher." I tried to hold back the tears. I failed.

When I am eighty years old and someone asks me what I did in life, I will remember those students holding those signs. I will straighten up and proudly say, "I was a teacher."

The powers that be threw two of us to the wolves. I was out in the cold among the hungry lupus [wolves]. I

(continues)

Teachers' *Voices*

Putting Research and Theory into Practice (*Continued*)

survived because of my defenders. My first stop was the campus rep of the Texas State Teachers Association. A lawyer in Austin jumped on a plane and arrived in El Paso just in time to quietly take notes at the Friday night district meeting. He was noticed. At every meeting, people were there to support me. When I walked into a potential ambush by district officials, I was accompanied by two union representatives who have spent a lifetime protecting teachers. And today, I am back in the classroom teaching the lessons of the last month.

Questions

1. What do you think of Flickinger's decision to send an e-mail "praising the actions" of Montwood students?

2. If the majority of teachers in a school or district are opposed to a reform mandated by their school board, what should they do?
3. Why do you think the school board decided to mandate block scheduling, in spite of the teachers' 149–13 vote against the change?
4. In what ways does this case support the observation that "politics . . . is typically informal, often clandestine, and frequently illegitimate. It is illegitimate because it is behavior usually designed to benefit the individual or group at the expense of the organization" (Hoy and Miskel 2001, 28)?

John Flickinger teaches English at Montwood High School in El Paso, Texas. The preceding is excerpted from his article that appeared in *NEA Today*, May 2003, p. 7.

In Defense of Our Children: When Politics, Profit, and Education Collide observed that "this letter carries with it the clear implication of a threat: 'Use what we approve, or don't get funded.' . . . [H]ere we have a letter essentially bullying the schools into using a program" (Garan 2004, 82).

Teacher Accountability

The preceding example of reading instruction and politics is just one instance of how political forces—from the national level to the within-school level—can place teachers "in the line of fire." Increasingly, politicians, business leaders, and citizens are joining the call to hold teachers accountable for student learning. As a result of this emphasis on **accountability**, teachers are expected to implement higher educational standards and to prepare students for tests that assess students' mastery of these standards.

Clearly, today's teachers are under intense pressure from many sectors of our society. As Joel Spring (1998, 25) noted in *Conflict of Interests: The Politics of American Education*: "Politicians compete among themselves for political positions, and workers and business people compete for higher wages and profits. Schools supply the arena for such competition." To be a teacher, then, is to experience these political pressures.

The Teachers' Voices feature on pages 11–12 in this chapter describes how one teacher came to be "in the line of fire" after publicly expressing his disagreement with an educational reform mandated by his school board.

What Groups Are Competing for Control of Schools in the United States?

Competition to influence schools in the United States is inevitable, and politics play an important role in this competition. Several groups try to gain the advantage in this competition. Their efforts to shape educational policies can have dramatic effects on the lives of teachers in the classroom, as Figure 1.4 illustrates. Among these groups, at least ten can be identified:

1. *Parents*—Concerned with controlling local schools so that quality educational programs are available to their children
2. *Students*—Concerned with policies related to freedom of expression, dress, behavior, and curricular offerings
3. *Teachers*—Concerned with their role in school reform, improving working conditions, terms of employment, and other professional issues
4. *Administrators*—Concerned with providing leadership so that various interest groups, including teachers, participate in the shared governance of schools and the development of quality educational programs
5. *Taxpayers*—Concerned with maintaining an appropriate formula for determining local, state, and federal financial support of schools
6. *Federal, state, and local authorities*—Concerned with the implementation of court orders, guidelines, and legislative mandates related to the operation of schools
7. *Ethnic and racial groups*—Concerned with the availability of equal educational opportunity for all and with legal issues surrounding administrative certification, terms of employment, and evaluation
8. *Educational theorists and researchers*—Concerned with using theoretical and research-based insights as the bases for improving schools at all levels
9. *Corporate sector*—Concerned with receiving from the schools graduates who have the knowledge, skills, attitudes, and values to help an organization realize its goals
10. *Special-interest groups*—Concerned with advancing educational reforms that reflect particular religious, philosophical, economic, and philosophical points of view

Figure 1.4 Competition to shape educational policies that impact the classroom teacher.

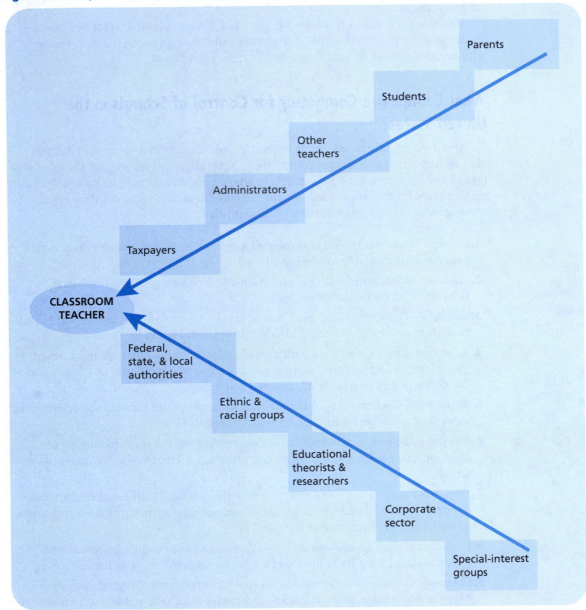

The Technology in Teaching feature in this chapter illustrates how one of the preceding groups—teachers—is using the Internet to influence educational policies. Out of the complex and often turbulent interactions of the groups illustrated in Figure 1.4, school policies are developed. And, as strange as it may seem, no one of

Technology in Teaching

How are teachers using the Internet to influence educational policies?

The results of "Speak Up Day for Teachers 2004" were presented on September 23, 2004, to policymakers and educators during a Capitol Hill briefing hosted by Senator Hillary Rodham Clinton (D-NY) and Senator Michael Enzi (R-WY). "Speak Up Day for Teachers" was the first nationwide online survey to give teachers an opportunity to express their views about the use of technology and the Internet. More than 11,000 teachers from 1,885 schools in fifty states completed the online survey. The National Education Association (NEA), in collaboration with Bell-South and NetDay (a nonprofit organization) sponsored "Teacher Speak Up Day."

The survey revealed that teachers are relying more on technology to meet the requirements of No Child Left Behind legislation. The "Speak Up Day" survey also made it clear that teachers desire a greater voice in technology-related decisions that impact schools. When asked, "Which of these education stakeholders (teachers, principals, students, technology administrators, or parents) do you think should have a greater voice in how technology is used in schools," survey respondents "chose [teachers] by an overwhelming response" (NetDay 2004, 12). In commenting on the survey, the president of the NEA said, "Teachers are telling us that they want to be involved in all stages of the decision-making to bring computers into the classroom. And we know from our own research and experiences that educators must be involved in this planning" (NetDay 2004, 12).

these groups can be said to control today's schools. As Seymour Sarason (1997, 36), author of several books on the complexities of educational change, points out, education in the United States "*is a system in which accountability is so diffused that no one is accountable*" (italics in original). Those who we might imagine control schools—principals, superintendents, and boards of education—are in reality responding to shifting sets of conditions created by those who are competing to have the greatest influence on schools.

Schools and teachers are also influenced by several out-of-school factors—what sociologists have termed *environmental press*. Schools, like society itself, are influenced directly and indirectly by societal and political forces at the local, state, national, and global levels. For example, in their controversial book, *Politics, Markets & America's Schools*, John Chubb and Terry Moe (1990) maintain that student achievement would increase if schools were free of bureaucratic control at the local, state, and federal levels. The best hope for reforming schools, they maintain, is to change how schools are controlled politically. Since educational reformers cannot change factors that contribute to low student achievement such as family background, they should focus on what they can change—namely, how schools are controlled. Instead of being controlled by bureaucracies, schools should be controlled by economic forces of the marketplace. Their proposal gives parents the right to choose the schools their children attend. In addition to bureaucratic

These teachers are acting politically to have a greater role in the development of educational policies. What are some other ways that teachers act politically to influence educational policies?

control, other forces that influence schools and teachers are prevailing attitudes and values, mass media, public opinion, current events, political climate, and population changes.

Clearly, it is difficult to untangle the web of political forces that influence schools. Figure 1.5 illustrates how school authorities are confronted with the difficult task of funneling input from various sources into unified, coherent school programs.

Figure 1.5   School politics.

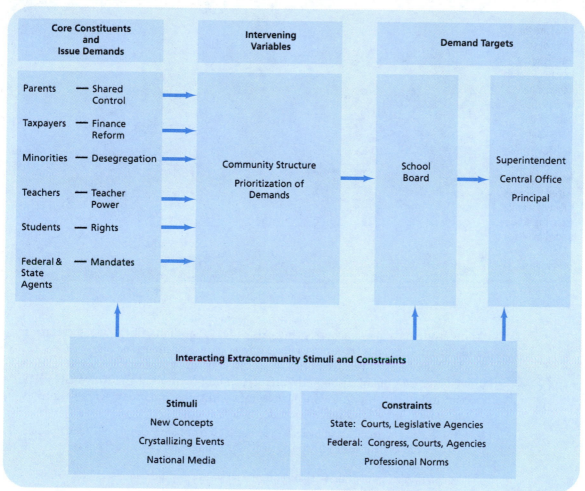

Source: Adapted from Frederick M. Wirt and Michael W. Kirst, *The Political Dynamics of American Education.* Berkeley, CA: McCutchan, 1997, p. 34. Used with permission.

How Is Restructuring Changing How Schools Are Controlled?

At many schools across the country, exciting changes are taking place in regard to how schools are controlled locally. To improve the performance of schools, to decentralize school governance, and to enhance the professional status of teachers, some districts are restructuring their school systems. **Restructuring** goes by several names: *shared governance, administrative decentralization, teacher empowerment, professionalization, bottom-up policymaking, school-based planning, school-based management,* and *shared decision making.* These approaches to school governance give those who

What are the goals of school restructuring? In school-based management, who participates in the governance and management of schools? How is school-based management different from the school board model of local governance?

know students best—teachers, principals, aides, custodians, librarians, secretaries, and parents—greater freedom to decide how to meet students' needs.

In a synthesis of research on school restructuring at more than 1,500 schools, the Center on Organization and Restructuring of Schools at the University of Wisconsin found that the following structural conditions enhance a school's "professional community" and increase students' learning:

- Shared governance that increases teachers' influence over school policy and practice
- Interdependent work structures, such as teaching teams, which encourage collaboration
- Staff development that enhances technical skills consistent with school missions for high-quality learning
- Deregulation that provides autonomy for schools to pursue a vision of high intellectual standards
- Small school size, which increases opportunities for communication and trust
- Parent involvement in a broad range of school affairs (Newmann and Wehlage 1995, 52)

School-Based Management

One of the most frequently used approaches to restructuring schools is **school-based management (SBM)**. Most SBM programs have three components in common:

1. Power and decisions formerly made by the superintendent and school board are delegated to teachers, principals, parents, community members, and students at

local schools. At SBM schools, teachers can become directly involved in making decisions about curriculum, textbooks, standards for student behavior, staff development, promotion and retention policies, teacher evaluation, school budgets, and the selection of teachers and administrators.

2. At each school, a decision-making body (known as a board, cabinet, site-based team, or council)—made up of teachers, the principal, and parents—implements the SBM plan.

3. SBM programs operate with the whole-hearted endorsement of the superintendent of schools.

The primary aim of SBM is to provide teachers, administrators, staff, and, indeed, the entire school community with a greater sense of ownership and efficacy in the operation of schools. Such empowerment, it is believed, will result in greater cooperation, satisfaction, and pride among those directly involved with educating children. The assumption is that if people have a greater say in the decisions that affect them, they will become more involved and, ultimately, their schools will become more successful.

SBM increases communication among teachers, principals, parents, students, and other groups concerned with the operation of schools. With increased communication comes a greater awareness of what needs to be done to improve education at the local school site.

The range of management decisions that can be made by teachers at SBM schools is very broad. Among the changes implemented at some SBM schools are the following:

- Offering Saturday classes to teach students in a more informal setting
- Initiating various before- and after-school programs
- Hiring aides instead of assistant principals
- Creating new positions, such as "discipline manager" and "enrichment coordinator"
- Having teachers give up some of their planning time to reduce class size during basic-skills instruction
- Creating a developmental program for five-year-olds that includes monthly "hands-on" workshops for parents
- Having teachers create their own report card to give parents more detailed information about their children
- Instituting a high school "teacher-as-advisor" program in the middle of the day to counsel students about suicide, drug abuse, and stress-related problems

Chicago's Approach to SBM

A pioneer in SBM has been the City of Chicago public schools. For years, the Chicago public school system faced an array of problems: low student achievement, periodic teacher strikes, budget crises, a top-heavy central bureaucracy, and

Case for Reflection

Parental Involvement and Politics

You are working at a school located on a quiet street in a city of about 100,000 people. It is early fall, and the morning air is filled with the sweet smell of fallen leaves.

Today, just before school starts, you are talking with another teacher in the teachers' lounge. A few months ago, the two of you developed a program to involve more parents in the school. You both took a course titled "Parent Involvement in Education" at the state university located in the city.

"I am so excited about how involved parents are becoming this year," your friend says. "Their involvement makes all the difference in the world, doesn't it?"

"I heard through the grapevine that a lot of parents are really getting involved and vocal in the PTA and on the parent advisory committee," you say. "In fact, I think the principal may be trying to prevent the PTA from becoming a political action group instead of a support group."

Two weeks later, at the request of the principal, you and your friend enter her office for a meeting at the end of the day. The principal closes the door and sits down at her desk. She frowns at you and your friend.

"Do the two of you know what happened at the parent advisory committee meeting last night?" she begins, visibly angered. "I don't suppose you do. I didn't see either of you there."

"No, what happened?" you ask.

"Well, a bunch of parents who participate in your parent involvement program presented a long list of complaints about how the school is run. They demanded to know what I was going to do about their complaints."

"I understand how you might feel put on the spot," you say. "Parents do have a lot of expectations of today's principals."

"Yes," your friend says. "They seem to think that principals can solve just about any problem. The reality is that a lot of things are beyond the principal's control. Principals have to deal with a lot of political pressures."

The fact that you and your friend understand the political pressures confronting today's principals has little influence on the principal's anger.

"Remember when I told you to move slowly with the parent advisory program?" she asks. "Instead, you rushed ahead, and now look what's happened. I should have said 'no' to the parent involvement program. These parents want to go over every inch of the school budget, and they want me to put together a summary of our students' test scores in relation to every other school in the city. Not only that, they want to get involved in developing guidelines for evaluating teachers. This is too much, too fast!"

Questions

1. How effective are the following forms of parental involvement: home visits, parent volunteers, parent advisory committees, parent-teacher organizations?
2. Can parental involvement have a negative influence on schools?
3. In this case, do you think the benefits of the parental involvement program outweigh its limitations?
4. What would you say to the principal?

schools in the decaying inner city that seemed beyond most improvement efforts. In response to these problems, the late Mayor Harold Washington appointed a fifty-five-member committee of business, education, and community leaders to develop a school reform proposal. Among the group's recommendations was the creation of a **local school council (LSC)** for each of the city's more than 550 schools, with the majority of council members being parents of schoolchildren.

In December 1988, the Illinois state legislature passed the **Chicago School Reform Act**, "a series of bold, original reforms [that] attracted intense nationwide interest, particularly because many of the problems faced by Chicago's schools are shared by schools throughout the nation" (Russo 2004, v). Among the provisions of the act were the following:

- School budgets would be controlled by an LSC made up of six parents, two community members, two school employees, and the principal.
- The LSC had the authority to hire and fire the principal.
- The LSC, with input from teachers and the principal, had the authority to develop an improvement plan for the local school.
- New teachers would be hired on the basis of merit, not seniority.
- Principals could remove teachers forty-five days after giving them official notice of unsatisfactory performance.
- A Professional Personnel Advisory Committee of teachers would have advisory responsibility for curriculum and instruction.

The first six years of the Chicago School Reform Act produced few concrete improvements. In 1995, frustrated with the district's chronic financial problems and inability to increase student achievement, the Illinois legislature gave Mayor Richard M. Daley control over Chicago's schools. Daley created a five-member "reform board of trustees" and appointed a chief executive officer (CEO) who advocated "a balance between local control and central-office control" (Hendrie 1999).

By many accounts, the Chicago reform efforts during the last half of the 1990s were a continuing "struggle about how to improve an urban school system" (Hendrie 1999). Friction between the mayor's management team and the parent-dominated LSCs intensified with each report that an LSC member had abused his or her authority.

In spite of ongoing conflicts over the governance of Chicago schools, the program resulted in modest increases in student achievement. In 1995, the percentage of students at or above the national norm in reading was 26.5 percent; by 2001 this percentage had risen to 37.6 percent (Hess 2004). In mathematics, scores improved even more—from 29.8 percent in 1995 to 43.5 percent in 2001 (Hess 2004). At the high school level, graduation rates for nineteen-year-olds increased slightly, and dropout rates for nineteen-year-olds decreased slightly (Miller, Allensworth, and Kochanek 2002).

The preceding gains, however, were not uniform in schools across the city; the city's lowest-performing schools, for example, showed little improvement

(Rosenkranz 2002). In addition, the Reform Act's goal for Chicago schools to reach national norms within five years was not reached.

In spite of modest results, however, the Chicago experiment is clearly one of the more dramatic efforts to empower parents and to make them full partners in school governance. In reflecting on the accomplishments of the Chicago School Reform Act, the chief academic officer during many years of the reform makes the following observation:

> There were three major accomplishments. The first was fiscal stability, being able to run a school system without worrying about funding. Fiscal stability led to union stability, which was number two, because we had contracts, no strikes, we knew that the schools were going to open each year, and people had confidence in the system. And the third was that we had an overarching academic program that addressed the needs of the students (Buckney 2004, 159).

Working in SBM schools such as those described in this section may be difficult for some teachers. The self-assessment shown in Table 1.1 is based on the author's experiences assisting with the implementation of SBM programs. It is designed to give you an opportunity to determine how suited you might be for working in an SBM school. For each item, circle a number to indicate to what extent each listed behavior would be difficult or easy for you.

Now add up your total score, which will range from 10 to 50. A score of 50 suggests that you would be "perfectly" suited for working at an SBM school. High

Table 1.1 Self-assessment for working in an SBM school					
	Very Difficult for Me to Do				Very Easy for Me to Do
1. Taking new risks	1	2	3	4	5
2. Sharing power with others	1	2	3	4	5
3. Willingly changing roles and responsibilities	1	2	3	4	5
4. Learning to trust others	1	2	3	4	5
5. Working in situations that may lack definition and clarity	1	2	3	4	5
6. Being willing to learn new skills	1	2	3	4	5
7. Doing more than is specified in a teaching contract	1	2	3	4	5
8. Assuming a leadership role	1	2	3	4	5
9. Being patient while waiting to see the result of one's efforts	1	2	3	4	5
10. Listening carefully to the opinions of those with whom I disagree	1	2	3	4	5

Total Score _____

scores on some items and low scores on others show your areas of strength and weakness in adapting and contributing to SBM programs.

How Is the Privatization Movement Changing School Governance?

One of the most dramatic reforms in U.S. education during the last decade has been the development of charter schools and for-profit schools, both of which were developed to provide an alternative to the perceived inadequacies of the public schools. On many different levels—governance, staffing, curricula, funding, and accountability—the **privatization movement** is a radical departure from schools as most people have known them. As a *New York Times* writer observes: "When it comes to reforming the nation's schools, these days the leading radicals are likely to be wearing pin-striped suits and come from oak-paneled boardrooms rather than the ivy-covered walls of academia" (Holmes 1990, D2).

Charter Schools

In 1991, Minnesota passed the nation's first charter school legislation calling for up to eight teacher-created and -operated, outcome-based schools that would be free of most state and local rules and regulations. When the St. Paul City Academy opened its doors in September 1992, it became the nation's first charter school.

Charter schools are independent, innovative, outcome-based, public schools.

> The charter school concept allows a group of teachers, parents, or others who share similar interests and views about education to organize and operate a school. Charters can be granted by a local school district, by the state, or by the national government. In effect, charter schools offer a model for restructuring that gives greater autonomy to individual schools and promotes school choice by increasing the range of options available to parents and students within the public schools system (Wohlstetter and Anderson 1994, 486).

For example, charter schools in Arizona range from those focusing on the fine arts to charter schools in remote regions of the state that serve Native American communities.

In return for freedom from rules and regulations that apply to "traditional" schools, charter schools are to be held accountable for student achievement. A school that fails to meet the academic criteria outlined in its charter or fails to follow relevant state and local laws can be closed by the agency that approved the school's charter.

Currently, thirty-six states, Puerto Rico, and the District of Columbia have adopted charter school legislation, and 3,300 schools serve almost one million students (Feller 2004). About 10 percent of the nation's charter schools are operated on a for-profit basis (Keller 2002).

To open a charter school, an original **charter** (or agreement) is signed by the school's founders and a sponsor (usually the local school board). The charter specifies the learning outcomes that students will master before they continue their studies. Charter schools, which usually operate in the manner of autonomous

What are the strengths and weaknesses of charter schools? Do you think charter schools are strengthening, or weakening, the U.S. system of public education?

school districts (a feature that distinguishes them from the alternative schools that many school districts operate), are public schools and must teach all students. If admission requests for a charter school exceed the number of available openings, students are selected by drawing.

Because charter schools are designed to promote the development of new teaching strategies that can be used at other public schools, they can prove to be an effective tool for promoting educational reform and the professionalization of teaching in the future. Moreover, as Milo Cutter, one of the two teachers who founded St. Paul City Academy points out, charter schools give teachers unprecedented leadership opportunities and the ability to respond quickly to students' needs:

> [We had] the chance to create a school that takes into account the approaches we know will work. We listen to what the students want and need, because we ask them. And each day we ask ourselves if we are doing things the best way we can. We also have the flexibility to respond. We can change the curriculum to meet these needs as soon as we see them. Anywhere else it would take a year to change. It is much better than anything we have known in the traditional setting (North Central Regional Education Laboratory 1993, 3).

Research on Charter Schools   In a report titled *Do Charter Schools Measure Up? The Charter School Experiment after 10 Years*, the American Federation of Teachers (AFT) suggested that, by mid-2002, charter schools had not lived up to the claims of their advocates. The following are among the shortcomings of charter schools, according to the AFT report:

- Charter schools contribute to the racial and ethnic isolation of students.
- Charter school teachers are less experienced and lower paid than teachers in other public schools.
- Charter schools generally score no better (and often do worse) on student achievement tests than other comparable public school students.
- Charter schools have not been held to the "bargain" they made—trading freedom from rules for increased accountability.
- Charter schools were supposed to experiment with new curricula and classroom practices, but they have proven no more innovative than other public schools (American Federation of Teachers 2002, 5–6).

Another study of charter schools compared reading and mathematics scores on the 2003 National Assessment of Educational Progress (NAEP) for fourth-grade students at 150 charter schools with students in other public schools. Results indicated that underprivileged students in charter schools do worse in reading and mathematics than students in other schools. However, students of the same race or ethnicity scored as well in either type of school. Overall, the NAEP assessment found that less than one-third of students, regardless of the type of school they attended, were "proficient" in mathematics or reading, according to federal standards (U.S. Department of Education, Institute for Education Sciences 2004).

On the other hand, another 2004 research report indicated that charter school students outperformed students in comparable traditional public schools in reading and mathematics (Hoxby 2004). The researcher compared the achievement of 99 percent of all elementary students enrolled in charter schools with that of students in neighboring public schools with similar racial composition. Results indicated that charter school students were 5.2 percent more likely to be proficient in reading and 3.2 percent more likely to be proficient in mathematics on their state's exam.

Regardless of the mixed results on the effectiveness of charter schools, few charter schools have been closed because of failure to meet academic outcomes. Instead, charter school closings are related to "low enrollment, facility problems, financial improprieties, or mismanagement" (F. M. Hess 2004, 509). By 2002, 194 (6.95 percent) of the nation's 2,790 charter schools had been closed, but only 0.005 percent were closed for failure to meet academic outcomes (F. M. Hess 2004).

For-Profit Schools

One of the hottest educational issues today is the practice of turning the operation of public schools over to private, for-profit companies. Advocates of privatization believe that privately operated schools are more efficient. Privately operated schools reduce costs and maximize "production"—that is, student achievement. In addition, advocates point out that private sector firms are typically more

productive and responsive to consumer demands than their public sector counter-
parts. Lastly, as the president of the National Center on Education and the Economy observes: "It is clear that business has an open door to the top policymakers,
including the President, in a way that professional educators would envy" (Weisman 1991, 1).

Opponents of privately operated schools are concerned that profit, rather than
increasing student achievement, is the real driving force behind **for-profit schools**.
For-profit education companies focusing on the preK–12 level had revenues of $58
billion in 2001 (Eduventures 2003). Critics of for-profit schools are also concerned
that school districts may not be vigilant enough in monitoring the performance of
private education companies.

Edison Schools, Inc.   Concerned about the slow pace of educational reform in the
United States, Christopher Whittle, the originator of Channel One, launched the $3
billion Edison Project in 1992—an ambitious plan to develop a national network
of more than one thousand for-profit secondary schools by 2010. As of 2001–02,
the Edison Project, now named Edison Schools, Inc., had become the largest company involved in the for-profit management of K–12 schools, and it served 74,000
students in 133 schools located in twenty-two states and the District of Columbia
(Edison Schools, Inc. 2004).

In 1999, Edison Schools, Inc., reported that achievement was steadily moving
upward at the "vast majority" of Edison Schools. At seventeen of the Edison
Schools that had been able to establish achievement trends, fourteen had records
the company labeled "positive" or "strongly positive," and three had records that
were labeled "weak" (Walsh 1999b). However, in a report analyzing the results
reported by Edison the previous year, the American Federation of Teachers claimed
that the company exaggerated achievement gains at many schools and downplayed
negative results at others. "On the whole, Edison results were mediocre" (American
Federation of Teachers 1998, 10).

Education Alternatives, Inc.   Another approach to for-profit schools was developed by
Education Alternatives, Inc. (EAI), a company that negotiates with school districts
to operate their public schools. Participating school districts give the company the
same per-pupil funding to operate the school that the district would have used.
The company, using its own curricula and cost-saving techniques, agrees to
improve student performance and attendance in return for the opportunity to
operate schools at a profit.

Education Alternatives, Inc., which began operating its first for-profit school in
Dade County, Florida, in 1991, became the first private company to run an entire
school district when the Duluth, Minnesota, school board awarded the company a
three-month contract in 1992 to serve as interim superintendent for the district.
In Baltimore, Maryland, and Hartford, Connecticut, where EAI operated several
schools in the mid-1990s, critics challenged the achievement gains the company
reported and accused the company of mismanaging finances. After numerous

disputes over the management of schools, both school systems eventually terminated their contracts with the company. In 1999, EAI moved its headquarters from Bloomington, Minnesota, to Scottsdale, Arizona, and became the Tesseract Group, Inc. At that time, the company operated forty schools serving more than six thousand students.

Teacher-Owned Schools?   An innovative approach to for-profit schools has been suggested by Richard K. Vedder (2003) in his book *Can Teachers Own Their Own Schools? New Strategies for Educational Excellence.* Vedder believes that for-profit public schools would benefit from competition and develop cost-effective ways to achieve educational quality. In addition, such schools would attract additional funding and expertise needed to revolutionize school systems.

Vedder's approach is patterned after Margaret Thatcher's privatization of government council housing in England, privatization reforms in Latin America, and the E.S.O.P. (Employee Stock Ownership Plan) movement in the United States. He suggests that teachers, administrators, and other educational stakeholders would become the owners of schools, acquiring an attractive financial stake in the process. Such privatization reforms could pave the way for new, cost-effective means of improving education for all students. Vedder believes that schools in which teachers, administrators, and parents have a significant financial stake would foster vibrant school communities with increased parental involvement and the innovation and efficiency essential to produce educational excellence.

Summary

Why Do You Need to Understand Educational Politics?

- Understanding educational politics is an important form of professional knowledge.

- *Politics* refer to how people use power, influence, and authority within an organization to persuade others to act in desired ways.

- Educators use within-school politics to influence instructional and curricular practices within a school.

- Five dimensions of educational politics influence teachers: (1) politics at the federal, state, and local levels; (2) legal rights and responsibilities of teachers;

(3) conflicting educational philosophies; (4) competition for educational resources; and (5) standards, mandated testing, and calls for accountability.

How Do Educational Politics Place Teachers "in the Line of Fire"?

- Political forces—from the national level to the within-school level—can place teachers "in the line of fire."

- Several professional associations and state departments of education have developed standards for teachers that include knowledge of the political influences on schools and teaching. Four associations have a significant impact on teacher education programs on teachers' professional development: Interstate New Teacher Assessment and Support Consortium (INTASC), National Council for Accreditation of Teacher Education (NCATE), Praxis Series: Professional Assessments for Beginning Teachers, and National Board for Professional Teaching Standards (NBPTS).

What Groups Are Competing for Control of Schools in the United States?

- Parents; students; teachers; administrators; taxpayers; federal, state, and local authorities; ethnic and racial groups; educational theorists and researchers; the corporate sector; and special-interest groups exert political influence on education.

- Schools reflect the society they serve and thus are influenced by out-of-school factors such as prevailing attitudes and values, mass media, public opinion, current events, political climate, and population changes.

How Is Restructuring Changing How Schools Are Controlled?

- As part of the restructuring movement, schools are changing their policies for governance, curricula, and community collaboration.

- The Chicago School Reform Act is one example of restructuring based on school-based management that empowers teachers, principals, parents, community members, and students at local schools.

How Is the Privatization Movement Changing School Governance?

- Charter schools and for-profit schools, both part of the privatization movement, were developed in response to perceived inadequacies of the public schools.

- Charter schools are independent, innovative, outcome-based public schools started by a group of teachers, parents, or others who obtain a charter from a local school district, a state, or the federal government.

- Research on charter schools is mixed—some studies show that charter school students outperform students at other schools, while other studies show the opposite.

- Very few charter schools have been closed because of failure to meet academic outcomes; about 7 percent have been closed because of low enrollment, facility problems, financial improprieties, or mismanagement.

- Edison Schools, Inc. (formerly the Edison Project) and the Tesseract Group, Inc. (formerly Education Alternatives, Inc.) are examples of for-profit schools operated by private corporations.

- For-profit schools owned by teachers, administrators, and other stakeholders have been suggested as one way to improve the quality of schools.

Key Terms and Concepts

accountability, 12
charter, 23
charter schools, 23
Chicago School Reform Act, 21
for-profit schools, 26
Interstate New Teacher Assessment and Support Consortium (INTASC), 7

local school council (LSC), 21
National Board for Professional Teaching Standards (NBPTS), 7
National Council for Accreditation of Teacher Education (NCATE), 7
political foundations of education, 4

Praxis Series: Professional Assessments for Beginning Teachers, 7
privatization movement, 23
restructuring, 17
school-based management (SBM), 18
within-school politics, 7

Reflective Application Activities

Discussion Questions

1. As this chapter points out, many individuals and groups believe that they should play an important role in school governance. Rank in order (from "greatest influence" to "least influence") the extent to which you think each of the following individuals or groups *should* control schools: students, teachers, administrators, parents, the school board, the local school district, the state government, and the federal government. Are there certain areas of schooling that should be controlled by these individuals and groups? Compare your rankings with those of your classmates. What differences do you note?

2. Reread the epigraph for this chapter on page 2. What should teachers do if they disagree with their principal about what should be taught to students or how it should be taught?

Professional Journal

1. Reflect on your experiences in schools and write a paragraph or two about a time when politics influenced the education you received. Why is it important for teachers to develop an understanding of how politics influence schools?

2. Imagine that you are going to open a charter school. How would this school differ from the schools in your community? What would you say to parents to convince them to send their children to your school?

Online Assignments

1. Use your favorite search engine to visit the websites for several charter schools. What do these schools have in common? How are they different?

2. Visit the U.S. Department of Education's charter school website and click on the "State Policies for Charter Schools" link. How do the states' charter school policies differ? How are they similar?

Observations and Interviews

1. Using Figure 1.3, interview a teacher in a local school about his or her perceptions of the political influences on education. Ask the teacher to select one influence and describe how it currently affects the school in which the teacher works.

2. Interview a teacher and ask him or her to rank in order (from "greatest influence" to "least influence") the extent to which each of the following individuals or groups *should* control schools: students, teachers, administrators, parents, the school board, the local school district, the state government, and the federal government. How do the teacher's beliefs compare with your own?

Professional Portfolio

Think of businesses and groups in your community that may make good candidates for a partnership with a school. Select one of them and develop a proposal outlining the nature, activities, and benefits of the partnership you envision.

Appendix 1.1
Guidelines for Teachers to Think and Act Politically

- Learn from those who have come before you.
- Find your main focus and organize around that.
- Provide leadership and direction.
- Build a coalition.
- Know who is making the decisions and who or what will influence them.
- Speak simply and forcefully.
- Be a lion.
- Look organized and be organized.
- Do it because it's the right thing to do.

TWENTY-FIVE WAYS TO BECOME INVOLVED

1. Attend organizational meetings.
2. Encourage others to become involved.
3. Organize a phone tree of supporters.
4. Keep each other informed on what is happening in individual schools and areas.
5. Get parents to agree to speak at school board meetings.
6. Provide transportation for parents and children to school board meetings.
7. Arrange for translators for limited-English-speaking parents at school board meetings.
8. Help parents and students prepare what they will say at school board meetings.
9. Attend school board meetings.
10. Write letters to parents.
11. Write letters to the superintendent.
12. Write letters to school board members.
13. Write letters to newspaper editors.
14. Write and send a survey to parents of present and former students.
15. Collect returned surveys to present to school board.
16. Call the school board members.
17. Call TV and radio stations.

Source: Adapted by permission of Barbara Keresty, Susan O'Leary, and Dale Wortley, *You Can Make a Difference: A Teacher's Guide to Political Action*. Portsmouth, NH: Heinemann, 1998, pp. 29–49, 58–59. Used by permission of the publisher Heinemann, a division of Reed Elsevier Inc.

18. Encourage parents to call school board members and the superintendent.
19. Encourage teachers in your school to call school board members and the superintendent.
20. Organize other teachers in your school to attend and to speak at school board meetings.
21. Be a liaison with specific school board members.
22. Work with your union.
23. Be creative.
24. Attend and speak at staff and committee meetings at the school and district level.
25. Provide refreshments.

2 Local, State, Regional, and Federal Influences on Education

*D*ear President,

The issue of education touches more of your fellow citizens—particularly the young, who are our most vulnerable citizens—than almost all other policy areas. At the start of your tenure, I beg you to take a step back, to put aside the familiar political and bureaucratic ways of addressing education policy, and to look afresh at what might and must be at its core if education is to improve our children's future and the state of our democracy.

—Theodore R. Sizer, "What We All Want for Each of Our Children," in Carl Glickman (ed.), *Letters to the Next President*, 2004

You and three other teachers are talking in a classroom at the end of the school day.

"I don't see how you can say we have the freedom to decide what to teach and how to teach it," says Kim, a language arts teacher who came to the school two years ago. "The books I use are chosen by a district textbook selection committee. Next April all my kids have to take a test mandated by the state. And. . . ."

"Hold it," says Betty, raising her hand to interrupt. "That doesn't mean that politicians control the schools. Unless I'm mistaken, I was the only teacher in my classroom today. I've been here eight years and no one's ever told me what to do." Betty takes a quick sip of her diet soda.

"Politicians are running the schools more and more," says Ralph, looking up from the mathematics book he is evaluating. "Look," he continues, "the politicians even set up a beginning teacher program that in reality tells this new teacher how to teach and what to teach." He looks toward you. Feeling a bit uncomfortable, you smile and nod in agreement.

"Ralph is right," says Kim. "The other day, John Matthews, who teaches over at Crestview, told me he figured out that teachers there have a total of over one hundred federal, state, and local guidelines they have to follow. Can you imagine that!" She rolls her eyes to emphasize the point.

"Right," Ralph says. "I'm surprised the number isn't higher—not only do you have state tests, you've got mandated standards for grading, for graduation, for athletic eligibility, for placement in special programs, for suspending kids, for just about anything you can think of."

"That's an exaggeration," says Betty. "We've got the freedom to decide what we want to teach and how we want to teach it. Sure, there are guidelines, but they help us and the kids."

"Help us?" says Kim, rolling her eyes again in a pained expression of disbelief. "How can you say that?"

"We've got a difficult enough job to do without the politicians making it harder," says Ralph.

"I hear what you're both saying," says Betty, "but you've got to remember why we're here—for the kids. The Feds, our legislators, the school board . . . they're just looking out for the kids."

"Well, who's looking out for us?" asks Kim. "If we meet all their guidelines, then we've got less time to teach the kids. Is that helping kids?"

"Well, I still think you're overreacting," says Betty. "Why don't we ask the new teacher here. What do you think?"

The three teachers look at you, awaiting your response. What do you say?

Guiding Questions

1. **How does the local community influence schools?**
2. **What powers and influence do states have in governing schools?**
3. **How do regional education agencies assist schools?**
4. **How does the federal government influence education?**

The preceding scenario illustrates how federal and state legislation, as well as local educational politics, can influence teachers' daily lives. Controversies abound in U.S. education, and politics at federal, state, and local levels clearly play an important role in identifying the steps taken to resolve these controversies. How should teachers be prepared? What should be included in the curriculum? How should schools be financed? How should they be governed? How should student learning be assessed? These and other questions are just a few of the issues that will impact your life as a teacher. Within this broad context of controversies about education and educational politics, this chapter examines how political forces at the local, state, regional, and federal levels will influence your future as a teacher.

How Does the Local Community Influence Schools?

While the Constitution does not address public education, the Tenth Amendment is used as the basis for giving states the legal authority to create and to manage school systems. In addition, as Chapter 1 pointed out, various individuals and groups, though not legally empowered, compete vigorously to influence those legally entitled to operate the schools (see Figure 1.4, page 14).

The Tenth Amendment gives to the states all powers not reserved for the federal government and not prohibited to the states. To provide public education, then, the states created local school districts, giving them responsibility for the daily operation of public schools. The number of local public school districts has declined from 119,001 in 1937–38 to 14,928 in 1999–2000, as a result of efforts to consolidate districts (National Center for Education Statistics 2002).

Local School District

Local school districts vary greatly in regard to demographics such as number of school-age children; educational, occupational, and income levels of parents; operating budget; number of teachers; economic resources; and number of school buildings. Some serve ultrawealthy communities, others impoverished ghetto neighborhoods or rural areas. Their operations include 423 one-teacher elementary schools in this country (National Center for Education Statistics 2002) as well as scores of modern, multibuilding campuses in heavily populated areas.

The largest school districts are exceedingly complex operations with multimillion-dollar annual operating budgets (see Table 2.1). The largest—the New York City school system—has more than a million pupils (from 190 countries), nearly 64,000 teachers (a number that exceeds the number of *students* in Cincinnati; Minneapolis; Portland, Oregon; Sacramento; Seattle; and St. Louis), 1,200 schools, and total annual expenditures of almost $11 billion. The New York system, overseen by a schools chancellor, consists of thirty-two community school districts, each with its own superintendent.

The organizational structures of school districts also differ. Large urban systems, which may contain several districts, tend to have more complex distribution of roles and responsibilities than do smaller districts. Appendix 2.1 presents a typical organizational structure for a school district of about 20,000 pupils.

Table 2.1   Selected data for the ten largest public school systems, 1999

School System	Total Enrollment	Number of Teachers[1]	Pupil/ Teacher Ratio	Number of Schools	Total Expenditures in Thousands[2]	Expenditure per Pupil[2]
New York City	1,075,710	63,989	16.8	1,207	$10,799,265	$8,106
Los Angeles Unified	710,007	33,754	21.0	655	$4,618,160	$6,010
City of Chicago	431,750	23,455	18.4	597	$3,446,592	$6,617
Miami-Dade County	292,023	18,104	19.9	350	$2,501,659	$5,952
Broward County, FL	241,094	11,322	21.3	234	$1,470,830	$5,453
Clark County, NV	217,526	10,838	20.1	246	$1,356,279	$5,108
Houston Independent School District	209,716	11,638	18.0	296	$1,231,086	$5,340
Philadelphia	205,199	11,423	18.0	259	$1,510,785	$5,702
Hawaii Public Schools	185,860	10,866	17.1	256	$1,266,378	$5,859
Detroit Public Schools	167,124	9,148	18.3	268	$1,345,361	$7,326

[1]Data exclude teachers reported as working in school district offices rather than in schools.
[2]Data are for 1997–98.

Sources: U.S. Department of Education, National Center for Education Statistics, Common Core of Data survey. (Table prepared October 2001.) Adapted from *Digest of Education Statistics 2002.* Washington, DC: National Center for Education Statistics, U.S. Department of Education, Tables 92 and 93.

Local Educational Politics

School districts not only differ in size and location, but they also are influenced by different types of local educational politics. Differences in local educational politics are related to "the type of community power structure, the nature of the local labor market, the power of the local educational bureaucracy, and the militancy of the local teachers' union" (Spring 1998, 157).

Local Community Power Structures   Studies of local communities and their influence on schools suggest that that there are four types of community power structures (McCarty and Ramsey 1971; Spring 1998). These structures can greatly influence local educational politics and the day-to-day lives of teachers. The four types are dominated, factional, pluralistic, and inert power structures.

In a community with a *dominated power structure*, one person or a few people have most of the political power. Typically, those in power are from the community's economic "elite." However, they may be leaders of ethnic, religious, or political groups. Dominated power structures are found primarily in small towns or in urban areas that have a labor market dominated by one industry. A dominated power structure seldom has to deal with strong opposition.

A community with a *factional power structure* has two factions that compete for political influence. Typically, the factions hold different values, especially religious values. Each faction usually has similar ability to influence the operation of schools in the community.

In a community with a *pluralistic power structure*, several interest groups compete, and no one group dominates policies for the operation of schools. Schools in such a community may reflect a high degree of community involvement. Pluralistic power structures are often characteristic of suburban school systems that place great emphasis on occupations that require a college degree.

Some communities have an *inert power structure*—that is, no power structure is visible. In such a community, there is little competition for positions on the school board. Public interest in the schools is low, and few students enter occupations that require a college degree. The schools tend to emphasize a general or vocational education for most students.

Local School Board

A local **school board** acts as an agent of the state. School boards are responsible for the following important activities: approving the teachers, administrators, and other school personnel hired by the superintendent; developing organizational and educational policies; and determining procedures for the evaluation of programs and personnel. Nearly all school board meetings are open to the public; in fact, many communities even provide radio and television coverage. Open meetings give parents and interested citizens an opportunity to express their concerns and to get more information about problems in the district.

In most communities, school board members are elected in general elections. In some urban areas, however, board members are selected by the mayor. Board members typically serve a minimum of three to five years, and their terms of office are usually staggered. School boards usually range in size from five to fifteen members, with five or seven frequently suggested as the optimum size. Board members in urban areas usually are paid, while members in most other areas are not.

Frequently, school board meetings can be "battle grounds for many special interests" (Cibulka 1996, 13). Special-interest groups may include "internal" groups such as teachers' unions, administrators, and other educational employees (custodians and bus drivers, for example). "External" groups may include spokespersons for business and industry, members of ethnic groups, or members of religious groups. School board meetings can evolve into heated debates over issues such as multicultural education, religion and the curriculum, and instructional activities.

School boards play a critical role in the U.S. education system. "The quality of school board governance effectiveness is the single most important determinant of school district success or failure," according to Rod Paige, former U.S. Secretary of Education under President George W. Bush (*School Board News* 2002).

Makeup of School Boards   A 2001 national survey of school board members revealed that women constituted 39 percent of school boards and men 61 percent. The survey also revealed that board membership does not reflect the growing diversity of students in the United States—minority membership on school boards was 13.6 percent, an increase of 2.7 percent compared to 1998.

The survey also revealed that school board members were more affluent than the general population. Twenty-four percent of board members had annual incomes of $50,000 to $74,999; 22 percent $75,000 to $99,000; and 21.3 percent $100,000 to $149,000 (*American School Board Journal* 2001). The economic backgrounds of today's board members perhaps reflects the concept of "democratic elitism" that first emerged early in the twentieth century.

> In the rhetoric of democratic elitism, only the "best"—the elite—should determine important public matters. . . . [A] factory worker would have less ability than a banker to decide the public interest regarding schooling. . . . [Schools] should be governed only by the "best" members of the community (Spring 1998, 13).

Criticism of School Boards   School boards have been criticized for not educating themselves about issues and education policymaking, being reluctant to seek input from their communities, not communicating a shared vision of educational excellence to their communities, and not developing positive, productive relationships with superintendents. In addition, as the director of the Center on Reinventing Education at the University of Washington suggests, some school boards are more interested in achieving political rather than educational goals.

> Local school boards are political bodies pursuing many agendas, of which educational effectiveness is only one. . . . School boards should have one job: making sure every child is receiving a good education. This means closing bad schools and creating options for students who are not learning. The cost of letting school boards become the political farm clubs and resume builders for ambitious people is too great (Hill 2003, A11).

Other critics have pointed out that school boards should focus more on removing barriers to student learning (Mental Health in Schools Center 1998). Instead, school boards often

- fail to provide far-reaching or politically risky leadership for reform;
- have become another level of administration, often micromanaging districts;
- are so splintered by members' attempts to represent special interests or meet their individual political needs that boards cannot govern effectively;
- are not spending enough time on educating themselves about issues or about education policymaking; and
- exhibit serious problems in their capacity to develop positive and productive, lasting relationships with superintendents (Danzberger 1994, 369).

Some states have taken steps to reform school boards. For example, Arkansas provides school board members with training in developing partnerships with their communities, creating a vision of educational excellence, and team-building (*School Board News* 2002). West Virginia implemented legislation in 1994 to restructure school boards "so that they become well-informed, responsive, policy-making bodies." Board members now serve for four years rather than six, and they must complete training focused on "boardmanship and governing effectiveness" (Danzberger 1994, 394).

Superintendent of Schools

Though school boards operate very differently, the **superintendent** is invariably the key figure in determining a district's educational policy. The superintendent is the chief administrator of the school district, the person charged with seeing to it that schools operate in accord with federal and state guidelines as well as policies set by the local school board. Though the board of education delegates broad powers to the superintendent, his or her policies require board approval.

The specific responsibilities of the superintendent are many. Among the most important are:

- To serve as professional advisor to the board of education and to make policy recommendations for improving curricular and instructional programs
- To act as employer and supervisor of professional and nonteaching personnel (janitors, cafeteria workers, etc.)
- To represent the schools in their relations with the community and to explain board of education policies to the community
- To develop policies for the placement and transportation of students within the district
- To prepare an annual school budget and adhere to the budget adopted by the school board

Superintendents and Local Educational Politics   How the superintendent and his or her board work together appears to be related to the size of the school district, with superintendents and school boards in larger districts more likely to be in conflict.

Case for Reflection

Teachers vs. the Board of Education

Near the end of your first month of teaching at a suburban school, the board of education has stated that it cannot provide the salary increases promised to teachers last year. The board says that the school system, like others in the state, must cope with a significant reduction in state funds for education.

Teachers at your school, most of whom belong to the teachers' union, are angry about the board's failure to live up to its promise. Most teachers believe that the board can find the money if it really wants to. Your school's union representative has just called a meeting of teachers to discuss the situation and to consider a possible strike. The day before the meeting he stops by your classroom to urge you to attend.

"This is an important meeting," he says. "As a new teacher, you need to find out how the board of education has treated teachers."

"Well," you begin, "I don't know about a strike. Like everyone, I'm concerned about salaries. But if we go on strike, what about the kids? We have a responsibility to them."

"This is not just about money," he says. "The board has a history of failing to live up to its promises. We're actually doing this for the kids. If the board gets away with this, a lot of good teachers are going to transfer out of the district. And that's going to hurt the kids."

You agree to attend the meeting; however, you're not sure how you feel about teacher unions in general and going on strike in particular. Prior to the meeting, several questions keep coming to mind. If teachers are professionals, should they belong to a union? Should I join the union? If teachers go on strike, will I honor the strike? Would I cross the picket line in order to teach?

Questions

1. What is your position regarding teacher strikes?
2. Other than going on strike, what other actions could teachers in the preceding case take?
3. Imagine that teachers in the preceding case met with a group of parents whose children attend the school. How might teachers justify going on strike? What concerns might parents express?

School boards in smaller districts, however, are more effective when they do oppose the superintendent. In large districts, the board's own divisiveness makes it less likely that the board will successfully oppose the superintendent (Wirt and Kirst 1997).

Optimally, the superintendent of schools and the elected or appointed school board work together to decide and implement educational policies. However, superintendents have observed how widely the political climate of school districts can vary. "In some schools, changing the location of a bicycle rack will cause parents to call the principal. In other schools, we can cut the school day from seven periods to six periods without neighborhood reaction" (Wirt and Kirst 1982, 145). In most cases, budget issues and school-community relations are the superintendent's greatest challenges.

Superintendents must have great skill to respond appropriately to the many external political forces that demand their attention, and conflict is inevitable. As one observer put it, "Conflict is the DNA of the superintendency" (Cuban 1985, 28). Effective superintendents demonstrate that they are able to play three roles simultaneously: politician, manager, and teacher. It is a demanding position, and turnover is high; for example, between 1980 and 1995, the New York City school system had ten chancellors (Hurwitz 1999). In an environment characterized by political turbulence and demands from competing interest groups, the superintendent cannot be an omnipotent, insensitive figure; he or she must be a "negotiator-statesman" (Wirt and Kirst 1982, 144).

The Role of Parents

Parents may not be involved legally in the governance of schools, but they do play an important role in education. One characteristic of successful schools is that they develop close working relationships with parents. Additionally, children whose parents or guardians support and encourage school activities have a definite advantage in school. The Teachers' Voices feature in this chapter illustrates how one teacher developed partnerships with the parents of her students.

These parents are making important contributions to improving schools in their local community. What motivates parents to become involved with the schools? How can parents help you to be successful as a teacher?

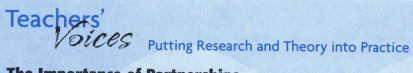

Teachers' *Voices*   Putting Research and Theory into Practice

The Importance of Partnerships

Karen M. Caruso

When I look back at my first year with Los Angeles Unified School District, I recall not only the students, but also the families I came to know. My class, in Room 17, was a combination second and third grade, which meant a wide range of learning abilities. Many new-to-the-school students were also added to the class. Despite these challenges, I was determined to make the year a special one.

As the year unfolded, I realized that many of the students in my class had emotional problems. Having recently completed my master's in psychology and an internship as a child therapist, I was able to apply my skills with the students at hand. I knew, though, that without families' support I couldn't be as successful as I hoped to be.

I began by setting up ongoing methods of communication with each of the families. There were obstacles: parents that needed to work late hours, split homes, and in some cases severe financial stress. In one situation, the parents had recently separated and Nat's mom, Holly, had relocated to New Mexico. In order to keep her informed and involved, every week I mailed her one of my home/school communication sheets that described what we had learned. I added a brief comment on Nat's progress. Holly often wrote back, and when Nat returned from his once-a-month visit he'd bring an artifact to share with the class. Because of the relationship, Holly knew she could contact me at any time about Nat. In another situation, Anthony's mom was single-handedly supporting her two children while attending school. We scheduled regular weekly morning appointments to talk about Anthony and his successes over the past week or to problem solve, if necessary. Anthony went from low performing to above grade level by the time the year was over. One of my second graders was having so many problems with self-control and violence that his

dad left his pager on for me. In addition to these individual meetings, I started Family Evenings. Once a month students and their families came to school for a potluck dinner and an educational activity. These events brought everyone together, thus fostering community among the families. All of these combined experiences made the school year memorable for all of us.

When the first day of a new school year or an open house fills your classroom with not only current students, but also past students and their parents, you understand that as a teacher you have an impact on the people involved in your students' lives. Years later I still recall that special group of parents and students who taught me that a teacher is someone who becomes part of the family when the family becomes part of the school.

Questions

1. How can partnerships with parents provide support for teachers?
2. Caruso developed her partnerships with parents by emphasizing home-school communication. What other approaches can teachers use to develop partnerships with parents?
3. What does Caruso mean when she says that "a teacher is someone who becomes part of the family when the family becomes part of the school"?
4. Reflect on the elementary and secondary schools you attended. What examples of parental partnerships do you recall?

Karen M. Caruso teaches at Third Street Elementary School in Los Angeles. Her comments were published in Adrienne Mack-Kirschner's *Powerful Classroom Stories from Accomplished Teachers* (Thousand Oaks, CA: Corwin, 2004), pp. 152–153.

Through participation on school advisory and site-based councils, parents are making an important contribution to restructuring and school reform efforts around the country. In addition, groups such as the Parent Teacher Association (PTA), Parent Teacher Organization (PTO), or Parent Advisory Council (PAC) give parents the opportunity to communicate with teachers on matters of interest and importance to them. Through these groups, parents can become involved in the life of the school in a variety of ways—from making recommendations regarding school policies, to providing much-needed volunteer services, to initiating school-improvement activities such as fund-raising drives.

A key element of parental involvement is communication between school and home. The Technology in Teaching feature in this chapter examines attitudes toward using the Internet to enhance school-home communication.

Many parents influence the character of education through involvement with the growing number of private, parochial, for-profit, and charter schools. In addition, many parents are activists and promote school choice, voucher systems, and home schooling. Some parents even join well-funded conservative interest groups that launch sophisticated national campaigns to remove from public schools practices and materials that they believe reflect secular humanism or New Age beliefs. According to a book titled *School Wars: Resolving Our Conflicts over Religion and Values*, educational reform initiatives targeted by activist parents have included "outcome-based education, the whole language approach [to teaching reading], thinking skills programs, imagery techniques, self-esteem programs, the teaching of evolution, global education and multiculturalism, and sex education" (Gaddy, Hall, and Marzano 1996, 93).

What Powers and Influence Do States Have in Governing Schools?

States have the legal authority to create and to manage school systems. Above the level of local control, states have a great influence on the governance of schools. Since the 1990s, the influence of the state on educational policy has increased steadily. For example, every state (except Iowa) has statewide academic standards, and every state has mandated a standardized test to assess students' mastery of academic standards. Currently, seventeen states require students to pass exit or end-of-course exams to receive a high school diploma, and seven more plan to do so in the future (Olson 2002). In addition, more than twenty states give state boards of education the authority to intervene in academically "bankrupt" schools whose students score too low as a group.

In response to criticisms of U.S. education, many of which pointed to the nation's frequent low ranking in international comparisons of achievement, many states launched extensive initiatives to improve education, such as the following:

- Increased academic standards
- Greater accountability for teachers
- Frequent assessments of students' mastery of basic skills

Political Foundations for Becoming a Teacher

Technology in Teaching

Can the Internet enhance school-home communication and parental involvement?

The following table shows that most teachers and members of the public believe that traditional forms of communication such as newsletters and open houses are much more effective than Internet chat rooms. Why do you think the Internet is not seen as more effective for school-home communica-tion? Do parents who have the ability to communicate with schools and teachers via the Internet have an unfair advantage over parents who do not have access to the Internet? What suggestions do you have for how schools might use the Internet more effectively to increase parental involvement?

Here are some ways in which public schools try to open lines of communication with citizens. In your opinion, how effective do you think each of the following would be?

	Very and Somewhat Effective		Very Effective	Somewhat Effective	Not Very Effective	Not at All Effective
	Teachers %	Public %	Teachers %	Teachers %	Teachers %	Teachers %
Public school newsletters	84	87 (2)	33	51	14	2
Public school open houses	81	89 (1)	35	46	15	3
Public school news hotlines	71	77 (5)	21	50	25	3
Neighborhood discussion groups	66	81 (4)	19	47	28	6
Open hearings	62	85 (3)	16	46	32	6
Televised school board meetings	60	74 (6)	16	45	33	7
Internet "chat rooms" set up by your local school	55	63 (7)	13	42	34	11

Numbers in parentheses indicate where the item ranks with the public. Not all rows add to 100% because of rounding.

Source: Carol A. Langdon, "The Fifth Phi Delta Kappa Poll of Teachers' Attitudes Toward the Public Schools," *Phi Delta Kappan*, April 1999, p. 618.

- Professional development as a criterion for continued employment of teachers
- Recertification of experienced teachers

As mentioned previously, the Tenth Amendment to the Constitution allows the states to organize and to administer education within their boundaries. To meet the responsibility of maintaining and supporting schools, the states have assumed several powers:

- The power to levy taxes for the support of schools and to determine state aid to local school districts
- The power to set the curriculum and, in some states, to identify approved textbooks
- The power to determine minimum standards for teacher certification
- The power to establish standards for accrediting schools
- The power to pass legislation necessary for the proper maintenance and support of schools

To carry out the tasks implied by these powers, the states have adopted a number of different organizational structures. Most states, however, have adopted a hierarchical structure similar to that presented in Figure 2.1.

The Role of State Government in Education

Various people and agencies within each state government play a role in operating the educational system within that state. Though state governments differ in many respects, the state legislature, the state courts, and the governor have a direct, critical impact on education in their state.

The State Legislature   In nearly every state, the legislature is responsible for establishing and maintaining public schools and for determining basic educational policies within the state. To accomplish these ends, the legislature has the power to enact laws related to education. Among the policies that the state legislature may determine are the following:

- How the state boards of education will be selected and what their responsibilities will be
- How the chief state school officer will be selected and what his or her duties will be
- How the state department of education will function
- How the state will be divided into local and regional districts
- How higher education will be organized and financed
- How local school boards will be selected and what their powers will be

In addition, the legislature may determine how taxes will be used to support schools, what will or will not be taught, the length of the school day and school year, how many years of compulsory education will be required, and whether or

Figure 2.1   Organizational structure of a typical state school system.

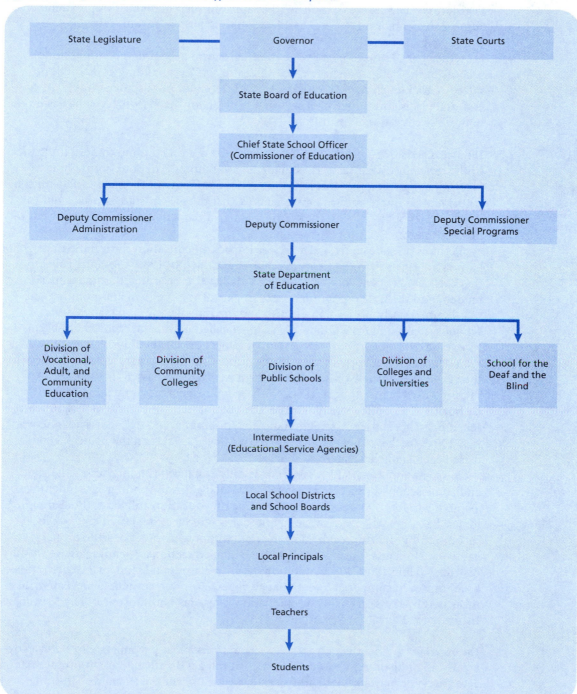

not the state will have community colleges and/or vocational/technical schools. Legislatures may also make policies that apply to such matters as pupil attendance, admission, promotion, teacher certification, teacher tenure and retirement, and collective bargaining.

Other policies developed by the state legislature may also apply to nonpublic schools in the state—policies related to health services, building construction, safety, school lunch services, textbooks, and testing of pupils, for example. In general, state legislatures may pass laws that provide for the reasonable supervision of nonpublic educational institutions.

The State Courts   From time to time, state courts are called on to uphold the power of the legislature to develop laws that apply to schools. The state courts must determine, however, that this power does not conflict with the state or federal constitution. It is important to remember, too, that the role of state courts is not to develop laws but to rule on the reasonableness of laws that apply to specific educational situations.

Perhaps no state court had a greater impact on education during the first half of the 1990s than the Kentucky Supreme Court. In 1989, the court ruled that the state's entire school system was "inadequate." Naming the state superintendent and the state education agency as part of the problem and pointing out that Kentucky schools were ineffective and inequitable, the court labeled the school system "unconstitutional." The court called on the governor and the legislature to develop an entirely new system of education for the state. A twenty-two-member task force, appointed by the governor and the legislature, then developed the 906-page **Kentucky Education Reform Act (KERA)** passed in 1990. KERA required each school to form a school-based management council by 1996 with authority to set policy in eight areas: curriculum, staff time, student assignment, schedule, school space, instructional issues, discipline, and extracurricular activities. Three teachers, two parents (elected by their peers), and the principal comprised each council.

Since its adoption, KERA has dramatically equalized funding across the state, and some school districts have made substantial gains in funding for students. Though variations among district spending on education still exist, these are no longer based on "the traditional determinants of educational financing . . . local income and property wealth. Now districts with low incomes or little property value per student are just as likely to have high educational spending as are wealthy districts" (Hoyt 1999, 36). In addition, teacher salaries and student-teacher ratios have improved compared to national averages. However, student achievement, as measured by test score gains or graduation rates, has not improved (The Kentucky Institute for Education Research 2001).

The Governor   While the powers of governors vary greatly from state to state, a governor can, if he or she chooses, have a great impact on education within the state. The governor may appoint and/or remove educators at the state level. In some states the governor may even appoint the chief state school officer. Furthermore, in every state except North Carolina, the governor may use his or her veto power to influence the legislature to pass certain laws related to education.

Governors are also extremely influential because they make educational budget recommendations to legislatures. In many states, they may also elect to use any accumulated balances in the state treasury for education. Governors can also significantly influence curriculum and instruction within the state and, indeed, across the nation. For example, Roy Romer, former governor of Colorado, was instrumental in organizing ACHIEVE, an effort by U.S. governors and corporate leaders to raise academic standards and to develop accountability systems for schools. In addition, the **National Governors' Association (NGA)** is active in teacher education and school reforms.

State Board of Education

The **state board of education**, acting under the authority of the state legislature, is the highest educational agency in a state. Every state, with the exception of Wisconsin, has a state board of education. Most states have two separate boards, one

Education is often at the center of the issues during election campaigns. Why is education such an important focal point for candidates and communities alike?

responsible for elementary through secondary education and the other for higher education.

The method of determining board members varies from state to state. In some states, the governor appoints members of the state board; in other states, members are selected through general elections. Two states have *ex officio* members who, by virtue of the positions they hold, automatically serve on the board. Most states have either seven- or nine-member boards.

People disagree on which is better: electing or appointing board members. Some believe that election to the state board may cause members to be more concerned with politics than with education. Others argue that elected board members are more aware of the wishes of the public whom the schools are supposed to serve. People in favor of appointing members to the state board suggest that appointment increases the likelihood that individuals will be chosen on the basis of merit rather than politics.

The regulatory and advisory functions generally held by state boards are as follows:

- Ensuring that local school districts adhere to legislation concerning educational policies, rules, and regulations
- Setting standards for issuing and revoking teaching and administrative certificates
- Establishing standards for accrediting schools
- Managing state monies appropriated for education
- Developing and implementing a system for collecting educational data needed for reporting and program evaluation
- Advising the governor and/or the state legislature on educational issues
- Identifying both short- and long-range educational needs in the state and developing plans to meet those needs
- Hearing all disputes arising from the implementation of its educational policies

In addition, a few state boards of education have instituted a statewide textbook adoption system. In the adoption system, boards choose a small number of titles for each subject area and grade level for all the state's schools. Individual schools and teachers then select their textbooks from this list.

North Carolina, for example, has created a 23-member Textbook Commission made up of teachers, principals, parents, and a local superintendent. The governor appoints members to serve four-year terms. Textbooks are evaluated using criteria based on the North Carolina Standard Course of Study. Adopted textbooks are placed on the statewide textbook list for five years.

Textbook adoptions have had a significant effect on the content of textbooks. Publishers have been responsive to the recommendations of textbook adoption states because of the attraction of statewide sales.

State Department of Education

The educational program of each state is implemented by the state's department of education, under the leadership of the chief state school officer. State departments of education have a broad set of responsibilities, and they affect literally every school, school district, and teacher education program in a state. In general, the state board of education is concerned with policymaking, the **state department of education** with the day-to-day implementation of those policies.

A great boost for the development of state departments of education came with the federal government's Elementary and Secondary Education Act of 1965. This act and its subsequent amendments required that local applications for federal funds to be used for innovative programs and for the education of disadvantaged, disabled, bilingual, and migrant students first receive approval from state departments of education.

Today, the responsibilities of state departments of education include the following:

- Certifying teachers
- Distributing state and federal funds to school districts
- Reporting to the public the condition of education within the state
- Ensuring that school districts adhere to state and federal guidelines
- Accrediting schools
- Monitoring student transportation and safety
- Sponsoring research and evaluation projects to improve education within the state

Perhaps the most significant index of the steady increase in state control since the 1980s is the fact that the states now supply the majority of funding for schools. Clearly, the power and influence of state departments of education will continue to be extensive.

Chief State School Officer

The **chief state school officer** (known as the commissioner of education or super-intendent of public instruction in many states) is the chief administrator of the state department of education and the head of the state board of education. In twenty-five states, the state board of education appoints the chief state school officer; in fifteen, the office is filled through a general election; and in the remaining ten, the governor appoints an individual to that position (personal communication, Council of Chief State School Officers June 7, 1999).

It is generally acknowledged that states with chief state school officers appointed by the board of education are more likely to attract individuals to that position who have the professional background and expertise necessary to provide effective leadership. In states where the office is filled through elections, the likelihood is increased that political connections, not professional qualifications, will determine who occupies the office.

While the responsibilities of chief state school officers vary from state to state, most hold several responsibilities in common:

- Serving as chief administrator of the state department of education and state board of education
- Selecting state department of education personnel
- Recommending educational policies and budgets to the state board
- Interpreting state school laws and state board of education policies
- Ensuring compliance with state school laws and policies
- Mediating controversies involving the operation of schools within the state
- Arranging for studies, committees, and task forces to address educational problems and recommend solutions
- Reporting on the status of education to the governor, legislature, state board, and public

As the preceding responsibilities indicate, the chief state school officer is a very influential person. He or she is frequently called upon to tell the governor, the legislature, the state board of education, and the people of the state what should be done to improve education.

How Do Regional Education Agencies Assist Schools?

When you think about how schools are governed and the political pressures applied to them, you probably think of influences from three levels: local, state, and federal. There is, however, an additional source of influence—the regional, or intermediate, unit.

The intermediate unit of educational administration, or the **Regional Educational Service Agency** (**RESA**), is the least understood branch of the state public school system. Through the intermediate unit, local school districts can receive supportive services that, economically and logistically, they could not provide for themselves.

Today, about half of the states have some form of intermediate or regional unit. The average unit is made up of twenty to thirty local school districts and covers a fifty-square-mile area. The intermediate or regional unit has many different names: educational service district (in Washington), county education office (in California), education service center (in Texas), intermediate school district (in Michigan), multicounty educational service unit (in Nebraska), and board of cooperative educational services (in New York).

The primary role of the intermediate unit is to provide assistance directly to districts in the areas of staff development, curriculum development, instructional media, and program evaluation. Intermediate or regional units also help school districts with their school improvement efforts by providing help in targeted areas such as bilingual education, vocational education, educational technology, and the education of gifted students and students with disabilities. Although intermediate units do monitor local school districts to see that they follow state educational guidelines, local districts, in fact, exert great influence over RESAs by identifying district-level needs that can be met by the intermediate unit.

How Does the Federal Government Influence Education?

Since the birth of the United States, the federal government has played a major role in shaping the character of schools. This branch of government has always recognized that the strength and well-being of the country are directly related to the quality of its schools. The importance of a quality education, for example, has been highlighted by many U.S. Supreme Court rulings supporting the free speech rights of teachers and students under the First Amendment and the right of all citizens to equal educational opportunity under the Fourteenth Amendment. While the future is impossible to predict, it is clear that the nation will face unprecedented levels of both global competition and the need for greater international cooperation. A rapidly changing, increasingly complex society will require a better-educated workforce to compete and to cooperate successfully.

Federal Initiatives

The federal government has taken aggressive initiatives to influence education at several points in U.S. history. For example, after Russia launched the world's first satellite in 1957, the federal government allocated federal money to improve science, mathematics, and foreign language education. During World War II, the federal government funded several new educational programs. One of these, the Lanham Act (1941), provided funding for (1) the training of workers in war plants by U.S. Office of Education personnel, (2) the construction of schools in areas where military personnel and workers on federal projects resided, and (3) the provision of child care for the children of working parents.

Another influential and extensive federal program in support of education was the Servicemen's Readjustment Act, popularly known as the **G.I. Bill of Rights**. Signed into law by President Franklin D. Roosevelt in 1944, the G.I. Bill has provided millions of veterans with payments for tuition and room and board at colleges and universities and at technical schools. Similar legislation was later passed to grant educational benefits to veterans of the Korean and Vietnam conflicts. Not only did the G.I. Bill stimulate the growth of colleges and universities in the United States, but it also opened higher education to an older and nontraditional student population.

The executive, legislative, and judicial branches of the federal government influence education in four ways:

1. *Exert moral suasion*—develop a vision and promote educational goals for the nation; for example, to honor public and private K–12 schools that are either academically superior in their states or that demonstrate dramatic gains in student

achievement, Rod Paige, former secretary of education under President George W. Bush, launched the No Child Left Behind—Blue Ribbon Schools Program (U.S. Department of Education 2002b).

2. *Provide categorical aid*—assist school systems with funding if they adopt federally endorsed programs, methods, or curricula

3. *Regulate*—withhold federal funds if a school system fails to follow legal statutes related to equal educational opportunity

4. *Fund educational research*—identify and then fund research projects related to federal goals for education

The federal government also disseminates research results and descriptions of exemplary educational programs. In addition, various branches of the federal government operate educational programs—for example, Department of Defense schools for children of military personnel, Bureau of Indian Affairs schools on reservations, and educational programs for the Department of Labor's Job Corps. Perhaps the federal government's most important role is to ensure, often through the intervention of the federal courts, that all students receive the equal educational opportunity guaranteed by the U.S. Constitution and federal laws.

The Impact of Presidential Policies

Presidential platforms on education often have a profound effect on education. Ronald Reagan's two terms of office (1980–88) and the first President Bush's term

How do federal education initiatives influence schools at the local level? How do these initiatives help reduce inequalities among schools?

(1988–92), for example, saw a significant shift in the federal government's role in education. In general, these two administrations sought to scale back what some viewed as excessive federal involvement in education. During Bill Clinton's two terms of office (1992–2000), the federal government assumed a more active role in ensuring equal educational opportunity. As President George W. Bush stated prior to his election to a second term in 2004, his educational platform would reflect a strong emphasis on standards and accountability:

> We are asking states and schools to set higher standards so that we can make sure that every student is learning. NCLB (No Child Left Behind) requires states to develop accountability plans to ensure that all students become proficient in reading and math and that achievement gaps between students of different socioeconomic backgrounds are closed.
>
> . . . Poor performance will no longer be hidden. Results will no longer be kept from parents. We will continue to work with schools that are performing poorly. Assessment results will be used to guide decisions, target resources, and reward success (Bush 2004, 119).

Advice to the President　One indicator of how a president can influence education is reflected in *Letters to the Next President: What We Can Do about the Real Crisis in Public Education* (Glickman 2004), a book that appeared just prior to the 2004 presidential election. The editor introduces the set of more than thirty-five letters from students, accomplished teachers, principals, parents, education scholars, and policymakers by making the following comments to the next president:

> MR. OR MS. NEXT PRESIDENT, read these letters while waking up in the morning, riding planes during the day to your next campaign stop, and in the quiet moments. Be thoughtful, be pragmatic, but please stand up and be articulate and committed to what must be an important part of your agenda—an education for each of our children that equips them to sit as equals at the table of American democracy (Glickman 2004, 6).

In the prologue he wrote for the same book, entertainer Bill Cosby, who received his doctorate in education from the University of Massachusetts, was more frank:

> I'm assuming that the President of the United States probably never went to a poor and neglected public school—where books have missing pages, walls have peeling paint, children have nothing to draw or write with, and where there is no library for reading a story or doing homework. These are the junkiest rooms: the poorest public schools where every year there are more cutbacks; where there's less money all the time.
>
> This time, on top of the mess is a new mess—a slew of new directives stretching budgets for more tests, more requirements, more unfunded programs—creating even more gaps in the education given to our wealthiest kids compared to our poorest kids.
>
> Wealthy people drive by the junky school and comfort themselves that money is not the issue. But nothing that is dear to America was ever maintained without it, from our nation's security to our communications systems, from our airlines to our highways. Believe this: the poor performance of schools and the lack of achievement

among many of our students is indeed about money. We need money to secure great teachers, money to update teaching methods, money for technology and supplies, and money for time. Time is a precious commodity and teachers need it to meet and plan with students, parents, principals, and citizens about how to take back their schools so that they can teach and kids can learn.

. . . We can sweep up all of this mess and get back to what education comes down to: caring, intelligent, trustworthy, and knowledgeable adults who will ensure that every student can learn (Cosby 2004, xii–xiii).

U.S. Department of Education

In 1979 President Carter signed a law creating the Department of Education. This new cabinet-level department assumed the responsibilities of the U.S. Office of Education, which had been formed in 1953 as a branch of the Department of Health, Education, and Welfare. Shirley Hufstedler, a state supreme court judge, became the first secretary of education when the new department opened in mid-1980. In 1983 President Reagan suggested that the Department of Education be dismantled and replaced with a Foundation for Education Assistance. However, public response to the reform report *A Nation at Risk* convinced the president that education was too important an issue not to be represented at the cabinet level.

A proposal to eliminate the Department of Education was soundly defeated at the 1984 Republican National Convention. So solid was the rejection of the proposal to eliminate the department that former secretary of education Terrel H. Bell was moved to comment that "dissolution of the department will not, in my opinion, ever again be a serious issue. . . . The Education Department is here to stay" (Bell 1986, 492). Today, the Department of Education employs about 5,000 people, with about one-third of them working at ten regional offices. Figure 2.2 shows the current organizational structure for the U.S. Department of Education.

In addition to supporting educational research, disseminating the results of research, and administering federal grants, the **U.S. Department of Education** advises the president on setting a platform for his educational agenda. For example, former U.S. Secretary of Education Rod Paige released a five-year strategic plan for the Department of Education, setting six goals for the agency and for the nation:

1. *Create a culture of achievement*—create a culture of achievement throughout the nation's education system by effectively implementing the new law, the No Child Left Behind Act of 2001, and by basing all federal education programs on its principles: accountability, flexibility, expanded parental options, and doing what works.
2. *Improve student achievement*—improve student achievement for all groups of students by putting reading first, expanding high-quality mathematics and science teaching, reforming high schools, and boosting teacher and principal quality, thereby closing the achievement gap.
3. *Develop safe schools and strong character*—establish disciplined and drug-free education environments that foster the development of good character and citizenship.
4. *Transform education into an evidence-based field*—strengthen the quality of education research.
5. *Enhance the quality of and access to postsecondary and adult education*—increase opportunities for students and the effectiveness of institutions.

Figure 2.2   Organizational chart: U.S. Department of Education.

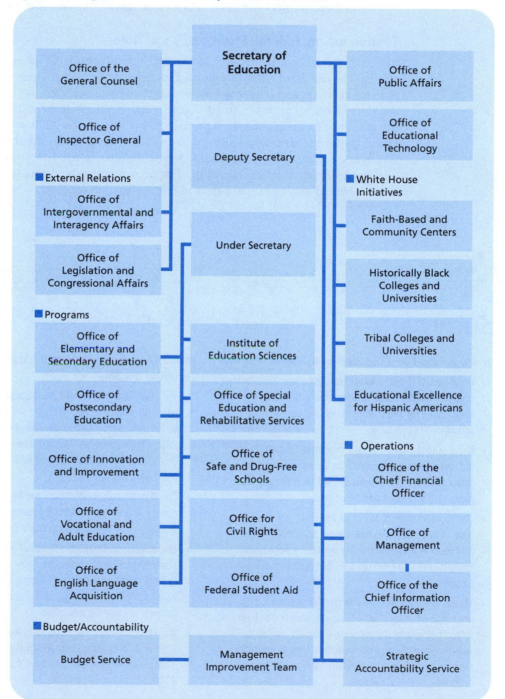

6. *Establish management excellence*—create a culture of accountability throughout the Department of Education (U.S. Department of Education 2002a).

Tension among Federal, State, and Local Roles

At times, the roles of the federal, state, and local governments in education are in conflict. As the trend continues toward increased state control over educational policies, teachers and students may be increasingly affected by partisan politics at the state level. For example, in 1996, legislators in one state were unable to override the governor's veto of the state's participation in the Goals 2000 program. The governor, claiming that Goals 2000 would give the federal government too much control over education in the state, said, "Our children's future is more important than a few pennies per child in federal funding accompanied by dictates. Now is no time to turn control of our reforms over to federal bureaucrats and politicians" (*Education Week* 1996, 14).

Summary

How Does the Local Community Influence Schools?

- Local school districts, which vary greatly in size, locale, organizational structure, demographics, and wealth, are responsible for the management and operation of schools.

- Local school boards, whose members are usually elected, set educational policies for a district; however, many people believe that boards should be reformed to be more well informed and responsive.

- The superintendent, the chief administrator of a local district, has a complex array of responsibilities and must work cooperatively with the school board and others in an environment that is often politically turbulent.

- Through groups like the PTA or PTO, some parents are involved in local school activities and reform efforts; others are involved with private schools; and some actively promote alternative approaches to education such as school choice, voucher systems, and home schooling.

What Powers and Influence Do States Have in Governing Schools?

- The state legislature, state courts, and the governor significantly influence education by setting policies related to the management and operation of schools within a state; many states have even passed legislation allowing them to take over academically failing school districts or individual schools.

- The state board of education, the highest educational agency in a state, regulates education and advises the governor and others on important educational policies.

- The state department of education implements policies related to teacher certification, allocation of state and federal funds, enforcement of state and federal guidelines, school accreditation, and research and evaluation projects to improve education.

- The chief state school officer oversees education within a state and, in collaboration with the governor, legislature, state board of education, and the public, provides leadership to improve education.

How Do Regional Education Agencies Assist Schools?

- The Regional Educational Service Agency (RESA), an intermediate unit of educational administration in about half of the states, provides assistance to two or more school districts for staff development, curriculum development, instructional media, and program evaluation.

How Does the Federal Government Influence Education?

- The federal government influences education at the state level through funding general and categorical programs, establishing and enforcing standards and regulations, conducting and disseminating educational research, providing technical assistance to improve education, and encouraging equity and excellence for the nation's schools.

- The national legislature, federal and Supreme courts, and the president significantly influence education by exerting moral suasion for the improvement of schools, providing categorical aid for federal programs, ensuring that school systems follow legal statutes, and funding educational research.

- The U.S. Department of Education supports and disseminates educational research, administers federal grants in education, and assists the president in developing and promoting a national agenda for education.

- At times, the roles of the federal, state, and local governments in education are in conflict.

Key Terms and Concepts

chief state school officer, 49
G.I. Bill of Rights, 51
Kentucky Education Reform Act (KERA), 46
local school districts, 34

National Governors' Association (NGA), 47
Regional Educational Service Agency (RESA), 50
school board, 36

state board of education, 47
state department of education, 49
superintendent, 38
U.S. Department of Education, 54

Reflective Application Activities

Discussion Questions

1. How can local educational politics enhance the effectiveness of schools and teachers? In what ways might local educational politics reduce the effectiveness of schools and teachers?

2. Imagine that you were able to arrange a 15-minute meeting with the chief state school officer in your state. What would you tell him or her about the concerns of prospective teachers?

Professional Journal

1. In the manner of Glickman's (2004) *Letters to the Next President* (see page 53), write a letter to the president of the United States describing a problem that might affect you as a professional educator. Make one or two key recommendations for actions the president might take to address that problem.

2. Describe some examples of how politicians are currently using schools to promote their interests within your

state. Which actions do you support? Which do you oppose?

Online Assignments

1. Use the Internet and the World Wide Web to gather information about the structure of education in your state. How many districts are in your state? Which is the largest? What are enrollment figures, trends, and projections for your state? What are the figures for household income and poverty rate? Begin your data search at the U.S. Department of Education's National Center for Education Statistics (NCES) where you will find NCES data from the *Digest of Education Statistics*, the *Condition of Education*, and *Projections of Education Statistics*.

2. Examine the website for your state's department of education. Based on your examination, are there politically "hot" issues in your state—for example, governance of schools, funding for schools, teacher accountability, or mandated testing of student achievement?

Observations and Interviews

1. Interview a teacher in a school about his or her perceptions of federal influences on education. Ask the teacher to select one influence and describe how it currently affects the school in which the teacher works.

2. Attend a meeting of the local school board and observe the communication and decision-making processes at that meeting. Note the following: topics on the agenda, who set the agenda, who participates in the discussion, how participation varies according to topic, who proposes policy, and the extent of agreement between superintendent and board. Note also the harmony or lack of harmony among board members. Finally, do you see evidence of single-issue interests?

Professional Portfolio

Prepare a profile of a school district. The district may be in your hometown, your college or university community, or a community in which you would like to teach. Information on the district may be obtained from your university library, public library, school district office, state board of education, or professional teacher associations.

Appendix 2.1

Typical Organizational Structure for a Medium-Size School District (20,000 Pupils)

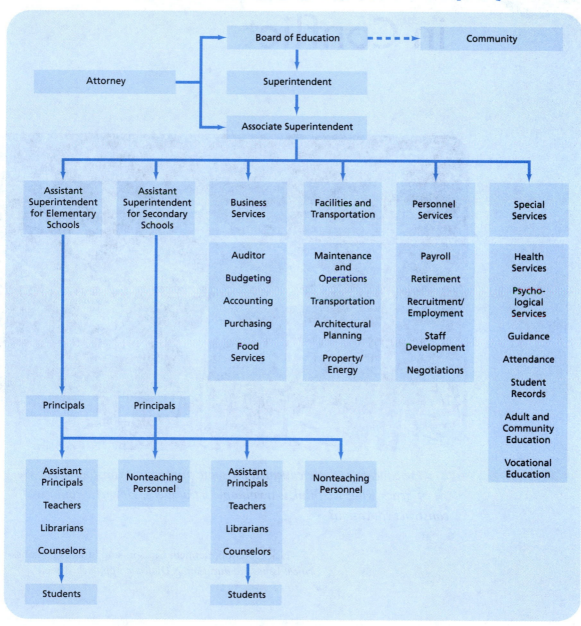

3 Educational Philosophies in Conflict

We educate and are educated for some purpose we consider good. We teach what we think is a valuable set of ideas. How else could we construct education?

—Jack L. Nelson, Kenneth Carlson, and Stuart B. Palonsky
Critical Issues in Education: A Dialectic Approach, 4th ed., 2000

Among the city's four high schools, Eastside High School has ranked highest on the annual standardized test of basic skills for the last three years. Eastside is in a middle-income area of the city and has an enrollment of about two thousand students.

Roberta Smith has been teaching English at Eastside for eight years. Roberta takes what she calls a critical approach to teaching—that is, she wants her students to question the status quo. She wants them to learn the important role they can play in improving the world.

To raise her students' level of awareness, Roberta has them think about how race, socioeconomic status, and gender are reflected in political events and in societal inequities. For example, after the outcome of the 2000 presidential election was finally determined, she spent several class sessions explaining to students how she believed the results "marginalized" African American voters in the state of Florida.

From time to time, Roberta also organizes her students to take action to address social problems. Last week, as part of a unit on the homeless in the city, her students spent a weekend helping at a neighborhood soup kitchen.

In the classroom, Roberta uses creative, occasionally risk-taking strategies. Students often participate in small group projects, simulations, role-plays, and classroom debates on societal issues.

Many of Roberta's colleagues are skeptical about her methods. They believe her teaching is "too political" and that she does her students a disservice by making them believe that they can change the world. These teachers also point out that Eastside parents want their children to learn the traditional basics rather than learn how to become social activists.

Today in the teachers' lunchroom, Roberta and two other English teachers are discussing how they teach writing. "My kids really got involved in the unit on the homeless," Roberta says. "Now they're working hard to express in writing what they experienced last week at the soup kitchen. They believe they have something to say. Two of my kids even plan to send their papers to the editorial page of the newspaper."

"I think assignments like that are pretty unrealistic," says the teacher seated across the table from Roberta. "That's not what our kids need to be doing—firing off letters to the editor, getting involved in all of these causes. We should just be teaching them how to write—period. Then if they want to focus on eliminating poverty, crime, or whatever, that should be their decision."

Do you agree or disagree with Roberta's approach to teaching? What do you think the purposes of education ought to be?

Guiding Questions

1. Why do you need to understand educational philosophy?
2. What is the nature of philosophy?
3. What determines your educational philosophy?
4. What are the branches of philosophy?
5. What are five modern philosophical orientations to teaching?
6. What psychological orientations have influenced teaching philosophies?
7. How can you develop your educational philosophy?

As the above scenario suggests, teachers can have conflicting views regarding how to answer two key questions about teaching: What should be the purposes of education? What knowledge is of most worth? In fact, the current system of public and private education in the United States is a reflection of how educators throughout our nation's history have answered these two important questions.

Today's teachers, however, must answer these two questions under the close scrutiny of numerous groups that desire to influence U.S. education. (Recall Chapter 1's discussion of ten groups, illustrated in Figure 1.4 on page 14, competing to influence schools). Not surprisingly, these groups frequently have conflicting points of view about education, as well as "various motives for engaging public schools in combat" (Bracey 2004, xi). Indeed, as suggested in Chapter 1, it is no exaggeration to say that conflicting points of view about education can place today's teachers "in the line of fire." The purpose of this chapter, then, is to examine the philosophical beliefs that underlie various perspectives on education in the United States today.

Why Do You Need to Understand Educational Philosophy?

Today's schools reflect the philosophical foundations and the aspirations and values brought to this country by its founders and generations of settlers. Understanding the philosophical ideas that have shaped education in the United States is an important part of your education as a professional. This understanding will enable you "to think clearly about what [you] are doing, and to see what [you] are doing in the larger context of individual and social development" (Ozmon and Craver 2003, 2).

Still, you may wonder, what is the value of knowing about the philosophy of education? Will that knowledge help you become a better teacher? An understanding of the philosophy of education will enhance your professionalism in three important ways. First, knowledge of philosophy of education will help you understand the complex political forces that influence schools. When people act politically to influence schools, their actions reflect their educational philosophies. Second, knowledge of how philosophy has influenced our schools will help you evaluate more effectively current proposals for change. You will be in a better position to evaluate changes if you understand how schools have developed and how current proposals might relate to previous change efforts. Lastly, awareness of how philosophy has influenced teaching is a hallmark of professionalism in education.

This chapter presents basic philosophical concepts that will help you answer five important questions teachers must consider as they develop an educational philosophy:

1. What should the purposes of education be?
2. What is the nature of knowledge?
3. What values should students adopt?
4. What knowledge is of most worth?
5. How should learning be evaluated?

What Is the Nature of Philosophy?

Philosophy is concerned with identifying the basic truths about being, knowledge, and conduct. While the religions of the world arrive at these truths based on supernatural revelations, philosophers use their reasoning powers to search out answers to the fundamental questions of life. Philosophers use a careful, step-by-step, question-and-answer technique to extend their understanding of the world. Through very exacting use of language and techniques of linguistic and conceptual analysis, philosophers attempt to describe the world in which we live.

The word *philosophy* may be literally translated from the original Greek as "love of wisdom." In particular, a philosophy is a set of ideas formulated to comprehend the world. Among the world's great philosophers have been Socrates, Plato, Aristotle, St. Thomas Aquinas, René Descartes, John Locke, David Hume, Jean-Jacques Rousseau, Immanuel Kant, Georg Hegel, John Stuart Mill, Karl Marx, John Dewey, Jean-Paul Sartre, and Mortimer Adler. They devoted their lives to pondering the significant questions of life: What is truth? What is reality? What life is worth living?

Philosophy is important to schools. Most likely, the school at which you will begin teaching will have a statement of philosophy to guide the actions of teachers, administrators, students, and parents. A school's philosophy is actually a public statement of what a school values—a description of the educational goals it seeks to attain. So important is a school's philosophy that school accrediting agencies evaluate schools partially on the basis of whether they achieve the goals set forth in their statements of philosophy.

What Determines Your Educational Philosophy?

In simplest terms, your **educational philosophy** consists of what you believe about education—the set of principles that guides your professional action. In other words, "stating the nature, the purpose, and the means for education, and then translating these principles into policies to implement them, has been the business of educational philosophy for the greater part of its history" (Power 1996, 191).

Each teacher, whether he or she recognizes it, has a philosophy of education—a set of beliefs about how human beings learn and grow and what one should learn in order to live the good life. To clarify their beliefs in these important areas, teachers must make use of philosophy. In fact, "all serious discussion of educational problems, no matter how specific, soon leads to consideration of educational aims, and becomes a conversation about the good life, the nature of man, the varieties of experience. . . . These are the perennial themes of philosophical investigation" (Black 1956, 154).

Teachers differ regarding the amount of effort they devote to developing their personal philosophy or educational platform. Some believe that philosophical reflections have nothing to contribute to the actual act of teaching. (This stance, of course, is itself a philosophy of education.) Other teachers recognize that teaching, because it is concerned with *what ought to be*, is basically a philosophical activity and requires philosophical "habits of mind." As the great educational philosopher John Dewey put it, to be concerned with education is to be concerned with philosophy: "If we are willing to conceive education as the process of forming fundamental dispositions, intellectual and emotional, toward nature and fellow men, philosophy may even be defined as *the general theory of education*" (1916, 383). This chapter's Relevant Standards feature stresses the importance of developing a thoughtful educational philosophy.

Educational philosophy is also concerned with improving all aspects of teaching. By putting your educational philosophy into practice, you can discover the solutions to problems you may encounter in the classroom. Five purposes of educational philosophy illustrate how it can help you solve problems of practice:

1. Educational philosophy is committed to laying down a plan for what is considered to be the best education absolutely.
2. Educational philosophy undertakes to give directions with respect to the kind of education that is best in a certain political, social, and economic context.
3. Educational philosophy is preoccupied with correcting violations of educational principle and policy.
4. Educational philosophy centers attention on those issues in educational policy and practice that require resolution either by empirical research or rational reexamination.

Relevant Standards

Developing Philosophical "Habits of Mind"

As the following standards illustrate, accomplished teachers understand the importance of having a carefully thought-out educational philosophy to guide their decision making in the classroom.

- "[Teacher candidates] understand and are able to apply knowledge related to the . . . philosophical foundations of education." (National Council for Accreditation of Teacher Education [NCATE] 2002, 196).

- "[N]ot only are thoughtful teachers able to teach more efficiently and effectively, they are also models for the critical, analytic thinking that they strive to develop in our youth. Teachers who are themselves exemplars of careful reasoning–considering purposes, marshaling evidence and balancing outcomes–are more likely to communicate to students the value and manner of such reasoning." (National Board for Professional Teaching Standards [NBPTS] 2002, 17. Supporting statement for Proposition #4: "Teachers think systematically about their practice and learn from experience.")

- "The teacher values critical thinking and self-directed learning as habits of mind." (Interstate New Teacher Assessment and Support Consortium [INTASC] 1992, 31. Disposition statement for Principle #9: "The teacher is a reflective practitioner who continually evaluates the effects of his/her choices and actions on others (students, parents, and other professionals in the learning community) and who actively seeks out opportunities to grow professionally.")

- "Teacher makes a thoughtful and accurate assessment of a lesson's effectiveness and the extent to which it achieved its goals, citing many specific examples from the lesson and weighing the relative strength of each." (Praxis Series, distinguished level of performance for Domain 4: Professional Responsibilities, Component 4a: Reflecting on Teaching.) (From Danielson 1996, 107)

5. Educational philosophy conducts an inquiry into the whole of the educational enterprise with a view toward assessing, justifying, and reforming the body of experience essential to superior learning (Power 1982, 15–16).

Your behavior as a teacher is strongly connected to your personal beliefs about the world and to your beliefs about the following five dimensions of education: teaching, learning, students, knowledge, and what is worth knowing (see Figure 3.1). Regardless of what you believe about these five dimensions, you should be aware of the need to reflect continually on *what* you believe and *why* you believe it.

Beliefs about Teaching and Learning

One of the most important parts of your educational philosophy is how you view teaching and learning. In other words, what do you think is the teacher's primary role? Is the teacher a subject matter expert who efficiently and effectively imparts knowledge to students? Is the teacher a helpful adult who establishes caring relationships with students and nurtures their growth in needed areas? Or is the teacher a skilled technician who manages the learning of many students at once?

Figure 3.1   The influence of the teacher's educational beliefs on teaching behavior.

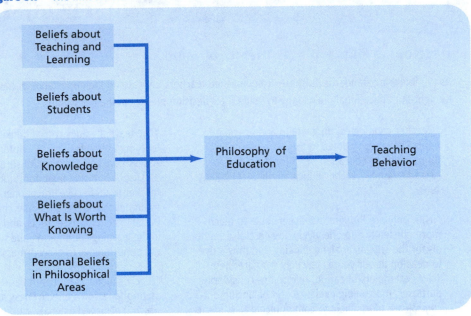

How we view the role of the teacher says a lot about our basic conception of teaching. Some people view teaching as a science—a complex activity that, nevertheless, can be reduced to a specific set of objectively measurable behaviors. For others, teaching is viewed as an art—a spontaneous, unrehearsed, and creative encounter between teacher and student. And for others, teaching is an activity that is both science and art; it requires the artistic (or intuitive) implementation of scientifically validated procedures.

Some teachers emphasize the individual student's experiences and cognitions. Others stress the student's behavior. Learning, according to the first viewpoint, is seen as changes in thought or action that result from personal experience. In other words, learning is largely the result of internal forces within the individual. In contrast, the other view defines learning as the associations between various stimuli and responses. Here, learning results from forces that are external to the individual.

Beliefs about Students

Your beliefs about students will have a great influence on how you teach. Each teacher formulates an image in his or her mind of what students are like—their dispositions, skills, motivation levels, and expectations. What you believe students are like is based on your unique life experiences, as well as your observations of young people and your knowledge of human growth and development.

This teacher is helping students connect with academic content. What beliefs about teaching and learning characterize this teacher?

Negative views of students often promote teacher–student relationships based on fear and coercion rather than on trust and helpfulness. Extremely positive views may risk not providing students with sufficient structure and direction and not communicating sufficiently high expectations. In the final analysis, the truly professional teacher—the teacher who has a carefully thought-out educational philosophy—understands that *all children can learn*, though they may differ in their predisposition to do so. To assess your beliefs about students, compare your beliefs with those of 1,273 elementary and secondary teachers who responded to the MetLife Survey of the American Teacher 2001 (see Figure 3.2).

Beliefs about Knowledge

How teachers view knowledge is directly related to how they go about teaching. If teachers view knowledge as the sum total of small bits of subject matter or discrete facts, their students will most likely spend a great deal of time learning that information in a straightforward, rote manner. For example, as students, we have all been directed to memorize certain information—the capitals of the fifty states, definitions for the eight parts of speech, the periodic table in chemistry, and so on.

Other teachers view knowledge more conceptually. They view knowledge as consisting of the "big ideas" that enable us to understand and to influence our environment. Such teachers might want students to be able to explain how legislative decisions are made in the state capital, how knowledge of the eight parts of

Figure 3.2 Teachers' expectations.

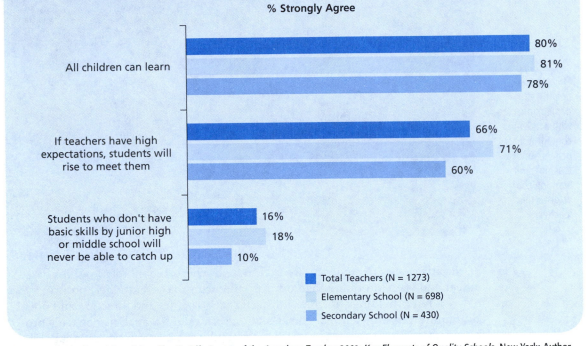

Question: *How much do you agree or disagree with the following?*

% Strongly Agree

All children can learn
- 80%
- 81%
- 78%

If teachers have high expectations, students will rise to meet them
- 66%
- 71%
- 60%

Students who don't have basic skills by junior high or middle school will never be able to catch up
- 16%
- 18%
- 10%

Total Teachers (N = 1273)
Elementary School (N = 698)
Secondary School (N = 430)

Source: Louis Harris and Associates, *The MetLife Survey of the American Teacher 2001: Key Elements of Quality Schools.* New York: Author, 2001, p.66. Used with permission.

speech can improve one's writing, or how chemical elements are grouped according to their atomic numbers.

Finally, teachers differ in their beliefs about whether students' increased understanding of their own experiences is a legitimate form of knowledge. Knowledge of self and one's experiences in the world is not the same as knowledge about a particular subject, yet personal knowledge is essential for a full, satisfying life. Teachers who primarily view knowledge as enabling students to understand their experiences in the world will provide them with learning activities that develop their abilities to acquire this understanding.

Beliefs about What Is Worth Knowing

Teachers have different ideas about what should be taught. One teacher might believe it is most important for students to learn the basic skills of reading, writing, and computation. Students will need these skills to be successful in their chosen occupations, and it is the school's responsibility to prepare students for the world of work.

Case for Reflection

What Knowledge Is of Most Worth?

As a first-year teacher, you are attending your school's open house held one evening during the early fall. From 7:30 to 8:30 P.M., teachers are required to stay in their classrooms and visit with parents as they drop by. Several parents have already visited your classroom and heard you explain your curriculum. Based on their comments and questions, they appear to be pleased with what their children are learning.

Near the end of the open house, the parents of one of your students enter the room. You greet them and then begin to explain the goals and objectives of your curriculum. They listen attentively. The father jots down a few notes on the cover of the open house program he received when he signed in at the office.

After a few minutes, you conclude your presentation by saying, "Overall, my curriculum has two primary goals: One is for students to go beyond the basics. I want them to know how to use the material they learn, how to solve problems. The second is for students to become self-actualized, to become all that they are capable of becoming. My biggest hope for students is that they see themselves as capable learners."

At this point, your student's mother says, "I'm not sure I agree. The purpose of the curriculum should be to learn the basics. We want our child to do well on the state's test of basic skills."

"Right," her husband says. "If kids don't do well on the test, they're less likely to continue their education. To focus on anything other than the basics is to emphasize needless frills. That may sound rather narrow, but that's what I believe."

Questions

1. How do you justify your educational philosophy to these parents?
2. Your view of the knowledge that is of most worth?

Another teacher might believe that the most worthwhile content is to be found in the classics or the Great Books. Knowledge of the "great ideas" from the sciences, mathematics, literature, and history best prepares students to deal with the world of the future.

A third teacher might be most concerned with developing the "whole child." This teacher wants students to become self-actualizing. To achieve this goal, the teacher designs curricula that are meaningful and contribute to students' efforts to become mature, well-integrated adults.

As Roberta and her colleagues illustrated in this chapter's opening scenario, there are no easy answers to the question "What knowledge is of most worth?" Your beliefs about teaching and learning, students, the nature of knowledge, and what knowledge is worth knowing, then, are the foundation of your educational philosophy.

What Are the Branches of Philosophy?

To provide you with additional knowledge to formulate and to clarify your educational philosophy, this section summarizes six areas of philosophy that are of central concern to teachers—metaphysics, epistemology, axiology, ethics, aesthetics, and logic. Each area focuses on one of the questions that have concerned the world's greatest philosophers for centuries: What is the nature of reality? What is the nature of knowledge, and is truth ever attainable? According to what values should one live? What is good and what is evil? What is the nature of beauty and excellence? What processes of reasoning will yield consistently valid results?

Metaphysics

Metaphysics is concerned with explaining, as rationally and as comprehensively as possible, the nature of reality (in contrast to how reality *appears*). What is reality? What is the world made of? These are metaphysical questions. Metaphysics also is concerned with the nature of being and explores questions such as: What does it mean to exist? What is humankind's place in the scheme of things? Metaphysical questions such as these are at the very heart of educational philosophy. As two educational philosophers put it: "Our ultimate preoccupation in educational theory is with the most primary of all philosophic problems: metaphysics, the study of ultimate reality" (Morris and Pai 1994, 28).

Metaphysics has important implications for education because the school curriculum is based on what we know about reality. And what we know about reality depends upon the kinds of questions we ask about the world. In fact, any position regarding what schools should teach has behind it a particular view of reality—a particular set of answers to metaphysical questions.

Epistemology

The next major set of philosophical questions that concerns teachers is called **epistemology**. These questions focus on knowledge: What knowledge is true? How does knowing take place? How do we know that we know? How do we decide between opposing views of knowledge? Is truth constant, or does it change from situation to situation? What knowledge is of most worth?

Your answers to the epistemological questions that confront all teachers will have significant implications for your teaching. First, you will need to determine what is true about the content you will teach. Then, you must decide on the most appropriate means of conveying this content to students. Even a casual consideration of epistemological questions reveals that there are many ways of knowing about the world. Five of these ways of knowing are of interest to teachers:

1. *Knowing based on authority*—for example, knowledge from the sage, the poet, the expert, the ruler, the textbook, or the teacher. In everyday conversations, people often refer to unnamed experts as sources of authoritative knowledge: "*They* say we'll have a manned flight to Mars by the middle of the century," for example.

2. *Knowing based on divine revelation*—for example, knowledge in the form of supernatural revelations from the sun god of early peoples, the many gods of the ancient Greeks, or the Judeo-Christian god. Throughout history, divine revelations have been a major source of knowledge about the world.

3. *Knowing based on empiricism (experience)*—for example, knowledge acquired through the senses, the informally gathered empirical data that direct most of our daily behavior. The term *empirical* refers to knowledge acquired through the senses. When we say that "experience is the best teacher," we refer to this mode of knowing.

4. *Knowing based on reason and logical analysis*—for example, knowledge inferred from the process of thinking logically. Much of our knowledge derives from our ability to reason and to use logical analysis. In schools, students learn to apply rational thought to solve mathematical problems, distinguish facts from opinions, or defend or refute a particular argument. Many students also learn a method of reasoning and analyzing empirical data known as the *scientific method*. Using this method, students identify a problem, gather relevant data, formulate a hypothesis based on the data, and empirically test the hypothesis.

5. *Knowing based on intuition*—for example, knowledge arrived at without the use of rational thought. Just about everyone has at some time acquired knowledge through intuition—a nondiscursive (beyond reason) way of knowing something. Intuition draws from our prior knowledge and experience and gives us an immediate understanding of the situation at hand. Our intuition convinces us that we know something, but we don't know *how* we came to have that knowledge. Our intuitive sense, it seems, is a mixture of instinct, emotion, and imagination.

Axiology

The next set of philosophical questions concerns values. Teachers are concerned with values because "school is not a neutral activity. The very idea of schooling expresses a set of values" (Nelson, Carlson, and Palonsky 2000, 304). Your decision to become a teacher reflects your values. Teachers teach toward purposes they consider to be good, and they teach what they think are good things.

Among the axiological questions teachers must answer are, What values should teachers encourage students to adopt? What values enable humanity to best express what it means to be human? What values does a truly educated person hold?

Axiology highlights the fact that teachers have an interest not only in the *quantity* of knowledge students acquire but also in the *quality* of life that becomes possible after they acquire that knowledge. Vast knowledge is of little use if an individual is unable to put that knowledge to good use. This point raises two additional questions: How do we define quality of life? What curricular experiences contribute most to that quality of life? All teachers must deal with the issues raised by these questions.

Ethics   While axiology addresses the question "What is valuable?", **ethics** focuses on "What is good and evil, right and wrong, just and unjust?"

Knowledge of ethics can help the teacher solve many of the dilemmas that arise in the classroom. Frequently, teachers must take action in situations in which they are unable to gather all of the relevant facts and in which no single course of action is totally right or wrong. Imagine, for example, that a student whose previous work was above average plagiarizes a term paper: Should the teacher fail the student for the course if the example of swift, decisive punishment will likely prevent other students from plagiarizing? Or should the teacher follow her hunches about what would be in the student's long-term interest and have the student redo the term paper, knowing that other students might get the mistaken notion that plagiarism has no negative consequences?

Consider another ethical dilemma. Is an elementary mathematics teacher justified in trying to increase achievement for the whole class by separating two disruptive girls and placing one in a mathematics group beneath her level of ability?

Ethics can provide teachers with ways of thinking about problems when it is difficult to determine the right course of action. This branch of philosophy also helps teachers to understand that "ethical thinking and decision making are not just following the rules" (Strike and Soltis 1985, 3).

The Teachers' Voices feature in this chapter illustrates how one teacher grappled with an ethical dilemma when he decided to give a student a grade of 50 for her final research paper because half of it was plagiarized. The research paper grade gave the student a six-weeks' grade of 69 (one point short of a passing grade of 70). The failing grade made the girl ineligible to compete in athletics. However, the teacher reflects on whether he has made the "right" decision, after meeting with the girl's upset parents and learning that the father has serious health problems. Unsure about how to solve his ethical dilemma, the teacher asks his principal and department head for advice.

Aesthetics   The branch of axiology known as **aesthetics** is concerned with values related to beauty and art. Naturally, we expect that teachers of music, art, drama, literature, and writing regularly require that students make judgments about the quality of works of art. However, we can easily overlook the role that aesthetics ought to play in *all* areas of the curriculum. Harry Broudy, a well-known educational philosopher, said that the arts are necessary, not "just nice" (1979, 347–350). Through developing their aesthetic perceptions, students can find increased meaning in all aspects of life.

Aesthetics can also help the teacher increase his or her effectiveness. Teaching, because it may be viewed as a form of artistic expression, can be judged according to artistic standards of beauty and quality. In this regard, the teacher is an artist whose medium of expression is the spontaneous, unrehearsed, and creative encounter between teacher and student.

Logic   If members of the public were to decide on a single goal for schools, it would most likely be to teach students how to think. Our extensive ability for vari-

Dollars and Points

Marcus Goodyear

After almost a week, I asked my principal for advice. What would he do? I asked my department head. Miraculously neither of them had ever become cynical, and so I trusted them. "Give her the point," they said. "It isn't worth it to hold the line. They'll drag you to the school board. They'll make you look like the villain. They'll examine every minor grade under a microscope. Just give her the point and let her have a 70."

On the grade change form I checked "teacher error." The student became eligible. She went on to the state competition that year. "What will you say to the people you beat?" I wanted to ask her. "What will you say to the students who had enough honor not to plagiarize their research papers?" But I swallowed my pride. I swallowed some of my moral self-righteousness. I even swallowed my anger at parents who will bully their way through teachers and administrators and anyone else standing between them and their entitlements. Because I hadn't known about her dad's health problems. If the girl had just told me that she thought her father might die, I would have given her extra time on the paper. I would have allowed more makeup work. I would have helped her. I should have helped her.

Part of me still felt like I was compromising academics for athletics. Part of me wanted to punish the student for the actions of her parents. But I learned an important lesson: Always err on the side of the student.

Because I do make mistakes, of course. I made a big mistake with that plagiarized paper—I assumed the worst of my student. I should have given the girl a chance to confess and rewrite the paper. Now I know to reward students for what they do well, rather than punish students for what they do poorly. Some students will need to face consequences for their mistakes, but that can never become my focus as a teacher. It would destroy me. It would make me shrivel up into bitterness and indignation that the students, the teachers, the whole educational system was just going to hell. Everyone makes mistakes in the classroom, even me. That is what the classroom is for.

And those mistakes will only make me worthless and vindictive if I remain proud and absolute. Like some one-room-schoolhouse tyrant. Or like the cynics down the hall.

During that conference [with the girl's parents] I also realized that no amount of points brings value to a student's education. Passing my class, passing the state achievement test, even passing the Advanced Placement test were all based on an economic view of the world. These things reduce human actions and feelings to a few numbers—either test scores or the price of a college class. These things work as external rewards, but the biggest rewards are always internal. In addition to points, I can give my students respect and trust and confidence and faith. They need to become adults; they need me to treat them like adults.

Why would I treat them any other way?

Above all I finally realized that I teach for the students. Not their parents. Not my peers. Not even for myself or the paycheck at the end of every month. I teach for my students to rise above their mistakes.

And the mistakes of their teachers.

Some of them will. I know it.

Questions

1. Based on his account of the plagiarism incident, how does Goodyear view the following elements of educational philosophy: Beliefs about teaching and learning? Beliefs about students? Beliefs about knowledge? Beliefs about what is worth knowing?
2. Why does Goodyear decide to change his student's grade? Do you agree or disagree with his decision?
3. What ethical dilemmas might you encounter when you begin to teach? How will you resolve those ethical dilemmas?

Marcus Goodyear teaches at O'Connor High School in San Antonio, Texas. The preceding is excerpted from his chapter that appeared in Molly Hoekstra's (ed.), *Am I Teaching Yet? Stories from the Teacher-Training Trenches* (Portsmouth, NH: Heinemann, 2002), pp. 70–75.

ous kinds of thinking is, after all, one of the major differences between us and other forms of animal life. **Logic** is the area of philosophy that deals with the process of reasoning and identifies rules that will enable the thinker to reach valid conclusions.

The two kinds of logical thinking processes that teachers most frequently have students learn are *deductive* and *inductive* thinking. The deductive approach requires the thinker to move from a general principle or proposition to a specific conclusion that is valid. On the other hand, inductive reasoning moves from the specific to the general. Here, the student begins by examining particular examples that eventually lead to the acceptance of a general proposition. Inductive teaching is often referred to as discovery teaching—by which students discover, or create, their own knowledge of a topic.

Socrates (ca. 470–399 B.C.)

Perhaps the best-known teacher to use the inductive approach to teaching was the Greek philosopher Socrates (ca. 470–399 B.C.). His method of teaching, known today as the Socratic method, consisted of holding philosophical conversations (dialectics) with his pupils. The legacy of Socrates lives in all teachers who use his questioning strategies to encourage students to think for themselves. Figure 3.3 presents guidelines for using **Socratic questioning** techniques in the classroom.

Figure 3.3 The spirit and principles of Socratic questioning.

The Spirit and Principles of Socratic Questioning

- Treat all thoughts as in need of development.
- Respond to all answers with a further question (that calls on the respondent to develop his or her thinking in a fuller and deeper way).
- Treat all assertions as a connecting point to further thoughts.
- Recognize that any thought can exist fully only in a network of connected thoughts. Stimulate students—by your questions—to pursue those connections.
- Seek to understand—where possible—the ultimate foundations for what is said or believed.
- Recognize that all questions presuppose prior questions and all thinking presupposes prior thinking. When raising questions, be open to the questions they presuppose.

Source: Richard Paul and Linda Elder, "The Art of Socratic Questioning," *Critical Thinking,* Fall 1995, 16.

What Are Five Modern Philosophical Orientations to Teaching?

Five major philosophical orientations to teaching have been developed based on the branches of philosophy we have just examined. These orientations, or schools of thought, are perennialism, essentialism, progressivism, existentialism, and social reconstructionism. The following sections present a brief description of each of these orientations, moving from those that are teacher-centered to those that are student-centered (see Figure 3.4). Each description concludes with a sample portrait of a teacher whose behavior illustrates that philosophical orientation in action.

Perennialism

Perennialism, as the term implies, views truth as constant, or perennial. The aim of education, according to perennialist thinking, is to ensure that students acquire knowledge of unchanging principles or "great ideas." Perennialists also believe that the natural world and human nature have remained basically unchanged over the centuries. Thus, the great ideas continue to have the most potential for solving the problems of any era. In addition, perennnialist philosophy emphasizes the rational thinking abilities of human beings; development of the intellect makes human beings truly human and differentiates them from other animals.

The curriculum, according to perennialists, should stress students' intellectual growth in the arts and sciences. To become "culturally literate," students should be exposed to the best, most significant works that humans have created in these areas. For any area of the curriculum, only one question needs to be asked: Are

Figure 3.4   Five philosophical orientations to teaching.

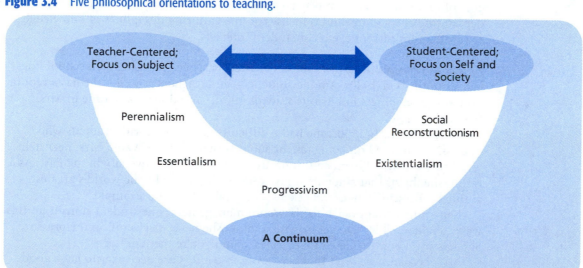

students acquiring content that represents the human race's most lofty accomplishments in that area? Thus, a high school English teacher would require students to read Melville's *Moby-Dick* or one of Shakespeare's plays rather than a novel on the current best-seller list. Similarly, science students would learn about the three laws of motion or the three laws of thermodynamics rather than build a model of the space shuttle.

Robert Maynard Hutchins (1899–1977)

Perennialist Educational Philosophers   Two of the best-known perennialist philosophers have been Robert Maynard Hutchins (1899–1977) and, more recently, Mortimer Adler. As president of the University of Chicago from 1929 to 1945, Hutchins (1963) developed an undergraduate curriculum based on the study of the Great Books and discussions of these classics in small seminars. Hutchins's perennialist curriculum was based on three assumptions about education:

1. Education must promote humankind's continuing search for truth. Whatever is true will always, and everywhere, be true. In short, truth is universal and timeless.

2. Because the mind's work is intellectual and focuses on ideas, education must also focus on ideas. The cultivation of human rationality is the essential purpose of education.

3. Education should stimulate students to think thoughtfully about significant ideas. Teachers should use correct and critical thinking as their primary method, and they should require the same of students.

Noted educational philosopher Mortimer Adler, along with Hutchins, was instrumental in organizing the Great Books of the Western World curriculum. The curriculum is based on more than one hundred enduring classics, from Plato to Einstein. Teachers can use the Great Books approach to achieve the perennialist goal of teaching students to become independent and critical thinkers. It is a demanding curriculum, and it focuses on the enduring disciplines of knowledge rather than on current events or student interests.

Portrait of a Perennialist Teacher   Mrs. Bernstein has been teaching high school English since the mid-1980s. Among students—and teachers as well—she has a reputation for demanding a lot. As one student put it, "You don't waste time in Mrs. Bernstein's class."

During the early 1990s, she had a difficult time dealing with students who aggressively insisted on being taught subjects that were "relevant." Mrs. Bernstein received a classical, liberal education from a prestigious university in the East. As a result, she insists that students study works of literature by the world's greatest authors—Beowulf, Chaucer, Dickens, and Shakespeare, for example.

Regarding her approach to classroom management, one student sums it up this way: "She doesn't let you get by with a thing; she never slacks off on the pressure. She lets you know that she's there to teach and you're there to learn."

Mrs. Bernstein believes that hard work and effort are necessary to get a good education. Accordingly, she gives students very few opportunities to misbehave, and she is immune to the grumblings of students who complain openly about the workload in her classes. She becomes very animated when she talks about the value of the classics for students who are preparing to live as adults in an increasingly complex, globally interdependent world:

> *The classics are unequaled in terms of the insights they can give students into the major problems they will confront during their lifetimes. Though our civilization has made impressive technological advances during the last two centuries, we have not really progressed that much in terms of improving the quality of our lives as human beings. The observations of a Shakespeare or a Dickens on the human condition are just as relevant today as they were when they were alive.*

Essentialism

William C.
Bagley
(1874–1946)

Essentialism has some similarities to perennialism. William C. Bagley (1874–1946), a professor of education at Teachers College, Columbia University, originally formulated essentialism as a criticism of progressive trends in schools. To promote the essentialist philosophy, Bagley founded the Essentialistic Education Society and the education journal, *School and Society*.

Bagley and other like-minded educators had become very critical of progressive educational practices, contending that the movement had diminished intellectual and moral standards among young people (Bagley 1934). Following World War II, criticism of progressive education became even more widespread and seemed to point to one conclusion: Schools were failing in their task of transmitting the country's social and intellectual heritage.

Essentialists believe that human culture has a core of common knowledge that schools are obligated to transmit to students in a systematic, disciplined way. Unlike perennialists, who emphasize a set of external truths, essentialists stress what they believe to be the essential knowledge and skills (often termed "the basics") that productive members of our society need to know. Several books have been written that lament the decline of rigorous schooling in the United States and call for an essentialist approach to schooling. Among them have been James D. Koerner's *The Case for Basic Education* (1959), H. G. Rickover's *Education and Freedom* (1959), and Paul Copperman's *The Literacy Hoax. The Decline of Reading, Writing, and Learning in the Public Schools and What We Can Do about It* (1978).

Like the teacher in this chapter's opening scenario who is critical of Roberta's emphasis on addressing social issues in the classroom, essentialist teachers believe that schooling should be practical and provide children with sound instruction that prepares them to live life. Schools should not try to influence or set social policies.

Critics of essentialism claim that such a tradition-bound orientation to schooling will indoctrinate students and rule out the possibility of change. Essentialists respond that, without an essentialist curriculum, students will be indoctrinated in humanistic or behavioral curricula that run counter to society's accepted standards and need for order.

The Back-to-Basics Movement   The **back-to-basics movement** that began in the mid-1970s and continues today is the most recent large-scale push to install essentialist programs in the schools. Above all else, the essentialists contend, the schools must train students to communicate clearly and logically. The core skills in the curriculum should be reading, writing, speaking, and computation, and the school has the responsibility for seeing that all students master these skills.

The essentialist curriculum emphasizes the teaching of facts. It has little patience with the indirect, introspective approaches promoted by progressivism. Some essentialists even view the arts and humanities as frills. They believe that the hard sciences and technical and vocational courses are the true essentials that students need to contribute to society.

Though the essentialist educator does not view the child as evil, neither does he or she view the child as naturally good. Unless children are actively and vigorously taught the value of discipline, hard work, and respect for authority, they will not become valuable members of society. The teacher's role, then, is to shape children, to hold their natural, nonproductive instincts (e.g., aggression, mindless gratification of the senses, etc.) in check until their education has been completed.

Portrait of an Essentialist Teacher   Mr. Chen teaches mathematics at a junior high school in a poor section of a major urban area. Prior to coming to this school six years ago, he taught at a rural elementary school.

Middle-aged and highly energetic, Mr. Chen is known around the school as a hardworking, dedicated teacher. His commitment to children is especially evident when he talks about preparing "his" children for life in high school and beyond. "A lot of teachers nowadays have given up on kids," he says with a touch of sadness to his voice. "They don't demand much of them. If we don't push kids now to get the knowledge and skills they're going to need later in life, we've failed them. My main purpose here is to see that my kids get the basics they're going to need."

Mr. Chen has made it known that he does not approve of the methods used by some of the younger, more humanistically oriented teachers in the school. At a recent faculty meeting, for example, he was openly critical of some teachers' tendency to let students do their own thing and spend time expressing their feelings. He called for all teachers to focus their energies on getting students to master subject matter content, "the things kids will need to know," rather than on helping students adjust to the interpersonal aspects of school life. He also reminded everyone that "kids come to school to learn." All students would learn, he pointed out, if "teachers based their methods on good, sound approaches that have always worked—not on the so-called innovative approaches that are based on fads and frills."

Mr. Chen's students have accepted his no-nonsense approach to teaching. With few exceptions, his classes are orderly, business-like operations. Each class period follows a standard routine. Students enter the room quietly and take their seats with a minimum of the foolishness and horseplay that mark the start of many other classes in the school. As the first order of business, the previous day's homework is returned and reviewed. Following this, Mr. Chen presents the day's lesson, usually a 15- to 20-minute explanation of how to solve a particular kind of math problem. His mini-lectures are lively, and his wide-ranging tone of voice and animated, spontaneous delivery convey his excitement about the material and his belief that students can learn. During large-group instruction, Mr. Chen also makes ample use of the blackboard, overhead transparencies, and various manipulatives such as a large abacus and colored blocks of different sizes and shapes.

Progressivism

Progressivism is based on the belief that education should be child-centered rather than focused on the teacher or the content area. The writing of John Dewey (1859–1952) in the 1920s and 1930s contributed a great deal to the spread of progressive ideas. Briefly, Deweyan progressivism is based on six central assumptions:

1. The content of the curriculum ought to be derived from students' interests rather than from the academic disciplines.

2. Effective teaching takes into account the whole child and his or her interests and needs in relation to cognitive, affective, and psychomotor areas.

3. Learning is essentially active rather than passive. Effective teachers provide students with experiences that enable them to learn by doing.

4. The aim of education is to teach students to think rationally so that they may become intelligent, contributing members of society.

5. At school, students learn personal, as well as social, values.

6. Humankind is in a constant state of change, and education makes possible a future that is better than the past.

The Technology in Teaching feature on page 80 in this chapter explains how you can use the Internet to learn more about progressive education and, more generally, enhance your study of and interest in the philosophy of education.

Progressive Strategies   The progressive philosophy also contends that knowledge that is true in the present may not be true in the future. Hence, the best way to prepare students for an unknown future is to equip them with problem-solving strategies that will enable them to discover meaningful knowledge at various stages of their lives.

Educators with a progressive orientation give students a considerable amount of freedom in determining their school experiences. Progressives believe that life is evolving in a positive direction and that human beings, young as well as adult, are good and may be trusted to act in their own best interests. Contrary to the perceptions of many, though, progressive education does not mean that teachers do not provide structure or that students are free to do whatever they wish. Progressive teachers begin where students are and, through the daily give-and-take of the classroom, lead students to see that the subject to be learned can enhance their lives.

In a progressively oriented classroom, the teacher serves as a guide or resource person whose primary responsibility is to facilitate student learning. The teacher

Technology in Teaching

How can the Internet enhance your study of and interest in the philosophy of education?

The Internet has increased dramatically the amount of information that is easily available to anyone with a computer. The Internet, in a manner perhaps more dramatic than the invention of the printing press in the middle of the fifteenth century, has brought limitless information and expertise to people around the globe.

However, you might wonder, is there any connection between the Internet and the philosophy of education? Can the Internet enhance your study of and interest in this area? Prior to the availability of the Internet, it may have been more difficult for a student to develop an interest in the philosophy of education and to see its relevance to becoming a teacher. Only the most diligent students had the time, energy, and interest to do library research in this area. Moreover, the outcomes of their research were limited to the size of the library collections they were using.

Today, however, the Internet makes available to you in a digitized form almost the entirety of human culture. This means that you can easily access more information that is more relevant to your interests, experiences, and professional goals. The Internet makes available to you not only vast information on the philosophy of education, but also an extensive collection of original primary sources. For example, you can learn more about progressive education by visiting the website for the Center for Dewey Studies maintained by Southern Illinois University. Established in 1961, the Center has a large collection of source materials about this leading U.S. philosopher-educator. The site includes an audio of Dewey reading from his work and links to the John Dewey Discussion Group on the Internet, the John Dewey Society, and the John Dewey Project on Progressive Education.

helps students learn what is important to them rather than passing on a set of so-called enduring truths. Progressive teachers provide students with learning experiences that replicate everyday life as much as possible. Students have many opportunities to work cooperatively in groups, often solving problems that the group, not the teacher, has identified as important.

Portrait of a Progressive Teacher   Mr. Barkan teaches social studies at a middle school in a well-to-do part of the city. Boyishly handsome and in his mid-thirties, Mr. Barkan usually works in casual attire—khaki pants, soft-soled shoes, and a sports shirt. He seems to get along well with students. Mr. Barkan likes to give students as much freedom of choice in the classroom as possible. Accordingly, his room is divided up into interest and activity centers, and much of the time students are free to choose where they want to spend their time. One corner at the back of the room has a library collection of paperback and hardcover books, an easy chair, and an area rug; the other back corner of the room is set up as a project area and has a worktable on which are several globes, maps, large sheets of newsprint, and assorted drawing materials. At the front of the room in one corner is a small media

How might you explain what is happening in this classroom from the perspective of progressivism? From the perspective of perennialism? From the perspective of essentialism?

center with three cassette tape recorders with headphones, a CD player, a television with VCR, and a computer.

Mr. Barkan makes it a point to establish warm, supportive relationships with his students. He is proud of the fact that he is a friend to his students. "I really like the kids I teach," he says in a soft, gentle voice. "They're basically good kids, and they really want to learn if we teachers, I mean, can just keep their curiosity alive and not try to force them to learn. It's up to us as teachers to capitalize on their interests."

The visitor to Mr. Barkan's class today can sense his obvious regard for students. He is genuinely concerned about the growth and nurturance of each one. As his students spend most of their time working in small groups at the various activity centers in the room, Mr. Barkan divides his time among the groups. He moves from group to group and seems to immerse himself as an equal participant in each group's task. One group, for example, has been working on making a papier-mâché globe. Several students are explaining animatedly to him how they plan to transfer the flat map of the world they have drawn to the smooth sphere they have fashioned out of the papier-mâché. Mr. Barkan listens carefully to what his students have to say and then congratulates the group on how cleverly they have engineered the project. When he speaks to his students, he does so in a matter-of-fact, conversational tone, as though speaking to other adults.

As much as possible, he likes to bring textbook knowledge to life by providing his students with appropriate experiences—field trips, small-group projects, simulation activities, role-playing, Internet explorations, and so on. Mr. Barkan believes that his primary function as a teacher is to prepare his students for an unknown future. Learning to solve problems at an early age is the best preparation for this future, he feels.

> *The increase in the amount of knowledge each decade is absolutely astounding. What we teach students as true today will most likely not be true tomorrow. Therefore, students have to learn how to learn and become active problem solvers. In addition, students need to learn how to identify problems that are meaningful to them. It doesn't make much sense to learn to solve problems that belong to someone else.*
>
> *To accomplish these things in the classroom, teachers have to be willing to take the lead from the students themselves—to use their lives as a point of departure for learning about the subject. What this requires of the teacher is that he or she be willing to set up the classroom along the lines of a democracy, a close community of learners whose major purpose for being there is to learn. You can't create that kind of classroom atmosphere by being a taskmaster and trying to force kids to learn. If you can trust them and let them set their own directions, they'll respond.*

Existentialism

Existential philosophy is unique in that it focuses on the experiences of the individual. Other philosophies are concerned with developing systems of thought for identifying and understanding what is common to *all* reality, human existence, and values. **Existentialism**, on the other hand, offers the individual a way of thinking about *his* life, what has meaning for *him*, what is true for *him*. In general, existentialism emphasizes creative choice, the subjectivity of human experiences, and concrete acts of human existence over any rational scheme for human nature or reality.

Jean-Paul
Sartre
(1905–1980)

The writings of Jean-Paul Sartre (1905–1980), well-known French philosopher, novelist, and playwright, have been most responsible for the widespread dissemination of existential ideas. According to Sartre (1972), every individual first exists and then he or she must decide what that existence is to mean. The task of assigning meaning to that existence is the individual's alone; no preformulated philosophical belief system can tell one who one is. It is up to each of us to decide who we are.

Two Existentialist Views   There are two schools of existential thought—one *theistic*, the other *atheistic*. Most of those belonging to the first school refer to themselves as Christian Existentialists and point out that humankind has a longing for an ultimate being, for God. Though this longing does not prove the existence of God, people can freely choose to live their lives as if there is a God (Morris and Pai 1994, 259–260). The Spanish philosopher Miguel de Unamuno expresses this position well: "Let life be lived in such a way, with such dedication to goodness and the highest values, that if, after all, it is annihilation which finally awaits us, that will be an injustice" (quoted in Morris and Pai 1994, 260).

Most existentialists, however, point out that it is demeaning to the human condition to say that we must entertain a fantasy in order to live a life of moral responsibility. Such a stance absolves humans of the responsibility for dealing with the complete freedom of choice that we all have. It also causes them to avoid the inescapable fact that "we are alone, with no excuses," and that "we are condemned to be free" (Sartre 1972, 101).

Life, according to existential thought, has no meaning, and the universe is indifferent to the situation humankind finds itself in. Moreover, "existentialists [believe] that too many people wrongly emphasize the optimistic, the good, and the beautiful—all of which create a false impression of existence" (Ozmon and Craver 2003, 253). With the freedom that we have, however, each of us must commit him- or herself to assign meaning to his or her *own* life. As Maxine Greene, who has been described as "the preeminent American philosopher of education today" (Ayers and Miller 1998, 4), states: "We have to know about our lives, clarify our situations if we are to understand the world from our shared standpoints" (1995b, 21). The human enterprise that can be most helpful in promoting this personal quest for meaning is the educative process. Teachers, therefore, must allow students freedom of choice and provide them with experiences that will help them find the meaning of their lives. This approach, contrary to the belief of many, does not mean that students may do whatever they please; logic indicates that freedom has rules, and respect for the freedom of others is essential.

Existentialists judge the curriculum according to whether it contributes to the individual's quest for meaning and results in a level of personal awareness that Greene (1995b) terms "wide-awakeness." As Greene (1995a, 149–150) suggests in the following, the ideal curriculum is one that provides students with extensive individual freedom and requires them to ask their own questions, conduct their own inquiries, and draw their own conclusions: "To feel oneself en route, to feel oneself in a place where there are always possibilities of clearings, of new openings, this is what we must communicate to the young if we want to awaken them to their situations and enable them to make sense of and to name their worlds."

Portrait of an Existentialist Teacher   Right after he first started teaching English eight years ago at a suburban high school, Richard Rodriguez began to have doubts about the value of what he was teaching students. Although he could see a limited, practical use for the knowledge and skills he was teaching, he felt he was doing little to help his students answer the most pressing questions of their lives. Also, Richard had to admit to himself that he had grown somewhat bored with following the narrow, unimaginative Board of Education curriculum guides.

During the next eight years, Richard gradually developed a style of teaching that placed emphasis on students finding out who they are. He continued to teach the knowledge and skills he was required to teach, but he made it clear that what students learned from him they should use to answer questions that were important to them. Now, for example, he often gives writing assignments that encourage students to look within in order to develop greater self-knowledge. He often uses assigned literature as a springboard for values clarification discussions. And, whenever possible, he gives his students the freedom to pursue individual reading and writing projects. His only requirement is that students be meaningfully involved in whatever they do.

Richard is also keenly aware of how the questions his students are just beginning to grapple with are questions that he is still, even in his mid-thirties, trying to answer for himself. Thoughtfully and with obvious care for selecting the correct words, he sums up the goals that he has for his students:

> I think kids should realize that the really important questions in life are beyond definitive answers, and they should be very suspicious of anyone—teacher, philosopher, or member of organized religion—who purports to have the answers. As human beings, each of us faces the central task of finding our own answers to such questions. My students know that I'm wrestling with the same questions they're working on. But I think I've taught them well enough so that they know that my answers can't be their answers.

Richard's approach to teaching is perhaps summed up by the bumper sticker on the sports car he drives: "Question authority." Unlike many of his fellow teachers, he wants his students to react critically and skeptically to what he teaches them. He also presses them to think thoughtfully and courageously about the meaning of life, beauty, love, and death. He judges his effectiveness by the extent to which students are able and willing to become more aware of the choices that are open to them.

Social Reconstructionism

As the name implies, **social reconstructionism** holds that schools should take the lead in changing or reconstructing society. Theodore Brameld (1904–1987), acknowledged as the founder of social reconstructionism, based his philosophy on two fundamental premises about the post–World War II era: (1) We live in a period of great crisis, most evident in the fact that humans now have the capability of destroying civilization overnight; and (2) humankind also has the intellectual, technological, and moral potential to create a world civilization of "abundance, health, and humane capacity" (Brameld 1959, 19). In this time of great need, then, schools should become the primary agent for planning and directing social change. Schools should not only *transmit* knowledge about the existing social order; they should seek to *reconstruct* it as well.

Social Reconstructionism and Progressivism   Social reconstructionism has clear ties to progressive educational philosophy. Both provide opportunities for extensive interactions between teacher and students and among students themselves. Furthermore, both place a premium on bringing the community, if not the entire world, into the classroom. Student experiences often include field trips, community-based projects of various sorts, and opportunities to interact with people beyond the four walls of the classroom.

According to Brameld and social reconstructionists such as George Counts, who wrote *Dare the School Build a New Social Order?* (1932), the educative process should provide students with methods for dealing with the significant crises that confront the world: war, economic depression, international terrorism, hunger, inflation, and ever-accelerating technological advances. The curriculum is arranged to highlight the need for various social reforms and, whenever possible, allow students to have firsthand experiences in reform activities. Teachers realize that they can play a significant role in the control and resolution of these problems, that they and their students need not be buffeted about like pawns by these crises.

The logical outcome of education based on social reconstructionist philosophy would be the eventual realization of a worldwide democracy (Brameld 1956). Unless we actively seek to create this kind of world through the intelligent application of present knowledge, we run the risk that the destructive forces of the world will determine the conditions under which humans will live in the future.

Portrait of a Social Reconstructionist Teacher   At the urban high school where she teaches social studies and history, Martha Vydra has the reputation for being a social activist. On first meeting her, she presents a casual and laid-back demeanor. Her soft voice and warm smile belie the intensity of her convictions about pressing world issues, from international terrorism and hunger to peaceful uses of space and the need for all humans to work toward a global community.

During the early 1970s, Martha participated as a high school student in several protests against the war in Vietnam. This also marked the beginning of her increased awareness of social injustice in general. Like many young people of that era, Martha vigorously supported a curriculum that focused on students understanding these inequities and identifying resources that might eliminate them from society. Before she graduated from high school, Martha had formulated a vision of a healthier, more just society, and she vowed to do what she could to make that vision become a reality during her lifetime.

Martha feels strongly about the importance of having students learn about social problems as well as discovering what they can *do* about them. "It's really almost immoral if I confront my students with a social problem and then we fail to do anything about it," she says. "Part of my responsibility as a teacher is to raise the consciousness level of my students in regard to the problems that confront all human beings. I want them to leave my class with the realization that they can make a difference when it comes to making the world a more humane place."

For Martha to achieve her goals as a teacher, she frequently has to tackle controversial issues—issues that many of her colleagues avoid in the classroom. She feels that students would not learn how to cope with problems or controversy if she were to avoid them.

I'm not afraid of controversy. When confronted with controversy, some teachers do retreat to the safety of the more "neutral" academic discipline. However, I try to get my students to see how they can use the knowledge of the discipline to attack the problem. So far, I've gotten good support from the principal. She's backed me up on several controversial issues that we've looked at in class: the war in Iraq, the nuclear energy plant that was to be built here in this county, the right to die, and absentee landlords who own property in the poorer sections of the city.

What Psychological Orientations Have Influenced Teaching Philosophies?

In addition to the five philosophical orientations to teaching described in previous sections of this chapter, several schools of psychological thought have formed the basis for teaching philosophies. These psychological theories are comprehensive worldviews that serve as the basis for the way many teachers approach teaching and the way many people take political action to influence education.

Psychological orientations to teaching are concerned primarily with understanding the conditions that are associated with effective learning. In other words, what motivates students to learn? What environments are most conducive to learning? Chief among the psychological orientations that have influenced teaching philosophies are humanistic psychology, behaviorism, and constructivism.

Humanistic Psychology

Humanistic psychology emphasizes personal freedom, choice, awareness, and personal responsibility. As the term implies, it also focuses on the achievements, motivation, feelings, actions, and needs of human beings. The goal of education, according to this orientation, is individual self-actualization.

Humanistic psychology is derived from the philosophy of **humanism**, which developed during the European Renaissance and Protestant Reformation and is based on the belief that individuals control their own destinies through the application of their intelligence and learning. People "make themselves." The term *secular humanism* refers to the closely related belief that the conditions of human existence relate to human nature and human actions rather than to predestination or divine intervention.

The Influence of Rousseau and Pestalozzi   After the Renaissance and Reformation, later expressions of humanism included Jean-Jacques Rousseau's (1712–1778) child-centered educational theories, in which children were to be viewed as naturally good individuals who learn best in nurturing environments. Rousseau, considered by some to be the "father of modern child psychology" (Mayer 1973), believed that children progressed through stages of growth and development that should guide the development of instructional strategies. Rousseau also believed in the innate goodness of children—a natural goodness that society corrupts. Rousseau's child-centered educational theories influenced many educators in France and beyond—for example, John Dewey, whose educational philosophy shaped the progressive education movement in the United States from 1920–45.

In his novel *Emile*, Rousseau set forth the ideal education for a youth named Emile. During the first five years of life, the child should be allowed to play freely in natural settings, and adults should "not treat the child to discourses which he cannot understand. No descriptions, no eloquence, no figures of speech. Be content to present to him appropriate objects" (Compayre 1888, 299). The next seven years should focus on concrete learning experiences, with abstract concepts and ideas

Jean-Jacques
Rousseau
(1712–1778)

emphasized between ages twelve and fifteen. These ideas match the principles of developmentally appropriate education that are observed today.

Johann Heinrich Pestalozzi (1746–1827) was a Swiss educator who implemented many of Rousseau's ideas. Noted educators worldwide, including Horace Mann from the United States, traveled to Pestalozzi's experimental school in Yverdun, Switzerland, to observe his methods and learn from him. His 1826 book, *How Gertrude Teaches Her Children*, contributed greatly to the development of elementary schools.

Like Rousseau, Pestalozzi believed that the innate goodness of children was corrupted by society and that instructional practices and curriculum materials should be selected in light of students' natural abilities and readiness to learn. Effective instruction, Pestalozzi believed, moved from concrete experiences to abstract concepts, from the simple to the complex. He also recognized that children's learning was enhanced by healthy self-esteem and feelings of emotional security. He was particularly concerned about poor children, whom he believed needed to feel loved by their teachers, as Ulich (1950, 264) points out: "In the studies of Old Swiss and German schoolmasters one could often find a reproduction of a painting of Pestalozzi in which we see him, with a profound expression of love on his ugly and wrinkled face, embracing the children of peasants who, clad in rags, enter the simple schoolroom."

Self-Actualization of Students   In the 1950s and 1960s, humanistic psychology became the basis of educational reforms that sought to enhance students' achievement of their full potential through self-actualization (Maslow 1954, 1962; Rogers 1961). According to this psychological orientation, teachers should not force students to learn; instead, they should create a climate of trust and respect that allows students to decide what and how they learn, to question authority, and to take initiative in "making themselves." Teachers should be what noted psychologist Carl Rogers calls

How has Pestalozzi's philosophy of education influenced the development of elementary education in the United States?

"facilitators," and the classroom should be a place "in which curiosity and the natural desire to learn can be nourished and enhanced" (1982, 31). Through their nonjudgmental understanding of students, humanistic teachers encourage students to learn and grow.

Portrait of a Humanistic Teacher   As an example of a humanist teacher, consider Carol Alshahwan, who ten years ago began teaching at a small rural middle school—a position she enjoys because the school's small size enables her to develop close relationships with her students and their families. Her teaching style is based on humane, open interpersonal relationships with her students, and she takes pride in the fact that students trust her and frequently ask her advice on problems common to children in early adolescence. The positive rapport Carol has developed with her students is reflected in the regularity with which former students return to visit or to seek her advice.

Carol is also committed to empowering her students, to giving them opportunities to shape their learning experiences. As she puts it: "I encourage students to give me feedback about how they feel in my classroom. They have to feel good about themselves before they can learn. Also, I've come to realize that students should help us plan. I've learned to ask them what they're interested in. 'What do you want to do?' 'How do you want to do it?' "

Much of Carol's teaching is based on classroom discussions in which she encourages students to share openly their ideas and feelings about the subject at hand. Carol's interactions with students reveal her skill at creating a conversational environment that makes students feel safe and willing to contribute. During discussions, Carol listens attentively to students and frequently paraphrases their ideas in a way that acknowledges their contributions. She frequently responds with short phrases that indicate support and encourage the student to continue the discussion such as the following: "I see . . . Would you say more about that?" "That is an interesting idea. Tell us more."

When Carol is not facilitating a whole-group discussion, she is more than likely moving among the small cooperative-learning groups she has set up. Each group decided how to organize itself to accomplish a particular learning task—developing a strategy for responding to a threat to the environment or analyzing a poem about brotherhood, for example. "I think it's important for students to learn to work together, to help one another, and to accept different points of view," says Carol.

Behaviorism

Behaviorism is based on the principle that desirable human behavior can be the product of design rather than accident. According to behaviorists, it is an illusion to say that humans have a free will. Although we may act as if we are free, our behavior is really *determined* by forces in the environment that shape our behavior. "We are what we are and we do what we do, not because of any mysterious power of human volition, but because outside forces over which we lack any semblance of control have us caught in an inflexible web. Whatever else we may be, we are not the captains of our fate or the masters of our soul" (Power 1982, 168).

Founders of Behavioristic Psychology   John B. Watson (1878–1958) was the principal originator of behavioristic psychology and B. F. Skinner (1904–1990) its best-known promoter. Watson first claimed that human behavior consisted of specific stimuli that resulted in certain responses. In part, he based this new conception of learning on the classic experiment conducted by Russian psychologist Ivan Pavlov (1849–1936). Pavlov had noticed that a dog he was working with would salivate when it was about to be given food. By introducing the sound of a bell when food was offered and repeating this several times, Pavlov discovered that the sound of the bell alone (a conditioned stimulus) would make the dog salivate (a conditioned response).

Watson came to believe that all learning conformed to this basic stimulus-response model (now termed classical or type S conditioning). In fact, Watson once boasted, "Give me a dozen healthy infants, well-formed, and my own specified world to bring them up in, and I'll guarantee to take any one at random and train him to become any type of specialist I might select—doctor, lawyer, artist, merchant-chief and, yes, even beggarman and thief, regardless of his talents, penchants, tendencies, abilities, vocations, and race of his ancestors" (1925, 82).

Skinner went beyond Watson's basic stimulus-response model and developed a more comprehensive view of conditioning known as operant (or type R) conditioning. Operant conditioning is based on the idea that satisfying responses are conditioned, but unsatisfying ones are not. In other words, "The things we call pleasant have an energizing or strengthening effect on our behaviour" (Skinner 1972, 74). For the teacher, this means that desired student behavior should be reinforced, but undesired behavior should not. Also, the teacher should be concerned with changing students' behavior rather than trying to alter their mental states.

In his novel *Walden Two* (1962), Skinner portrayed how "behavioral engineering" could lead to the creation of a utopian society. The book describes how a community with a desirable social order was created by design rather than by accident. In much the same way, educators can create learners who exhibit desired behaviors by carefully and scientifically controlling the educative process. The teacher need merely recognize that all learning is conditioning and adhere to the following four steps:

1. Identify desired behaviors in concrete (observable and measurable) terms.
2. Establish a procedure for recording specific behaviors and counting their frequencies.
3. For each behavior, identify an appropriate reinforcer.
4. Ensure that students receive the reinforcer as soon as possible after displaying a desired behavior.

Portrait of a Behaviorist Teacher   Jane Henriques teaches fourth grade at a school with an enrollment of about five hundred in a small midwestern town. Now in her fifth year at the school, Jane has spent the last three years developing and refining a systematic approach to teaching. Last year, the success of her methods was confirmed when her students received the highest scores on the state's annual basic skills test.

Her primary method is individualized instruction wherein students proceed at their own pace through modules she has put together. The modules cover five major areas: reading, writing, mathematics, general science, and spelling. She is working on a sixth module, geography, but it won't be ready until next year.

She has developed a complex point system to keep track of students' progress and to motivate them to higher levels of achievement. The points students accumulate entitle them to participate in various in-class activities: free reading, playing with the many games and puzzles in the room, drawing or painting in the art corner, or playing video games on one of the two personal computers in the room.

Jane has tried to convert several other teachers at the school to her behavioristic approach, and she is eager to talk to anyone who will listen about the effectiveness of her systematic approach to instruction. When addressing this topic, her exuberance is truly exceptional: "It's really quite simple. Students just do much better if you tell them exactly what you want them to know and then reward them for learning it."

In regard to the methods employed by some of her colleagues, Jane can be rather critical. She knows some teachers in the school who teach by a trial-and-error method and "aren't clear about where they're going." She is also impatient with those who talk about the "art" of teaching; in contrast, everything that she does as a teacher is done with precision and a clear sense of purpose. "Through careful design and management of the learning environment," she says, "a teacher can get the results that he or she wants."

Constructivism

In contrast to behaviorism, **constructivism** focuses on processes of learning rather than on learning behavior. According to constructivism, students use cognitive processes to *construct* understanding of the material to be learned—in contrast to the view that they *receive* information transmitted by the teacher. Constructivist approaches support student-centered rather than teacher-centered curriculum and instruction. The student is the key to learning.

Unlike behaviorists who concentrate on directly observable behavior, constructivists focus on the mental processes and strategies that students use to learn. Our understanding of learning has been extended as a result of advances in **cognitive science**—the study of the mental processes students use in thinking and remembering. By drawing from research in linguistics, psychology, anthropology, neurophysiology, and computer science, cognitive scientists are developing new models for how people think and learn.

Teachers who base classroom activities on constructivism know that learning is an active, meaning-making process, that learners are not passive recipients of information. In fact, students are continually involved in making sense out of activities around them. Thus the teacher must *understand students' understanding*

What are some ways in which teachers of young children might use behaviorist strategies in their teaching?

and realize that students' learning is influenced by prior knowledge, experience, attitudes, and social interactions.

Portrait of a Constructivist Teacher   In *Models of Teaching*, Bruce Joyce and Marsha Weil (2004, 42–43) provide the following description of a constructivist teacher:

> Jack Wu is a year one teacher in Cambridge, England. He meets daily for reading instruction with a group of children who are progressing quite well. He is studying how his students attack unknown words. He believes that they do well when they sound out words and recognize them as being in their listening-speaking vocabulary. For example, when they find "war" they are fine. However, a word like "postwar" appears to stop them. He decides that they have trouble with morphological structures where elements like prefixes and suffixes add to the root meanings of words. So, he plans the following sequence of lessons.
>
> Jack prepares a deck of cards with one word on each card. He selects words with particular prefixes and suffixes, and he deliberately puts in words that have the same root words but different prefixes and suffixes. He picks prefixes and suffixes because they are very prominent morphological structures—very easy to identify. (He will later proceed to more subtle features.) Jack plans a series of learning activities over the next several weeks using the deck of cards as a data set. Here are some of the words:

set	reset	heat	preheat	plant	replant
run	rerun	set	preset	plan	preplan

When the group of students convenes on Monday morning, Jack gives several cards to each student. He keeps the remainder, intending to gradually increase the amount of information. Jack has each student read a word on one of the cards and describe something about the word. Other students can add to the description. In this way the structural properties of the word are brought to the students' attention. The discussion surfaces features like initial consonants (begins with an "s," vowels), pairs of consonants ("pl"), and so on.

After the students have familiarized themselves with the assortment of words, Jack asks them to put the words into groups. "Put the words that go together in piles," he instructs. The students begin studying their cards, passing them back and forth as they sort out the commonalities. At first the students' card groups reflected only the initial letters or the meanings of the words, such as whether they referred to motion or warmth. Gradually, they noticed the prefixes, how they were spelled, and looked up their meanings in the dictionary, discovering how the addition of the prefixes affected the meanings of the root words.

When the students finished sorting the words, Jack asked them to talk about each category, telling what the cards had in common. Gradually, because of the way Jack had selected the data, the students could discover the major prefixes and suffixes and reflect on their meaning. Then he gave them sentences in which words not in their deck began and ended, using those same prefixes and suffixes, and asked them to figure out the meanings of those words, applying the concepts they had formed to help them unlock word meanings. He found that he had to teach them directly to identify the root word meaning and then add the meaning of the prefix or suffix.

By selecting different sets of words, Jack led the students through the categories of consonant and vowel sounds and structures they would need to attack unfamiliar words, providing students with many opportunities to practice inductive learning. Jack studied their progress and adjusted the classification tasks to lead them to a thorough understanding and the ability to use their new knowledge to attack unfamiliar words.

How Can You Develop Your Educational Philosophy?

As you read the preceding brief descriptions of five educational philosophies and three psychological orientations to teaching, perhaps you felt that no single philosophy fit perfectly with your image of the kind of teacher you want to become. Or there may have been some element of each approach that seemed compatible with your own emerging philosophy of education. In either case, don't feel that you need to identify a single educational philosophy around which you will build your teaching career.

In reality, few teachers follow only one educational philosophy. As Figure 3.5 shows, educational philosophy is only one determinant of the professional goals a teacher sets. Other influences include political dynamics, social forces, the expectations of one's immediate family or community, and economic conditions.

Most teachers develop an *eclectic* philosophy of education, which means they develop their own unique blending of two or more philosophies. A teacher's personal educational philosophy is reflected in the many decisions he or she makes regarding how to teach—how to arrange the classroom as a learning environment, how to plan for teaching, how to interact with students, or how to assess student

Figure 3.5 The relationship of philosophy to educational practice.

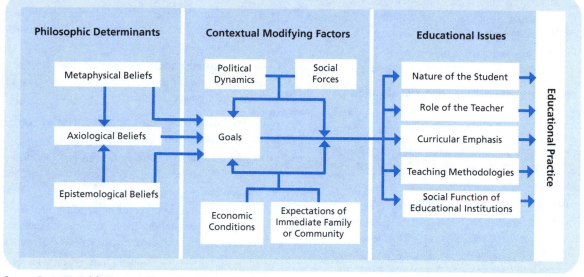

Source: George R. Knight, *Issues & Alternatives in Educational Philosophy,* 3rd ed. Berrien Springs, MI: Andrews University Press 1998, p. 34.

learning, for example. One characteristic of the professional teacher is that he or she continually tries to arrive at clearer, more comprehensive answers to basic philosophical questions: Why do I teach the way I do? Is my teaching practice consistent with my beliefs and values about educational goals, curriculum, and teachers' and students' roles in learning? To help you identify the philosophies most consistent with your beliefs and values about educational goals, curriculum, and teachers' and students' roles in learning, complete the Philosophic Inventory found in Appendix 3.1 at the end of this chapter. The Philosophic Inventory can also help you identify the educational philosophies of people who act politically to influence education.

Summary

Why Do You Need to Understand Educational Philosophy?

- Knowledge of educational philosophy enables teachers to understand the complex political forces that influence schools, to evaluate more effectively current proposals for change, and to grow professionally.

What Is the Nature of Philosophy?

- Philosophy, which means "love of wisdom," is concerned with pondering the fundamental questions of life: What is truth? What is reality? What life is worth living?

- Most schools have a statement of philosophy that describes important educational values and goals.

What Determines Your Educational Philosophy?

- An educational philosophy is a set of beliefs about education, a set of principles to guide professional action.

- A teacher's educational philosophy is made up of personal beliefs about teaching and learning, students, knowledge, and what is worth knowing.

What Are the Branches of Philosophy?

- The branches of philosophy and the questions they address are (1) metaphysics (What is the nature of reality?), (2) epistemology (What is the nature of knowledge and is truth attainable?), (3) axiology (What values should one live by?), (4) ethics (What is good and evil, right and wrong?), (5) aesthetics (What is beautiful?), and (6) logic (What reasoning processes yield valid conclusions?).

What Are Five Modern Philosophical Orientations to Teaching?

- *Perennialism*—Students should acquire knowledge of enduring great ideas.

- *Essentialism*—Schools should teach students, in a disciplined and systematic way, a core of "essential" knowledge and skills.

- *Progressivism*—The aim of education should be based on the needs and interests of students.

- *Existentialism*—In the face of an indifferent universe, students should acquire an education that will enable them to assign meaning to their lives.

- *Social reconstructionism*—In response to the significant social problems of the day, schools should take the lead in creating a new social order.

What Psychological Orientations Have Influenced Teaching Philosophies?

- *Humanism*—Children are innately good, and education should focus on individual needs, personal freedom, and self-actualization.

- *Behaviorism*—By careful control of the educational environment and with appropriate reinforcement techniques, teachers can cause students to exhibit desired behaviors.

- *Constructivism*—Teachers should "understand students' understanding" and view learning as an active process in which learners construct meaning.

How Can You Develop Your Educational Philosophy?

- Instead of basing their teaching on only one educational philosophy, most teachers develop an eclectic educational philosophy.

- Professional teachers continually strive for a clearer, more comprehensive answer to basic philosophical questions.

Key Terms and Concepts

Reflective Application Activities

Discussion Questions

1. Review the five philosophical orientations discussed in this chapter. With reference to today's schools, what is the current "status" of each—i.e., is it widespread or not? Which orientation is most popular among teachers today? Least popular?

2. What specific steps can you take throughout your teaching career to ensure that your philosophical orientation to teaching remains dynamic and growing rather than becoming static and limited?

Professional Journal

1. Imagine that you are a colleague of Roberta, who was profiled in this chapter's opening scenario. Write a memo to her in which you react to her philosophical orientation to teaching.

2. Recall one of your favorite teachers in grades K–12. Which of the educational philosophies or psychological orientations to teaching described in this chapter best captures that teacher's approach to teaching? Write a descriptive sketch of that teacher "in action."

Online Assignments

1. Visit the home page of the American Philosophical Association (APA), Philosophy in Cyberspace, The History of Education Site, or another professional organization devoted to educational philosophy or history and compile a list of online publications, associations, and reference materials you could use in developing your educational philosophy further.

2. Explore encyclopedias, bibliographies, periodicals, news sources, and other online reference works to research in greater detail the contributions of one of the educational philosophers included in this chapter.

Observations and Interviews

1. Interview a teacher for the purpose of understanding his or her educational philosophy. Formulate your interview questions in light of the philosophical concepts discussed in this chapter. Discuss your findings with classmates.

2. Observe the class of a teacher at the level at which you plan to teach. Which of the five philosophies or three psychological orientations to teaching discussed in this chapter most characterizes this teacher?

Professional Portfolio

Prepare a written (or videotaped) statement in which you describe a key element of your educational philosophy. To organize your thoughts, focus on *one* of the following dimensions of educational philosophy:

- Beliefs about teaching and learning
- Beliefs about students
- Beliefs about knowledge
- Beliefs about what is worth knowing
- Personal beliefs about the six branches of philosophy

Develop your statement of philosophy throughout the course, covering all dimensions. On completion of your teacher-education program, review your portfolio entry and make any appropriate revisions. Being able to articulate your philosophy of education and your teaching philosophy will be an important part of finding your first job as a teacher.

Appendix 3.1
Philosophic Inventory

The following inventory is to help identify your educational philosophy. Respond to the statements on the scale from 5 "Strongly Agree" to 1 "Strongly Disagree" by circling the number that most closely fits your perspective.

	Strongly Agree				Strongly Disagree
1. The curriculum should emphasize essential knowledge, *not* students' personal interests.	5	4	3	2	1
2. All learning results from rewards controlled by the external environment.	5	4	3	2	1
3. Teachers should emphasize interdisciplinary subject matter that encourages project-oriented, democratic classrooms.	5	4	3	2	1
4. Education should emphasize the search for personal meaning, *not* a fixed body of knowledge.	5	4	3	2	1
5. The ultimate aim of education is constant, absolute, and universal: to develop the rational person and cultivate the intellect.	5	4	3	2	1
6. Schools should actively involve students in social change to reform society.	5	4	3	2	1
7. Schools should teach basic skills, *not* humanistic ideals.	5	4	3	2	1
8. Eventually, human behavior will be explained by scientific laws, proving there is no free will.	5	4	3	2	1
9. Teachers should be facilitators and resources who guide student inquiry, not managers of behavior.	5	4	3	2	1
10. The best teachers encourage personal responses and develop self-awareness in their students.	5	4	3	2	1
11. The curriculum should be the same for everyone: the collective wisdom of Western culture delivered through lecture and discussion.	5	4	3	2	1
12. Schools should lead society toward radical social change, *not* transmit traditional values.	5	4	3	2	1
13. The purpose of schools is to ensure practical preparation for life and work, *not* to encourage personal development.	5	4	3	2	1
14. Good teaching establishes an environment to control student behavior and to measure learning of prescribed objectives.	5	4	3	2	1
15. Curriculum should emerge from students' needs and interests; therefore, it *should not* be prescribed in advance.	5	4	3	2	1

Source: Prepared by Robert Leahy for *Becoming a Teacher*, 3d ed. Boston: Allyn and Bacon, 1995. Used by permission of the author.

		Strongly Agree				Strongly Disagree
16.	Helping students develop personal values is more important than transmitting traditional values.	5	4	3	2	1
17.	The best education consists primarily of exposure to great works in the humanities.	5	4	3	2	1
18.	It is more important for teachers to involve students in activities to criticize and transform society than to teach the Great Books.	5	4	3	2	1
19.	Schools should emphasize discipline, hard work, and respect for authority, *not* encourage free choice.	5	4	3	2	1
20.	Human learning can be controlled: Anyone can be taught to be a scientist or a thief; therefore, personal choice is a myth.	5	4	3	2	1
21.	Education should enhance personal growth through problem solving in the present, *not* emphasize preparation for a distant future.	5	4	3	2	1
22.	Because we are born with an unformed personality, personal growth should be the focus of education.	5	4	3	2	1
23.	Human nature is constant—its most distinctive quality is the ability to reason; therefore, the intellect should be the focus of education.	5	4	3	2	1
24.	Schools perpetuate racism and sexism camouflaged as traditional values.	5	4	3	2	1
25.	Teachers should efficiently transmit a common core of knowledge, *not* experiment with curriculum.	5	4	3	2	1
26.	Teaching is primarily management of student behavior to achieve the teacher's objectives.	5	4	3	2	1
27.	Education should involve students in democratic activities and reflective thinking.	5	4	3	2	1
28.	Students should have significant involvement in choosing what and how they learn.	5	4	3	2	1
29.	Teachers should promote the permanency of the classics.	5	4	3	2	1
30.	Learning should lead students to involvement in social reform.	5	4	3	2	1
31.	On the whole, school should and must indoctrinate students with traditional values.	5	4	3	2	1
32.	If ideas cannot be proved by science, they should be ignored as superstition and nonsense.	5	4	3	2	1
33.	The major goal for teachers is to create an environment in which students can learn on their own by guided reflection on their experiences.	5	4	3	2	1
34.	Teachers should create opportunities for students to make personal choices, *not* shape their behavior.	5	4	3	2	1
35.	The aim of education should be the same in every age and society, *not* differ from teacher to teacher.	5	4	3	2	1
36.	Education should lead society toward social betterment, *not* confine itself to essential skills.	5	4	3	2	1

PHILOSOPHIC INVENTORY SCORE SHEET

In the space available, record the number you circled for each statement (1–36) from the inventory. Total the number horizontally and record it in the space on the far right of the score sheet. The highest total indicates your educational philosophy.

Essentialism

Essentialism was a response to progressivism and advocates a conservative philosophic perspective. The emphasis is on intellectual and moral standards that should be transmitted by the schools. The core of the curriculum should be essential knowledge and skills. Schooling should be practical and not influence social policy. It is a back-to-basics movement that emphasizes facts. Students should be taught discipline, hard work, and respect for authority. Influential essentialists include William C. Bagley, H. G. Rickover, Arthur Bestor, and William Bennett. E. D. Hirsch's Cultural Literacy could fit this category.

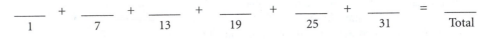

| ____ | + | ____ | + | ____ | + | ____ | + | ____ | + | ____ | = | ____ |
| 1 | | 7 | | 13 | | 19 | | 25 | | 31 | | Total |

Behaviorism

Behaviorism denies free will and maintains that behavior is the result of external forces that cause humans to behave in predictable ways. It is linked with empiricism, which stresses scientific experiment and observation; behaviorists are skeptical about metaphysical claims. Behaviorists look for laws governing human behavior the way natural scientists look for empirical laws governing natural events. The role of the teacher is to identify behavioral goals and establish reinforcers to achieve goals. Influential behaviorists include B. F. Skinner, Ivan Pavlov, John B. Watson, and Benjamin Bloom.

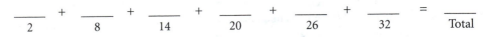

| ____ | + | ____ | + | ____ | + | ____ | + | ____ | + | ____ | = | ____ |
| 2 | | 8 | | 14 | | 20 | | 26 | | 32 | | Total |

Progressivism

Progressivism focuses on the child rather than the subject matter. The students' interests are important; integrating thinking, feeling, and doing is important. Learners should be active and learn to solve problems by reflecting on their experience. The school should help students develop personal and social values. Because society is always changing, new ideas are important to make the future better than the past. Influential progressivists include John Dewey and Francis Parker.

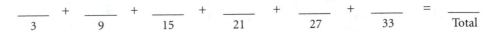

| ____ | + | ____ | + | ____ | + | ____ | + | ____ | + | ____ | = | ____ |
| 3 | | 9 | | 15 | | 21 | | 27 | | 33 | | Total |

Existentialism

Existentialism is a highly subjective philosophy that stresses the importance of the individual and emotional commitment to living authentically. It emphasizes individual choice over the importance of rational theories. Jean-Paul Sartre, the French philosopher, claimed that "existence precedes essence." People are born, and each person must define him- or herself through choices in life. Influential existentialists include Jean-Paul Sartre, Soren Kierkegaard, Martin Heidegger, Gabriel Marcel, Albert Camus, Carl Rogers, A. S. Neill, and Maxine Greene.

$$\underline{\qquad} + \underline{\qquad} + \underline{\qquad} + \underline{\qquad} + \underline{\qquad} + \underline{\qquad} = \underline{\qquad}$$

4   10   16   22   28   34   Total

Perennialism

The aim of education is to ensure that students acquire knowledge about the great ideas of Western culture. Human beings are rational, and it s this capacity that needs to be developed. Cultivation of the intellect is the highest priority of an education worth having. The highest level of knowledge in each field should be the focus of curriculum. Influential perennialists include Robert Maynard Hutchins, Mortimer Adler, and Allan Bloom.

$$\underline{\qquad} + \underline{\qquad} + \underline{\qquad} + \underline{\qquad} + \underline{\qquad} + \underline{\qquad} = \underline{\qquad}$$

5   11   17   23   29   35   Total

Reconstructionism

Reconstructionists advocate that schools should take the lead to reconstruct society. Schools have more than a responsibility to transmit knowledge, they have the mission to transform society as well. Reconstructionists go beyond progressivists in advocating social activism. Influential reconstructionists include Theodore Brameld, Paulo Freire, and Henry Giroux.

$$\underline{\qquad} + \underline{\qquad} + \underline{\qquad} + \underline{\qquad} + \underline{\qquad} + \underline{\qquad} = \underline{\qquad}$$

6   12   18   24   30   36   Total

4

Legal Issues in U.S. Education

In today's litigious society, educators must have a solid understanding of the laws that affect them and their institutions. Every day educators make decisions, many of which may have significant legal implications.

—Susan D. Looney
Education and the Legal System: A Guide to Understanding the Law, 2004, p. 1

The day has ended and you are grading papers while waiting to meet with Cassandra, one of your fifth-grade students, and her mother. Cassandra's mother called you at home yesterday to arrange the meeting. When you asked her about the purpose of the meeting, she was vague and offered only that Cassandra had recently had "some trouble" with one of her classmates, Robert.

A quick glance at the clock tells you they should arrive at any moment. To prepare for the meeting, you stop grading papers and reflect on what you know about the situation between Cassandra and Robert.

Because he was held back in the third grade, Robert is almost two years older than his classmates. Though physically more mature than the other boys in your class, Robert's social skills are less developed. Although he acts silly and immature from time to time, Robert has not been a behavior problem—at least not until a week ago, when Cassandra told you what happened on the playground.

Last Monday at the end of the day, Cassandra told you that Robert had "talked mean" to her during recess on the playground. When you questioned Cassandra to find out exactly what Robert said, her answers were hard to follow. At first, it seemed that, whatever words were exchanged, they were not unlike the taunts boys and girls hurl back and forth daily on playgrounds across the country. As you continued to press for details, however, Cassandra began to talk, again vaguely, about how Robert had "talked dirty" to her. Further questioning of Cassandra still failed to give you a clear picture of what happened on the playground.

Based on what you learned from talking with Cassandra, you decided to give Robert a stern reminder about appropriate ways of talking to other people. The following morning you did just that.

Robert listened respectfully and seemed genuinely contrite. He promised to leave Cassandra alone while they were on the playground. The conversation ended with you telling Robert that his behavior on the playground and in the classroom would be monitored closely.

During the following week, it appeared that the friction between Robert and Cassandra had ended. As far as you could tell, the matter was over.

When Cassandra and her mother entered the room, you knew immediately that both were upset. Cassandra looked like she was on the verge of tears, and her mother looked angry.

"Tell your teacher what you told me," Cassandra's mother began, as she and her daughter seated themselves at two student desks in front of your desk.

"Well," Cassandra began slowly, almost whispering, "Robert bothered me on the playground yesterday." Cassandra started breathing more deeply as she struggled to continue. "He came over to me and . . ." Cassandra stared at the top of her desk while searching for additional words to express what she wanted to say.

"What she means to tell you," said Cassandra's mother, "is that Robert rubbed up against her and said he wanted to have sex with her. She was sexually harassed."

On hearing what Robert is alleged to have done, you are shocked. What should you do? How does a teacher tell the difference between sexual harassment and the teasing and name calling that are an inescapable part of growing up? Should you try to determine the truth of the allegations before involving the principal? What are your responsibilities to Cassandra and her mother? What are your responsibilities to Robert? How should your school handle the matter?

Guiding Questions

1. **Why do you need a professional code of ethics?**

2. **What are your legal rights as a teacher?**

3. **Do student teachers have the same rights?**

4. **What are your legal responsibilities as a teacher?**

5. **What are the legal rights of students and parents?**

6. **What are some issues in the legal rights of school districts?**

The preceding scenario, based partially on actual events that culminated with the filing of a lawsuit against a school board (*Davis v. Monroe County Board of Education* 1999) and a U.S. Supreme Court ruling in 1999, highlights the role that legal issues can play in the lives of teachers and students. In this instance, a fifth-grade Georgia girl said she endured a five-month "barrage of sexual harassment and abuse" from a classmate. The boy allegedly touched the girl's breasts, rubbed against her suggestively, and repeatedly said he wanted to have sex with her. The lawsuit claimed that the girl's mother reported each incident to school officials but the boy was never disciplined; as a result, the girl's grades fell and she became mentally and emotionally upset. The sharply divided Supreme Court (five majority and four dissenting) ruled that school districts can be sued under Title IX in cases involving student-on-student sexual harassment, if the district acts with "deliberate indifference" to the harassment. (Title IX prohibits discrimination on the basis of sex in programs that receive federal money.)

Relevant Standards

Education and the Law

As the following standards indicate, teachers must act in accord with a wide range of federal and state legislation and court decisions—in short, they must understand the legal responsibilities that accompany their profession.

- "[Teacher candidates] understand and are able to apply knowledge related to . . . professional ethics, law, and policy." (National Council for Accreditation of Teacher Education [NCATE] 2002, 19. Supporting Explanation for Standard 1: Candidate Knowledge, Skills, and Dispositions.")

- "Professional practice requires that teachers be knowledgeable about their legal obligations to carry out public policy as represented by state statute and regulation, school board directives, court decisions and other policies." (National Board for Professional Teaching Standards [NBPTS] 2002, 18–19. Supporting statement for Proposition #5: "Teachers are members of learning communities.")

- "The teacher understands and implements laws related to students' rights and teacher responsi-

bilities (e.g., for equal education, appropriate education for handicapped students, confidentiality, privacy, appropriate treatment of students, reporting in situations related to possible child abuse." (Interstate New Teacher Assessment and Support Consortium [INTASC] 1992, 33. Knowledge statement for Principle #10: "The teacher fosters relationships with school colleagues, parents, and agencies in the larger community to support students' learning and well-being.")

- "The professional nature of the role imposes responsibilities on teachers. . . . [I]f [teaching] is to be treated as a profession, then the responsibilities as well as the benefits deriving from that status must apply." (Praxis Series, The Nature of Professionalism.) (From Danielson 1996, 27)

This chapter examines significant ethical and legal issues that affect the rights and responsibilities of teachers, administrators, students, and parents. A wide range of federal and state legislation and court decisions will affect your life as a teacher. As a teacher, you may need to deal with such legal issues as the teacher's responsibility for accidents, discriminatory employment practices, freedom of speech, desegregation, student rights, and circumstances related to job termination or dismissal. Without knowledge of the legal dimensions of such issues, you will be ill-equipped to protect your rights and the rights of your students. This chapter's Relevant Standards feature attests to the importance of understanding how the law will affect your future as a teacher.

Why Do You Need a Professional Code of Ethics?

Your actions as a teacher will be determined not only by what is legally required of you, but also by what you know you *ought* to do. You must do what is legally right, and you must *do the right thing*. A specific set of values will guide you. A deep and lasting commitment to professional practice should characterize your role as a teacher. You will need to adopt a high standard of professional ethics and model behaviors that are in accord with that code of ethics.

At present, the teaching profession does not have a uniform **code of ethics** similar to the Hippocratic Oath, which all doctors are legally required to take when they begin practice. However, the largest professional organization for teachers, the National Education Association (NEA), has a code of ethics for its members (see Appendix 4.1) that includes the following statement: "The educator accepts the responsibility to adhere to the highest ethical standards."

Ethical Teaching Attitudes and Practices

Teaching is an ethical enterprise—that is, a teacher has an obligation to act ethically, to follow what he or she knows to be the most appropriate professional action to take. The best interests of students, not the teacher, provide the rule of thumb for determining what is ethical and what is not. Behaving ethically is more than a matter of following the rules or not breaking the law—it means acting in a way that promotes the learning and growth of students and helps them realize their potential.

Unethical acts break the trust and respect on which good student-teacher relationships are based. An example of unethical conduct would be to talk publicly about Cassandra's allegations against Robert (described in this chapter's opening scenario). Other examples would be using grades as a form of punishment, expressing rage in the classroom, or intentionally tricking students on tests. You could no doubt think of other examples from your own experience as a student.

Ethical Dilemmas in the Classroom and School

As a teacher, you will probably encounter **ethical dilemmas** in the classroom and in the school. You will have to take action in situations in which all the facts are not known or for which no single course of action can be called *right* or *wrong*. At these times it can be quite difficult to decide what an ethical response might be. Dealing satisfactorily with ethical dilemmas in teaching often requires the ability to see beyond short-range consequences to consider long-range consequences.

An important part of responding to an ethical dilemma is identifying possible consequences of one's actions. Consider, for example, the following three questions based on actual case studies. On the basis of the information given, how would you respond to each situation? What might be the consequences of your actions?

1. Should the sponsor of the high school literary magazine refuse to print a well-written story by a budding writer if the piece appears to satirize a teacher and a student?

2. Is a mathematics teacher justified in trying to increase achievement for an entire class by separating two disruptive students and placing one in a math group beneath his reading level?

3. Should a chemistry teacher punish a student (on the basis of circumstantial, inconclusive evidence) for a laboratory explosion if the example of decisive, swift

What ethical dilemmas might this experiment pose for a teacher? How might you respond? On what moral or ethical grounds would you base your response? What legal concerns might be involved?

punishment will likely prevent the recurrence of a similar event and thereby ensure the safety of all students?

What Are Your Legal Rights as a Teacher?

It is frequently observed that with each freedom comes a corresponding responsibility to others and to the community in which we live. As long as there is more than one individual inhabiting this planet, there is a need for laws to clarify individual rights and responsibilities. This necessary balance between rights and responsibilities is perhaps more critical to teaching than to any other profession. As education law experts Martha McCarthy, Nelda Cambron-McCabe, and Stephen Thomas (1998, 309) point out: "Although public educators do not shed their constitutional rights as a condition of public employment, under certain circumstances restrictions on these freedoms are justified by overriding governmental interests."

While schools do have limited "power over" teachers, teachers' rights to **due process** cannot be violated. Teachers, like all citizens, are protected from being treated arbitrarily by those in authority. A principal who disagrees with a teacher's methods cannot suddenly fire that teacher. A school board cannot ask a teacher to resign merely by claiming that the teacher's political activities outside of school are "disruptive" of the educational process. A teacher cannot be dismissed for "poor" performance without ample documentation that the performance was, in fact, poor and without sufficient time to meet clearly stated performance evaluation criteria.

Certification

Karla Brown is a junior high school English teacher and lives in a state with a law speci-fying that a teacher must show proof of five years of successful teaching experience for a teaching certificate to be renewed. Last year was Karla's fifth year of teaching, and her principal gave her an unsatisfactory performance rating. Karla's principal told her that her teaching certificate cannot be renewed. Is the principal correct?

Karla's principal is mistaken about the grounds for nonrenewal of a teaching certificate. According to the state's law, *unsuccessful* performance, or a failure to complete the school year, is grounds for nonrenewal of a certificate—not perform-ance that is judged to be *unsatisfactory*. Because state laws vary and unsuccessful performance is defined differently in different states, however, Karla's principal might have been correct if she taught in another state.

No teacher who meets all of a state's requirements for initial certification can arbitrarily be denied a certificate. "However, obtaining a certificate does not guar-antee the right to retain it" (Imber and van Geel 2001, 192). For a certificate to be revoked, the reason must be job-related and demonstrably impair the teacher's ability to perform satisfactorily. In this regard, the case of a California teacher whose certificate was revoked because someone admitted to having a homosexual relationship with the teacher is often cited. The court determined that the teacher's homosexual conduct was not an impairment to the teacher's performance and ordered the certificate restored (*Morrison v. State Board of Education* 1969). When courts have upheld the refusal to hire and the right to terminate homosexual teach-ers, these decisions have been influenced by factors such as sexual involvement with students or public acts of indecency (McCarthy, Cambron-McCabe, and Thomas 1998). Several states (California, Connecticut, Hawaii, Massachusetts, Minnesota, New Jersey, and Wisconsin) and the District of Columbia have laws that prohibit discrimination on the basis of sexual orientation in regard to employ-ment, housing, and education. States that have such antidiscrimination laws "make it difficult, if not impossible . . . to uphold the denial of employment or the dis-charge of homosexuals" (LaMorte 2002, 227).

Teachers' Rights to Nondiscrimination

George, who pled guilty to possession of marijuana and cocaine in a criminal trial, was not reinstated to his teaching position after his criminal record was expunged. George claims that he is being discriminated against because of his past. Is he right?

States may impose certain limitations on initial certification as long as those limitations are not discriminatory in regard to race, religion, ethnic origin, sex, or age. Nearly all the states, for example, require that applicants for a teaching certifi-cate pass a test that covers basic skills, professional knowledge, or academic subject areas. Qualifications for initial certification may also legally include certain personal qualities. The case of George at the beginning of this section, for example, is based on a Louisiana case involving a man who was not reinstated to his teaching position even though his criminal record had been expunged. The court maintained that he had committed the act, and that expungement did not erase that fact, nor did it erase the "moral turpitude" of the teacher's conduct (*Dubuclet v. Home Insurance Company* 1995).

The right to **nondiscrimination** in regard to employment is protected by Title VII of the Civil Rights Act of 1964, which states:

> It shall be an unlawful employment practice for an employer (1) to fail or refuse to hire or to discharge any individual, or otherwise to discriminate against any individual with respect to his compensation, terms, conditions, or privileges of employment, because of such individual's race, color, religion, sex, or national origin; or (2) to limit, segregate, or classify his employees or applicants for employment in any way which would deprive or tend to deprive any individual of employment opportunities or otherwise adversely affect his status as an employee, because of such individual's race, color, religion, sex, or national origin.

Teaching Contracts

A **teaching contract** represents an agreement between the teacher and a board of education. For a contract to be valid, it must contain these five basic elements:

1. *Offer and acceptance*—The school board has made a formal offer and the employee has accepted the contract terms.
2. *Competent parties*—The school board is not exceeding the authority granted to it by the state and the teacher meets the criteria for employment.
3. *Consideration*—Remuneration is promised to the teacher.
4. *Legal subject matter*—The contract terms are neither illegal nor against public policy.
5. *Proper form*—The contract adheres to state contract laws.

Before you sign a teaching contract, it is important that you read it carefully and be certain that it is signed by the appropriate member(s) of the board of education or board of trustees. Ask for clarification of any sections you don't understand. It is preferable that any additional nonteaching duties be spelled out in writing rather than left to an oral agreement. Because all board of education policies and regulations will be part of your contract, you should also read any available teacher handbook or school policy handbook.

The importance of carefully reading a contract and asking for clarification is illustrated in the following case:

> *Victor Sanchez had just begun his first year as an English teacher at a high school in a city of about 300,000. Victor became quite upset when he learned that he had been assigned by his principal to sponsor the poetry club. The club was to meet once a week after school. Victor refused to sponsor the club, saying that the contract he had signed*

referred only to his teaching duties during regular school hours. Could Victor be compelled to sponsor the club?

Certain assignments, though not specified in a contract, may be required of teachers in addition to their regular teaching load, as long as there is a reasonable relationship between the teacher's classroom duties and the additional assignment. Furthermore, such assignments can include supervision of school events on weekends as well. Though Victor's contract did not make specific reference to club sponsorship, such a duty would be a reasonable addition to his regular teaching assignment.

When school authorities have assigned teachers to additional duties not reasonably related to their teaching, the courts have tended to rule in favor of teachers who file suit. For example, a school's directive to a tenured teacher of American history to assume the additional role of basketball coach was not upheld by a court of appeals (*Unified School District No. 241 v. Swanson* 1986).

Due Process in Tenure and Dismissal

Tenure is a policy that provides the individual teacher with job security by (1) preventing his or her dismissal on insufficient grounds and (2) providing him or her with due process in the event of dismissal. Tenure is granted to teachers by the local school district after a period of satisfactory teaching, usually two to five years. In most cases, tenure may not be transferred from one school district to another.

The following case highlights the importance of tenure to a teacher's professional career:

> *A teacher was dismissed from his teaching position by the school board after it learned that the teacher was a homosexual. The teacher filed suit in court, claiming that his firing was arbitrary and violated the provisions of tenure that he had been granted. The school board, on the other hand, maintained that his conduct was inappropriate for a teacher. Was the school board justified in dismissing the teacher?*

The events in this case were actually heard by a court, which ruled that the teacher was unfairly dismissed (*Burton v. Cascade School District Union High School No. 5* 1975). The court said that the board violated the teacher's rights as a tenured employee by failing to show "good and just cause" for dismissal. The teacher was awarded the balance due under his contract and an additional one-half year's salary. In a similar case, however, a court upheld the dismissal of a teacher whose sexual orientation was the target of parents' complaints and students' comments. The court ruled that the teacher could no longer effectively carry out his teaching duties (*Gaylord v. Tacoma School District No. 10* 1977).

The practice of providing teachers with tenure is not without controversy. Some critics point out that tenure policies make it too difficult to dismiss incompetent teachers and that performance standards are high in many other fields that do not provide employees with job security. Generally, however, the courts have held the position that tenure is a property right "from which students ultimately benefit" (Essex 1999, 179).

Just about every state today has a tenure law that specifies that a teacher may be dismissed with good cause; what counts as a good cause varies from state to state. The courts have ruled on a variety of reasons for **dismissal**: (1) insubordination, (2) incompetence or inefficiency, (3) neglect of duty, (4) conduct unbecoming a teacher, (5) subversive activities, (6) retrenchment or decreased need for services, (7) physical and/or mental health, (8) age, (9) causing or encouraging disruption, (10) engaging in illegal activities, (11) using offensive language, (12) personal appearance, (13) sex-related activities, (14) political activities, and (15) use of drugs or intoxicants.

For a tenured teacher to be dismissed, a systematic series of steps must be followed so that the teacher receives due process and his or her constitutionally guaranteed rights are not violated. Due process involves a careful, step-by-step examination of the charges brought against a teacher. Most states have outlined procedures that adhere to the following nine steps:

1. The teacher must be notified of the list of charges.
2. Adequate time must be provided for the teacher to prepare a rebuttal to the charges.
3. The teacher must be given the names of witnesses and access to evidence.
4. The hearing must be conducted before an impartial tribunal.
5. The teacher has the right to representation by legal counsel.
6. The teacher (or legal counsel) can introduce evidence and cross-examine adverse witnesses.
7. The school board's decision must be based on the evidence and findings of the hearing.
8. A transcript or record must be maintained of the hearing.
9. The teacher has the right to appeal an adverse decision.

These steps notwithstanding, it should be noted that "the definition [of due process] in each instance depends largely on a combination of the specific facts in a situation, the law governing the situation, the particular time in history in which judgment is being rendered, and the predilections of the individual judge(s) rendering the decision" (LaMorte 2002, 6), as the following case illustrates:

Near the start of his fifth year of teaching at an elementary school in a small city, and two years after earning tenure, Mr. Mitchell went through a sudden and painful divorce. A few months later a woman whom he had met around the time of his divorce moved into the house he was renting.

For the remainder of the school year, he and the woman lived together. During this time, he received no indication that his lifestyle was professionally unacceptable, and his teaching performance remained satisfactory.

At the end of the year, however, Mr. Mitchell was notified that he was being dismissed because of immoral conduct; that is, he was living with a woman he was not married to. The school board called for a hearing, and Mr. Mitchell presented his side of the case. The board, nevertheless, decided to follow through with its decision to dismiss him. Was the school board justified in dismissing Mr. Mitchell?

Though at one time teachers could readily be dismissed for living, unmarried, with a member of the opposite sex, a lifestyle such as Mr. Mitchell's is not that unusual today. Because the board had not shown that Mr. Mitchell's alleged immoral conduct had a negative effect on his teaching, his dismissal would probably not hold up in court, unless the community as a whole was upset by his behavior. Moreover, Mr. Mitchell could charge that his right to privacy as guaranteed by the Ninth Amendment to the Constitution had been violated. Overall, it appears that the decision to dismiss Mr. Mitchell was arbitrary and based on the collective bias of the board. Nevertheless, teachers should be aware that courts frequently hold that teachers are role models, and the local community determines "acceptable" behavior both in school and out of school.

Teachers also have the right to organize and to join teacher organizations without fear of dismissal. In addition, most states have passed **collective bargaining** laws that require school boards to negotiate contracts with teacher organizations. Usually, the teacher organization with the most members in a district is given the right to represent teachers in the collective bargaining process.

An important part of most collective bargaining agreements is the right of a teacher to file a **grievance**, a formal complaint against his or her employer. A teacher may not be dismissed for filing a grievance, and he or she is entitled to have the grievance heard by a neutral third party. Often, the teachers' union or professional association that negotiated the collective bargaining agreement will provide a teacher who has filed a grievance with free legal counsel.

One right that teachers are not granted by collective bargaining agreements is the right to strike. Like other public employees, teachers do not have the legal right to strike in most states. Although teachers have a limited right to strike in a few states, "extensive restrictions have been placed on its use" (McCarthy, Cambron-McCabe, and Thomas 1998, 433). Teachers who do strike run the risk of dismissal (*Hortonville Joint School District No. 1 v. Hortonville Education Association* 1976), though when teacher strikes occur a school board cannot possibly replace all the striking teachers.

Academic Freedom

A teacher of at-risk students at an alternative high school used a classroom management/motivational technique called Learnball. The teacher divided the class into teams, allowed students to elect team leaders and determine class rules and grading exercises, and developed a system of rewards that included listening to the radio and shooting baskets with a foam ball in the classroom. The school board ordered the teacher not to use the Learnball approach. Did the teacher have the right to continue using this teaching method?

This case is based on actual events involving a teacher in Pittsburgh. The teacher brought suit against the board to prevent it from imposing a policy that banned Learnball in the classroom. The teacher cited the principle of **academic**

freedom and claimed that teachers have a right to use teaching methods and materials to which school officials might object. A U.S. district court, however, upheld the school board policy against Learnball (*Murray v. Pittsburgh Board of Public Education* 1996).

Although the courts have held that teachers have the right to academic freedom, it is not absolute and must be balanced against the interests of society. In fact, education law expert Michael LaMorte (2002, 200) suggests that the concept of academic freedom "is no longer as strong a defense as it once was"; for this defense to prevail, "it must be shown that the teacher did not defy legitimate state and local curriculum directives; followed accepted professional norms for that grade level and subject matter; discussed matters which were of public concern; and acted professionally and in good faith when there was no precedent or policy."

Famous Cases   A landmark case involving academic freedom focused on John Scopes, a biology teacher who in 1925 challenged a Tennessee law that made it illegal to teach in a public school "any theory which denies the story of the Divine Creation of man as taught in the Bible, and to teach instead that man is descended from a lower order of animals." Scopes maintained that Darwin's theory about human origins had scientific merit and that the state's requirement that he teach the biblical account of creation violated his academic freedom.

Scopes's trial, which came to be known as the Monkey Trial, attracted national attention. Prosecuting Scopes was the "silver-tongued" William Jennings Bryan, a famous lawyer, politician, and presidential candidate. The defending attorney was Clarence Darrow.

Scopes believed strongly in academic freedom and his students' right to know about scientific theories. He expressed his views in his memoirs, *Center of the Storm:*

> Especially repulsive are laws restricting the constitutional freedom of teachers. The mere presence of such a law is a club held over the heads of the timid. Legislation that tampers with academic freedom is not protecting society, as its authors piously proclaim. By limiting freedom they are helping to make robot factories out of schools; ultimately, this produces nonthinking robots rather than the individualistic citizens we desperately need—now more than ever before (1966, 277).

The Monkey Trial ended after eleven days of heated, eloquent testimony. Scopes was found guilty of violating the Butler Act and was fined $100. The decision was later reversed by the Tennessee Supreme Court on a technicality.

Since the Scopes trial, controversy has continued to surround the teaching of evolution. In many states during the 1980s, for example, religious fundamentalists won rulings that required science teachers to give equal time to both creationism and evolutionism in the classroom. The Supreme Court, however, in *Edwards v. Aguillard* (1987) ruled that such "balanced treatment" laws were unconstitutional: "Because the primary purpose of the [Louisiana] Creationism Act is to advance a particular religious belief, the Act endorses religion in violation of the First Amendment." In 1996, controversy over evolution again emerged in Tennessee when lawmakers defeated, by a twenty-to-thirteen vote, legislation that would allow districts to dismiss teachers for "insubordination" if they taught evolution as fact.

Another case suggesting that a teacher's right to academic freedom is narrow and limited is *Krizek v. Cicero-Stickney Township High School District No. 201* (1989). In this instance, a district court ruled against a teacher whose contract was not renewed because she showed her students an R-rated film (*About Last Night*) as an example of a modern-day parallel to Thornton Wilder's play *Our Town*. Although the teacher told her students that they would be excused from viewing the film if they or their parents objected, she did not communicate directly with their parents. The teacher's attempt to consider the objections of students and parents notwithstanding, the court concluded that

> the length of the film indicates that its showing was more than an inadvertent mistake or a mere slip of the tongue, but rather was a planned event, and thus indicated that the teacher's approach to teaching was problematic.

Though concerned more with the right of a school to establish a curriculum than with the academic freedom of teachers per se, other cases have focused on the teacher's use of instructional materials. In *Mozert v. Hawkins County Board of Education* (1987, 1988), for example, a group of Tennessee parents objected to "secular humanist" reading materials used by their children's teachers. In *Smith v. Board of School Commissioners of Mobile County* (1987), 624 parents and teachers initiated a court suit alleging that forty-four history, social studies, and home economics texts used in the Mobile County, Alabama, public schools encouraged immorality, undermined parental authority, and were imbued with the "humanist" faith. In both cases, the courts supported the right of schools to establish a curriculum even in the face of parental disapproval. In *Smith v. Board of School Commissioners of Mobile County* (1987), the Eleventh Circuit Court stated that "[i]ndeed, given the diversity of religious views in this country, if the standard were merely inconsistency with the beliefs of a particular religion there would be very little that could be taught in the public schools."

States' Rights   The preceding cases notwithstanding, the courts have not set down specific guidelines to reconcile the teacher's freedom with the state's right to require teachers to follow certain curricular guidelines. Another federal court, for example, heard a similar case regarding a high school teacher who wrote a vulgar word for sexual intercourse on the blackboard during a discussion of socially taboo words. The court actually sidestepped the issue of academic freedom and ruled instead that the regulations authorizing teacher discipline were unconstitutionally vague and, therefore, the teacher could not be dismissed. The court, however, did observe that a public school teacher's right to traditional academic freedom is "qualified," at best, and the "teacher's right must yield to compelling public interests of greater constitutional significance." In reviewing its decision, the court also said, "Nothing herein suggests that school authorities are not free after they have learned that the teacher is using a teaching method of which they disapprove, and which is not appropriate to the proper teaching of the subject, to suspend him [or her] until he [or she] agrees to cease using the method" (*Mailloux v. Kiley* 1971).

Although some teachers have been successful in citing academic freedom as the basis for teaching controversial subjects, others have been unsuccessful. Teachers have been dismissed for ignoring directives regarding the teaching of controversial topics related to sex, polygamy, race, and religion. Though the courts have not been able to clarify just where academic freedom begins and ends, they have made it clear that the state does have a legitimate interest in what is taught to impressionable children.

Do Student Teachers Have the Same Rights?

Do student teachers have the same legal status as certified teachers? Read the following case:

> *Lakeisha Grant had really looked forward to the eight weeks she would spend as a student teacher in Mrs. Walker's high school English classes. Lakeisha knew that Mrs. Walker was one of the best supervising teachers she might have been paired with, and she was anxious to do her best.*
>
> *In Mrs. Walker's senior class, Lakeisha planned to teach* Brave New World. *Mrs. Walker pointed out to Lakeisha that this book was controversial and some parents might object. She asked Lakeisha to think about selecting an additional title that students could read if their parents objected to* Brave New World. *Lakeisha, however, felt that Mrs. Walker was bowing to pressure from conservative parents, so she decided to go ahead and teach the book.*
>
> *Two weeks later Lakeisha was called down to the principal's office where she was confronted by an angry father who said, "You have no right to be teaching my daughter this Communist trash; you're just a student teacher." What should Lakeisha do? Does she have the same rights as a fully certified teacher?*

In some states, a student teacher such as Lakeisha might have the same rights and responsibilities as a fully certified teacher; in others, her legal status might be that of an unlicensed visitor. The most prudent action for Lakeisha to take would be to apologize to the father and assure him that if any controversial books are assigned in the future, alternative titles would be provided. In addition, Lakeisha should learn how important it is for a student teacher to take the advice of his or her supervising teacher.

"The legal status of the student teacher is a perennial question with both student teachers and cooperating teachers" (Wentz 2001, 55). One study found that the authority of student teachers to teach was established by law in only forty states, and no state had a statutory provision regulating the dismissal of a student teacher, the assignment of a student teacher, or the denial of the right to student teach (Morris and Curtis 1983). Nevertheless, student teachers should be aware that a potential for liability exists with them just as it does with certified teachers.

One area of debate regarding student teachers is whether they can act as substitutes for their cooperating teachers or even other teachers in a school building.

Figure 4.1 Legal advice for student teachers.

Legal Advice for Student Teachers

1. Read the teacher's handbook, if one is available, and discuss its contents with the cooperating teacher. Be sure you understand its requirements and prohibitions.

2. Thoroughly discuss school safety rules and regulations. Be certain you know what to do in case of emergency, before assuming complete control of the classroom.

3. Be aware of the potential hazards associated with any activity and act accordingly to protect children from those dangers.

4. Be certain you know what controls the district has placed on the curriculum you will be teaching. Are there specific texts and/or methodologies that district policy requires or prohibits?

5. Be certain that student records are used to enhance and inform your teaching. Make certain that strict confidentiality is respected.

6. Document any problems you have with students, or as a teacher, in case you are called upon to relate details at a later time.

Source: Julie Mead and Julie Underwood, "A Legal Primer for Student Teachers," in Gloria Slick (Ed.), *Emerging Trends in Teacher Preparation: The Future of Field Experiences.* Thousand Oaks, CA: Corwin Press, 1995, pp. 49–50.

Unfortunately, many school districts have no policy regarding this practice. Depending on statutes in a particular state, however, a student teacher may substitute under the following conditions:

- A substitute teacher is not immediately available.
- The student teacher has been in that student teaching assignment for a specified minimum number of school days.
- The supervising teacher, the principal of the school, and the university supervisor agree that the student teacher is capable of successfully handling the teaching responsibilities.

- A certified classroom teacher in an adjacent room or a member of the same teaching team as the student teacher is aware of the absence and agrees to assist the student teacher if needed.
- The principal of the school or the principal's representative is readily available in the building.
- The student teacher is not paid for any substitute service. (This matter is negotiable in some jurisdictions.) (Dunklee and Shoop 2002, 89–90)

Given the ambiguous status of student teachers, it is important that you begin your student teaching assignment with a knowledge of the legal aspects of teaching and a clear idea of your rights and responsibilities. To accomplish this, read the NEA Bill of Rights for Student Teachers in Appendix 4.2 and follow the recommendations in Figure 4.1 made by school law experts Julie Mead and Julie Underwood.

What Are Your Legal Responsibilities as a Teacher?

Teachers are, of course, responsible for meeting the terms of their teaching contracts. As noted previously, teachers are responsible for duties not covered in the contract if they are reasonably related to teaching. Among these duties may be club sponsorship; lunchroom, study hall, or playground duty; academic counseling of students; and record keeping.

Teachers are also legally responsible for the safety and well-being of students assigned to them. Although it is not expected that a teacher be able to control completely the behavior of young, energetic students, a teacher can be held liable for any injury to a student if it is shown that the teacher's negligence contributed to the injury. The Teachers' Voices feature on pages 116–117 in this chapter illustrates one teacher's concern about the safety and well-being of her students during a field trip.

Avoiding Tort Liability

An eighth-grade science teacher in Louisiana left her class for a few moments to go to the school office to pick up some forms. While she was gone, her students continued to do some laboratory work that involved the use of alcohol-burning devices. Unfortunately, one girl was injured when she tried to relight a defective burner. Could the teacher be held liable for the girl's injuries?

The events described above actually occurred in 1974 (*Station v. Travelers Insurance Co.*). The court that heard the case determined that the teacher failed to provide adequate supervision while the students were exposed to dangerous conditions. Considerable care is required, the court observed, when students handle inherently dangerous objects, and the need for this care is magnified when students are exposed to dangers they don't appreciate.

At times, teachers may have concerns about their liability for damages as a result of their actions. The branch of law concerned with compensating an individual who suffers losses resulting from another's negligence is known as tort law. "A tort is a civil wrong in which one suffers loss as a result of the improper conduct of

Teachers' Voices
Putting Research and Theory into Practice

Opening the Door to Possibilities

Mary Hanson

As a third-grade teacher in a metropolitan city in Southern California, I have made efforts to be more than just "the teacher" or "la maestra" to my students—I have tried to be a mentor who provides more than reading, writing, and math lessons. You see, most of my students come from low-income families, where their view of their place in the community has not only been defined by their economic status, but also by the fact that extracurricular activities are limited and their exposure to many things we take for granted (like "take your daughter to work" day) are practically non-existent. So, whenever possible, I seize any opportunity to bring community members to my classroom to share their experiences with my third-graders.

This year, I was fortunate enough to have a Junior Achievement volunteer teach four lessons on business: the business of running a city, a bank, a newspaper, and a restaurant. The students were so engaged by this last unit that we became immersed in the business of being restaurateurs. The JA volunteer . . . arranged for us to visit a local Italian restaurant in Old Town. This was going to be the chance for them to see how a real restaurant works!

I must admit I had reservations about this trip. Our volunteer was so confident, and here I was thinking about things like forty busy little hands near boiling kettles and sharp objects, or worse, someone blurting out some embarrassing remark, but I just put in my paperwork to district transportation and kept my fingers crossed. I gave the students firm reminders to wash their hands and mind their manners. I reminded them that they were representing our school. . . .

At the restaurant, Mr. Chavez, the sous chef, greeted us at the door. Walking inside the closed restaurant (they are open only for dinner), each child was wide-eyed. The restaurant, famous for its photo-covered walls, was mesmerizing. There were hundreds upon hundreds of pictures, each conveying some aspect of Italian culture: families eating mounds of spaghetti, pictures of the Pope, the statues and fountains of Rome. After the initial shock wore off, the students passed through the kitchens and were seated in the largest seating area in the restaurant. Like magic, they transformed into curious little restaurant specialists. . . .

Too soon, [our visit ended] and we had to return to the bus. Mr. Chavez was sad to see us go since there were so many more questions. He called to a worker in the kitchen, "Make those pizzas TO GO!" The next thing I knew, we were back on the bus and I was carrying a gift from the restaurant for each child and pizza for 20. Tired, I slumped in the front seat, realizing we had gotten through this with no mishaps, no burned fingers, no embarrassing comments, and I was prouder than I ever thought I could be.

After we wolfed down the pizza and drank half my case of bottled water, we debriefed. We talked about what we'd learned. The third-graders talked about figuring out how to make a profit if you prepare a meal. They talked about the COLD freezer and how buying one costs a lot of money. They talked about a lot of things that they saw, including the pictures on the walls. But the part I liked most was that they talked about the possibilities. I can't count how many times I've heard these low-income kids, whose parents are working at low-paying, dead-end jobs, talk about the low-paying, dead-end jobs they will take when they turn eighteen. At least four kids have continued to talk about going to cooking school, and two more thought it would be cool going around to restaurants and fixing the refrigerators and freezers. Brenda, who had told me more than once that when she grew up she was going to clean houses like her mom, told me that when she was eighteen, she was going to go to Bucca di Beppo and ask for a job as a pasta chef. "I'd have to start as a helper, I think," she said with serious eyes, "But I could get better!" She smiled and ran out to recess.

Questions

1. Assume that one of Hanson's students was cut by a sharp object while in the restaurant's kitchen. Under what circumstances would Hanson not be liable for the student's injury?

2. Based on the situation above, under what circumstances would Hanson be liable for the student's injury?

3. When arranging field trips similar to Hanson's, what steps can a teacher take to minimize the possibility of being liable for a student's injury?

Mary Hanson is a National Board Certified Teacher in the Pasadena Unified School District, Pasadena, CA. The preceding is excerpted from her contribution to Adrienne Mack-Krisher's *Powerful Classroom Stories from Accomplished Teachers* (Thousand Oaks, CA: Corwin, 2004), pp. 156–159.

another" (LaMorte 2002, 383). The harm inflicted on the injured party may be the result of "intentional wrongdoing, recklessness, or simple carelessness" (Imber and van Geel 1993, 575). According to **tort liability** law, an individual who is negligent and at fault in the exercise of his or her legal duty may be required to pay monetary damages to an injured party. Generally, the standard of behavior applied by the courts is that the injury "must be avoidable by the exercise of reasonable care" (McCarthy, Cambron-McCabe, and Thomas 1998, 436). However, teachers are held to a higher standard than ordinary citizens, and certain teachers (e.g., physical education and chemistry teachers) are held to an even higher standard because of the increased risk of injury involved in the classes they teach. Table 4.1 presents several examples of cases in which students were injured and educators were found to have breached their duty of care.

Negligence   In contrast to the decision reached by the Louisiana court in *Station v. Travelers Insurance Co.*, the courts have made it clear that there are many accidents that teachers cannot reasonably foresee that do result in student injuries. For example, a teacher on playground duty was found to be not negligent when a student threw a rock that struck another student in the eye. After the teacher walked past a group of boys, one boy threw a small rock that hit a larger rock on the ground and then bounced up to hit the other boy in the eye. The court ruled that "[w]here the time between an act of a student and injury to a fellow student is so short that the teacher had no opportunity to prevent injury, it cannot be said that negligence of the teacher is a proximate cause of the injury" (*Fagen v. Summers* 1972). In another case, the court ruled that a New York teacher could not have anticipated that the paper bag she asked a student to pick up contained a broken bottle upon which the student cut herself (*West v. Board of Education of City of New York* 1959). In two almost identical cases, the courts ruled that a teacher of a class with a good behavior record could not reasonably be expected to anticipate that a student would be injured by a pencil thrown by a classmate while the teacher was momentarily out of the room attending to her usual duties (*Ohman v. Board of Education* 1950; *Simonetti v. School District of Philadelphia* 1982).

When a court considers a case involving tort liability, evidence is examined to determine whether the responsible party (the school district, the administrator, or

Table 4.1	Selected court decisions in which school personnel were found negligent for failure to meet a "standard of care"

1. A woodworking instructor allowed a student to operate a table saw without the use of a safeguard, which resulted in serious damage to his proximal interphalangeal joint. *Barbin v. State,* 506 So. 2d 88 (1st Cir. 1987).

2. A student dislocated his shoulder during an intramural football game, when the school provided no protective equipment and improper supervision of the game. *Locilento v. John A. Coleman Catholic High School,* 523 N.Y.S.2d 198 (A.D. 3d Dept. 1987).

3. An eleven-year-old student suffered serious head injuries from a blow in the head during a kick game and was without medical attention for more than an hour. The one-hour delay caused a hematoma to grow from the size of a walnut to that of an orange. *Barth v. Board of Education,* 490 N.E.2d 77 (Ill. App. 186 Dist. 1986).

4. An eight-year-old girl was seriously burned when her costume caught fire from a lighted candle on her teacher's desk. *Smith v. Archbishop of St. Louis,* 632 S.W.2d 516 (Mo. App. 1982).

5. A twelve-year-old boy was killed when he fell through a skylight at school while retrieving a ball. *Stahl v. Cocalico School District,* 534 A.2d 1141 (Pa. Cmwlth. 1987).

6. A boy was seriously injured while playing on school grounds when he fell into a hole filled with glass, trash, and other debris, due to the absence of school officials to warn him of the dangerous condition. *Dean v. Board of Education,* 523 A.2d 1059 (Md. App. 1987).

7. A female student was in route to class when she pushed her hand through a glass panel in a smoke-colored door, causing severe and permanent damage. *Bielaska v. Town of Waterford,* 491 A.2d 1071 (Conn. 1985).

8. A high school student was seriously injured when he was tackled and thrown to the ground during a touch football game in gym class, based on inadequate supervision when the players began to use excessive force. *Hyman v. Green,* 403 N.W.2d 597 (Mich. App. 1987).

Source: From Nathan L. Essex, *School Law and the Public Schools: A Practical Guide for Educational Leaders.* Boston: Allyn and Bacon, 1999, pp. 110, 126. Copyright © 1999 by Allyn and Bacon. Reprinted by permission.

the teacher) acted negligently. For a school official to be considered liable, the following must be shown to be present:

- A legal duty to conform to a standard of conduct for the protection of others
- A failure to exercise an appropriate standard of care
- A causal connection, often referred to as "proximate cause," between the conduct and the resultant injury
- Actual loss or damage as a result of the injury (LaMorte 2002, 406)

As a teacher, you should be especially alert when conditions exist that might lead to accidental injury of one or more students. You will have a duty in regard to your pupils, and you could be held liable for injuries that students incur as a result of your **negligence**. This does not mean, however, that your liability extends to any and all injuries your students might suffer; only if you fail to provide the same degree of care for pupils that a reasonable and prudent person would have shown in similar circumstances can you be held liable. A review of court cases involving

Should this teacher/coach have any concerns about tort liability? How might this teacher reduce the risk of liability?

the tort liability of teachers suggests that most cases involve at least one of the following:

- Inadequate supervision
- Inadequate instruction
- Lack of or improper medical treatment of pupils
- Improper disclosure of defamatory information concerning pupils—for example, release of school records that contain negative statements about a student

Teachers' concern about their potential monetary liability for failing to act reasonably and prudently in preventing injury to their students has been lessened by the availability of liability insurance. Many professional organizations for teachers offer liability coverage as part of their membership benefits, and teachers may also purchase individual liability insurance policies. In addition, some states that provide school districts with full or partial immunity from tort liability are considering extending the same protection to school employees. Georgia, for example, has extended immunity to teachers and principals (LaMorte 2002).

Educational Malpractice   Since the mid-1970s, several plaintiffs have charged in **educational malpractice** suits that schools should be responsible for a pupil whose failure to achieve is significant. In the first of such cases, the parents of Peter W. Doe charged that the San Francisco Unified School District was negligent because it allowed him to graduate from high school with a fifth-grade reading level and this handicap would not enable him to function in adult society. In particular, they charged that the "defendant school district, its agents and employees, negligently and carelessly failed to provide plaintiff with adequate instruction, guidance, counseling and/or supervision in basic academic skills such as reading and writing, although said school district had the authority, responsibility, and ability [to do so]." They sought $500,000 for the negligent work of the teachers who taught Peter.

In evaluating the claim of Peter W. Doe and his parents, the court pointed out that the alleged injury was not within the realm of tort law and that many factors beyond a school's responsibility or control can account for lack of achievement. The court did not hold the school responsible for Peter's lack of achievement and made it clear that to do so would be to set a precedent with potentially drastic consequences: "To hold [schools] to an actionable duty of care, in the discharge of their academic functions, would expose them to the tort claims—real or imagined—of disaffected students and parents in countless numbers. . . . The ultimate consequences, in terms of public time and money, would burden them—and society—beyond calculation" (*Peter Doe v. San Francisco Unified School District* 1976).

Reporting Child Abuse

As a teacher, you are *required* by law to report any suspected child abuse. You will be in a position to monitor and to work against the physical, emotional, and sexual abuse and the neglect and exploitation of children. Teachers' professional journals and information from local, state, and federal child welfare agencies encourage teachers to be more observant of children's appearance and behavior in order to detect symptoms of child abuse. Such sources often provide lists of physical and behavioral indicators of potential child abuse, similar to that shown in Table 4.2. Many communities, through their police departments or other public and private agencies, provide programs adapted for children to educate them about their rights in child-abuse situations and to show them how to obtain help.

On occasion, parents and guardians have alleged a Fourth Amendment (protection against search and seizure) violation, claiming that school personnel should not have questioned or examined a student to determine if child abuse had occurred. In a Pennsylvania case, the court concluded that the Fourth Amendment had not been violated as a result of school personnel questioning a student about

Table 4.2	Physical and behavioral indicators of child abuse and neglect	

Type of Child Abuse/Neglect	Physical Indicators	Behavioral Indicators
Physical abuse	Unexplained bruises and welts: • on face, lips, mouth • on torso, back, buttocks, thighs • in various stages of healing • clustered, forming regular patterns • reflecting shape of article used to inflict (electric cord, belt buckle) • on several different surface areas • regularly appear after absence, weekend, or vacation • human bite marks • bald spots Unexplained burns: • cigar, cigarette burns, especially on soles, palms, back, or buttocks • immersion burns (sock-like, glove-like, doughnut-shaped on buttocks or genitalia) • patterned like electric burner, iron, etc. • rope burns on arms, legs, neck, or torso Unexplained fractures: • to skull, nose, facial structure • in various stages of healing • multiple or spiral fractures Unexplained lacerations or abrasions: • to mouth, lips, gums, eyes • to external genitalia	Wary of adult contacts Apprehensive when other children cry Behavioral extremes: • aggressiveness • withdrawal • overly compliant Afraid to go home Reports injury by parents Exhibits anxiety about normal activities, e.g., napping Complains of soreness and moves awkwardly Destructive to self and others Early to school or stays late as if afraid to go home Accident prone Wears clothing that covers body when not appropriate Chronic runaway (especially adolescents) Cannot tolerate physical contact or touch
Physical neglect	Consistent hunger, poor hygiene, inappropriate dress Consistent lack of supervision, especially in dangerous activities or long periods Unattended physical problems or medical needs Abandonment Lice Distended stomach, emaciated	Begging, stealing food Constant fatigue, listlessness, or falling asleep States there is no caretaker at home Frequent school absence or tardiness Destructive, pugnacious School dropout (adolescents) Early emancipation from family (adolescents)

(continued)

Table 4.2   Continued

Type of Child Abuse/Neglect	Physical Indicators	Behavioral Indicators
Sexual abuse	Difficulty in walking or sitting Torn, stained, or bloody underclothing Pain or itching in genital area Bruises or bleeding in external genitalia, vaginal, or anal areas Venereal disease Frequent urinary or yeast infections Frequent unexplained sore throats	Unwilling to participate in certain physical activities Sudden drop in school performance Withdrawal, fantasy, or unusually infantile behavior Crying with no provocation Bizarre, sophisticated, or unusual sexual behavior or knowledge Anorexia (especially adolescents) Sexually provocative Poor peer relationships Reports sexual assault by caretaker Fear of or seductiveness toward males Suicide attempts (especially adolescents) Chronic runaway Early pregnancies
Emotional maltreatment	Speech disorders Lags in physical development Failure to thrive (especially in infants) Asthma, severe allergies, or ulcers Substance abuse	Habit disorders (sucking, biting, rocking, etc.) Conduct disorders (antisocial, destructive, etc.) Neurotic traits (sleep disorders, inhibition of play) Behavioral extremes: • compliant, passive • aggressive, demanding Overly adaptive behavior: • inappropriately adult • inappropriately infantile Developmental lags (mental, emotional) Delinquent behavior (especially adolescents)

Sources: Adapted from Cynthia Crosson Tower, *The Role of Educators in the Prevention and Treatment of Child Abuse and Neglect,* The User Manual Series, 1992. Washington, DC: U.S. Department of Health and Human Services. Derry Koralek, *Caregivers of Young Children: Preventing and Responding to Child Maltreatment,* The User Manual Series, 1992. Washington, DC: U.S. Department of Health and Human Services.

suspected abuse. According to the court, Pennsylvania's Child Protective Services Law required teachers and administrators to determine if there was "reason to believe" that a student had been abused (*Picarella v. Terrizzi* 1995).

Schools usually have a specific process for dealing with suspected abuse cases, involving the school principal and nurse as well as the reporting teacher. Because a child's physical welfare may be further endangered when abuse is reported, caution and sensitivity are required. Teachers are in a unique position to help students who are victims of child abuse, both because they have daily contact with them and because children learn to trust them.

Observing Copyright Laws

The continuing rapid development of technology has resulted in a new set of responsibilities for teachers in regard to observing **copyright laws** pertaining to the use of photocopies, videotapes, and computer software programs. In 1976, Congress revised the Copyright Act by adding the doctrine of **fair use**. Although the fair use doctrine cannot be precisely defined, it is generally interpreted as it was in *Marcus v. Rowley* (1983)—that is, one may "use the copyrighted material in a reasonable manner without [the copyright holder's] consent" as long as that use does not reduce the demand for the work or the author's income.

To "move the nation's copyright law into the digital age," the **Digital Millennium Copyright Act (DMCA)** amended the Copyright Act in 1998. The DMCA makes it illegal to circumvent copy-blocking measures (encryption and encoding, for example) that control access to copyrighted works. However, according to the statute, educational institutions may circumvent access control measures "solely for the purpose of making a good faith determination as to whether they wish to obtain authorized access to the work."

With the vast amount of material (in text, audio, video, and graphic formats) now distributed in digital form over the Internet, teachers must consider copyright laws and restrictions that apply to the use of this material. Unfortunately, the Copyright Act does not provide guidelines for the use of intellectual property found on the Internet. In any case, teachers should understand that "when [their] computer displays a home page on the Internet, [the] computer is presenting a copy of the page that 'exists' on a remote computer. . . . [They] are viewing a published copy of an original document" (Schwartz and Beichner 1999, 199), and the doctrine of fair use applies to the use of such materials.

Photocopies   To clarify the fair use doctrine as it pertained to teachers photocopying instructional materials from books and magazines, Congress endorsed a set of guidelines developed by educators, authors, and publishers. These guidelines allow teachers to make single copies of copyrighted material for teaching or research but are more restrictive regarding the use of multiple copies. The use of multiple copies of a work must meet the tests of brevity, spontaneity, and cumulative effect.

- *Brevity* means that short works can be copied. Poems or excerpts cannot be longer than 250 words, and copies of longer works cannot exceed 1,000 words or

10 percent of the work (whichever is less). Only one chart or drawing can be reproduced from a book or an article.

- The criterion of *spontaneity* means that the teacher doing the copying would not have time to request permission from the copyright holder.
- The criterion of *cumulative effect* limits the use of copies to one course and limits the material copied from the same author, book, or magazine during the semester. Also, no more than nine instances of multiple copying per class are allowed during a semester.

Videotapes   Guidelines for the use of videotapes made by teachers of television broadcasts were issued by Congress in 1981. Videotaped material may be used in the classroom only once by the teacher within the first ten days of taping. Additional use is limited to reinforcing instruction or evaluation of student learning, and the tape must be erased within forty-five days.

Computer Software   With the explosion of computer-based technology in schools, teachers face a new ethical and legal issue—adhering to copyright laws as they relate to computer software. Making an illegal copy of software on a computer hard drive—in effect, stealing another person's "intellectual property"—is quite easy. In fact, "It is very common for otherwise ethical and moral people to ask for and/or offer illegal copies of software to one another" (Schwartz and Beichner 1999, 193). It is therefore important that, as a teacher, you be an exemplar of ethical behavior regarding copyrighted computer software. Just as you would not allow students to plagiarize written material or submit work that was not their own, you should follow the same standard of behavior regarding the use of computer software.

Computer software publishers have become concerned about the abuse of their copyrighted material. Limited school budgets and the high cost of computer software have led to the unauthorized reproduction of software. To address the problem, the Copyright Act was amended in 1980 to apply the fair use doctrine to software. Accordingly, a teacher may now make one backup copy of a program. If a teacher were to make multiple copies of software, the fair use doctrine would be violated because the software is readily accessible for purchase and making multiple copies would substantially reduce the market for the software. Software publishers have several different options for licensing their software to schools (see Table 4.3), and teachers should be aware of the type of license that has been purchased with each software program they use.

The increased practice of networking computer programs—that is, storing a copy of a computer program on a network file server and serving the program to a computer on the network—is also of concern to software publishers. As yet, the practice has not yet been tested in the courts. As more public schools develop computer networks, however, the issue of networked software will most likely be debated in the courts.

Currently, the Copyright Act is being revised to reflect how the doctrine of fair use should be applied to digital data. Two questions currently not answered by

Table 4.3	Common types of commercial software licenses		
License Type	**What Is Permitted**	**Suitability for Schools**
Single-user license	Permits installation on one and only one computer.	Not usually economical for schools.
Multiple-user license (sometimes called a "Lab Pack")	Permits installation on up to a specified number of computers (typically 5, 10, 50, etc.).	Economical and commonly found in K–12 schools.
Network license	Permits installation on a network. License will specify the maximum number of simultaneous users.	Economical and commonly found in larger K–12 schools if they are networked.
Site license	Permits installation on any and all computers owned by the institution.	Not typically used in K–12 schools. More common for college campuses.

Source: From James E. Schwartz and Robert J. Beichner, *Essentials of Educational Technology.* Boston: Allyn and Bacon, 1999, p. 195. Copyright © 1999 by Allyn and Bacon.

copyright law as it pertains to the educational use of computer software are the legality of (1) installing a single program on several computers in a laboratory and (2) modifying the program for use in a computer network. The Copyright Act specifies four factors that are used to determine whether use of copyrighted material constitutes fair use or an infringement: (1) the purpose and character of the use, including whether such use is of a commercial nature or is for nonprofit educational purposes; (2) the nature of the copyrighted work; (3) the amount and substantiality of the portion used in relation to the copyrighted work as a whole; and (4) the effect of the use on the potential market for or value of the copyrighted work.

E-mail and the Internet   With the huge increase in the transmission of documents via e-mail and the Internet, copyright laws have been extended to cyberspace. Material "published" online may include a statement by the author that the material is copyright protected and may not be duplicated without permission. In other cases, the material may include a statement such as the following: "Permission is granted to distribute this material freely through electronic or by other means, provided it remains completely intact and unaltered, the source is acknowledged, and no fee is charged for it." If the material is published without restrictions on the Internet, one may assume that the author waives copyright privileges; however, proper credit and a citation should accompany the material if it is reproduced. The Technology in Teaching feature in this chapter examines how the Digital Millennium Copyright Act (DMCA) is being applied to distance-learning programs.

Publishing on the Internet   Thousands of teachers and their students around the globe are publishing material at their home pages on the Internet. Teacher- and

Technology in Teaching

How does the Digital Millennium Copyright Act apply to distance-learning programs?

Increasingly, teachers and schools are using the Internet to transmit and receive distance-learning programs. Rural schools, for example, often use distance learning to import courses in specialized subjects, such as Advanced Placement courses, that they otherwise could not offer.

The DMCA currently allows distance-learning educators to display, without fees, pages of a book or other material via analog media such as television. Educators believe the fee exemption should also apply to digital media. However, publishers, who project tremendous growth in distance-learning programs, support the idea of licensing fees for use of their materials.

To address this issue, the U.S. Copyright Office prepared a *Report on Copyright and Digital Distance Education* (1999) (the full report is available at http://www.copyright.gov/reports/de_rprt.pdf). The report acknowledges the rapidly changing digital environment and recommends "improv[ing] distance education and maintain[ing] an appropriate balance between users and owners of copyrighted works."

The report recommends eliminating the "physical classroom" requirement that currently allows the display of distance-education programs only in a classroom setting or to persons unable to attend a classroom. Eliminating the "physical classroom" requirement would make it easier for students to participate in distance-learning programs. On the other hand, the report recommends that distance-learning transmissions are made available only to officially enrolled students.

The report also recommends that Congress clarify the fair use doctrine with respect to distance education. According to the report, Congress should reaffirm that fair use principles apply to digital learning environments and provide examples of acceptable use.

student-produced materials can be copyright protected by including a statement that the materials may not be duplicated without permission. In addition, teachers should be careful not to include information that would enable someone to identify children in a class. Children's last names should never be published, nor should photos of children be published with any identifying information.

What Are the Legal Rights of Students and Parents?

As a prospective teacher, you have an obligation to become familiar with the rights of students. Since the 1960s, students have increasingly confronted teachers and school districts with what they perceived to be illegal restrictions on their behavior. This section presents brief summaries of selected major court decisions that have clarified students' rights related to freedom of expression, suspension and expulsion, search and seizure, privacy, and nondiscrimination.

Case for Reflection

Parental Objection to the Curriculum

After a year of open meetings for teachers, administrators, parents, and students, the school district in which you work narrowly approved a proposal requiring students at the district's three high schools to complete forty hours of community service during high school and to participate in reflective classroom discussions on those experiences. The new program has no opt-out feature; however, students may select from a wide array of preapproved service projects, or they may develop their own.

Students in your third-period high school class have just returned to the classroom after attending an assembly at which the principal introduced the mandatory community service project. You ask if any students have decided upon a service-learning project for the year.

"I'm gonna work on the stream," Dave says excitedly, referring to a clean-up project for the stream that runs behind the school.

"Me too," Carol says, smiling at Dave. A few students giggle, amused at Carol's willingness to acknowledge the close friendship that has begun to develop recently between her and Dave.

"Hank, what are you going to do?" you ask, turning to acknowledge the waving hand to your left.

"I want to work at the after-school day care center," Hank says. "I think that'd be a trip. Like, help'n those little kids and everything."

"Well, I ain't gonna do nothin'," Richard suddenly blurts out from the back of the room. He scowls and emits a long groan before continuing. "I ain't gonna be nobody's servant."

"Hey, chill out," Frank says, turning in his seat to address his classmate. "Nobody wants you to be a servant. The whole idea is just to help somebody out . . . you know, improve things."

"Yeah, it's not a big deal," says Carol.

"Now, let's give him a chance to speak," you say, responding to the murmurs of several students who obviously disagree with Richard.

"That's a violation of my rights," Richard continues. "It's like slavery or something . . . makin' him (Dave) pick up garbage down at the stream."

"Well, that's not the district's intention," you say. At this point, you decide to refocus the discussion on students' choices for their service-learning projects. "Okay, let's hear what some other people are going to do." You look toward Jane seated next to the window and invite her to speak.

After allowing the discussion to continue for a few minutes, you turn the class's attention to the review. As you proceed with the lesson, you wonder, "Does Richard have a right not to participate in the service-learning project?"

Note: The preceding case is based on actual events that culminated in the filing of a lawsuit against a school district. In this instance, a student filed a lawsuit claiming that the mandatory service-learning project violated his rights under the Thirteenth and Fourteenth Amendments. The student's parents joined the lawsuit, claiming that they had a constitutional right to direct their son's education. A U.S. district court ruled in favor of the school district. (*Immediato v. Rye Neck School District* 1996).

Freedom of Expression

The case of *Tinker v. Des Moines Independent Community School District* (1969) is perhaps the most frequently cited case concerning students' **freedom of expression**. The Supreme Court ruled in *Tinker* that three students, ages thirteen, fifteen, and sixteen, had been denied their First Amendment freedom of expression when they were suspended from school for wearing black arm bands in protest of the Vietnam War. The court ruled that neither teachers nor students "shed their rights to freedom of speech or expression at the schoolhouse gate." In addition, the court found no evidence that the exercise of such a right interfered with the school's operation.

Censorship One area of student expression that has generated frequent controversy is that of student publications. Prior to 1988, the courts generally made it clear that student literature enjoyed constitutional protection, and it could only be regulated if it posed a substantial threat of school disruption, if it was libelous, or if it was judged vulgar or obscene *after publication*. However, school officials could use "prior **censorship**" and require students to submit literature before publication if such controls were necessary to maintain order in the school.

Within these guidelines, students frequently successfully defended their right to freedom of expression. For example, the right of high school students to place in the school newspaper an advertisement against the war in Vietnam was upheld (*Zucker v. Panitz* 1969). Students were also upheld in their right to distribute information on birth control and on laws regarding marijuana (*Shanley v. Northeast Independent School District* 1972). And other cases upheld the right of students to publish literature that was critical of teachers, administrators, and other school personnel (*Scoville v. Board of Education of Joliet Township High School District 204* 1970; *Sullivan v. Houston Independent School District* 1969).

In January 1988, however, the Supreme Court, in a five-to-three ruling in *Hazelwood School District v. Kuhlmeier*, departed from the earlier *Tinker* decision and gave public school officials considerable authority to censor school-sponsored student publications. The case involved a Missouri high school principal's censorship of articles in the school newspaper, the *Spectrum*, on teenage pregnancy and the impact of divorce on students. The principal believed the articles were inappropriate because they might identify pregnant students and because references to sexual activity and birth control were inappropriate for younger students. Several students on the newspaper staff distributed copies of the articles on their own and later sued the school district, claiming that their First Amendment rights had been violated.

Writing for the majority in *Hazelwood School District v. Kuhlmeier*, Justice Byron White (who had voted with the majority in *Tinker*) said school officials could bar "speech that is ungrammatical, poorly written, inadequately researched, biased or prejudiced, vulgar or profane, or unsuitable for immature audiences." White also pointed out that *Tinker* focused on a student's right of "personal expression," and the Missouri case dealt with school-sponsored publications that were part of the curriculum and bore the "imprimatur of the school." According to White, "Educators do not offend the First Amendment by exercising editorial control over the style and content of student speech in school-sponsored expressive activities so long as their actions are reasonably related to legitimate pedagogical concerns."

A case involving an attempt to regulate an "underground" student newspaper entitled *Bad Astra*, however, had a different outcome. Five high school students in Renton, Washington, produced a four-page newspaper at their expense, off school property, and without the knowledge of school authorities. *Bad Astra* contained articles that criticized school policies, a mock poll evaluating teachers, and several poetry selections. The students distributed 350 copies of the paper at a senior class barbecue held on school grounds.

After the paper was distributed, the principal placed letters of reprimand in the five students' files, and the district established a new policy whereby student-written, nonschool-sponsored materials with an intended distribution of more than ten were subject to predistribution review. The students filed suit in federal district court, claiming a violation of their First Amendment rights. The court, however, ruled that the new policy was "substantially constitutional." Maintaining that the policy was unconstitutional, the students filed an appeal in 1988 in the Ninth Circuit Court of Appeals and won. The court ruled that *Bad Astra* was not "within the purview of the school's exercise of reasonable editorial control" (*Burch v. Barker* 1987, 1988).

Dress Codes   Few issues related to the rights of students have generated as many court cases as have dress codes and hairstyles. The demand on the courts to hear such cases prompted Supreme Court Justice Hugo L. Black to observe that he did not believe "the federal Constitution imposed on the United States Courts the burden of supervising the length of hair that public school students should wear" (*Karr v. Schmidt* 1972). In line with Justice Black's observation, the Supreme Court has repeatedly refused to review the decisions reached by the lower courts.

In general, the courts have suggested that schools may have dress codes as long as such codes are clear and reasonable, and students are notified. However, when the legality of such codes has been challenged, the rulings have largely indicated that schools may not control what students wear unless it is immodest or is disruptive of the educational process.

Students in private schools, however, do not have First Amendment protections provided by *Tinker v. Des Moines Independent Community School District* because private schools are not state affiliated. As a result, students at private schools can be required to wear uniforms, and "[d]isagreements over 'student rights' . . . are generally resolved by applying contract law to the agreement governing the student's attendance" (LaMorte 2002, 105).

At one time, educators' concerns about student appearance may have been limited to hairstyles and immodest dress; however, today's educators, as Michael

LaMorte (2002, 156) points out, may be concerned about "T-shirts depicting violence, drugs (e.g., marijuana leaves), racial epithets, or characters such as Bart Simpson; ripped, baggy, or saggy pants or jeans; sneakers with lights; colored bandannas, baseball or other hats; words shaved into scalps, brightly colored hair, distinctive haircuts or hairstyles, or ponytails for males; exposed underwear; Malcolm X symbols; Walkmen, cellular phones, or beepers; backpacks; tatoos, unusual-colored lipstick, pierced noses, or earrings; and decorative dental caps."

Since gangs, hate groups, and violence in and around public schools have become more prevalent during the last decade, rulings that favor schools are becoming more common when the courts "balance the First Amendment rights of students to express themselves against the legitimate right of school authorities to maintain a safe and disruption-free environment" (LaMorte 2002, 156). This balance is clearly illustrated in *Jeglin v. San Jacinto Unified School District* (1993). In this instance, a school's dress code prohibiting the wearing of clothing with writing, pictures, or insignia of professional or college athletic teams was challenged on the grounds that it violated students' freedom of expression. The court acknowledged that the code violated the rights of elementary and middle school students, but not those of high school students. Gangs, known to be present at the high school, had intimidated students and faculty in connection with the sports-oriented clothing. The court ruled that the curtailment of students' rights did not "demand a certainty that disruption will occur, but only the existence of facts which might reasonably lead school officials to forecast substantial disruption."

After the Columbine, Colorado, high school shootings in 1999—which left fourteen students and a teacher dead, including the two gunmen who were members of a clique called the "Trench Coat Mafia"—many school districts made their rules for student dress more restrictive. Ten days after the shootings, a federal judge who upheld a school's decision to suspend a student for wearing a T-shirt that said "Vegan" (a vegetarian who doesn't eat animal products) said that "gang attire has become particularly troubling since two students wore trench coats in the Colorado shooting." And, in Jonesboro, Arkansas, where four students and a teacher were shot and killed the previous year, a group of boys and girls identifying themselves as the "Blazer Mafia" were suspended for ten days (Portner 1999).

To reduce disruption and violence in schools, some school districts now require younger students to wear uniforms. In 1994, the 90,000-student Long Beach, California, school system became the first in the nation to require K–8 students to wear uniforms. Currently, the Birmingham, Alabama; Chicago; Dayton, Ohio; Oakland, California; and San Antonio public schools require elementary-age students to wear uniforms. At the beginning of the 2002–03 school year, Memphis took steps to become the nation's first large urban district to require all students to wear uniforms when school commissioners voted eight to one to implement a school uniform policy for the district's 175 schools (Richard 2002).

Currently, half the states have school districts with mandatory school uniform requirements, and "estimates suggest that over the next several years, one in four public school students may be wearing uniforms" (LaMorte 2002, 158). Courts have upheld mandatory school uniform policies. For example, a court ruled against a parent who challenged New York City's school uniform policy for preK through eighth-grade students. The parent claimed that the opt-out provision would make his daughter "stick out," while the New York City Board of Education stated that the policy would "promote a more effective learning climate; foster school unity and pride; improve student performance; foster self-esteem; eliminate label competition; simplify dressing and minimize costs to parents; teach children appropriate dress and decorum in the 'workplace'; and help to improve student conduct and discipline" (*Lipsman v. New York City Board of Education* 1999).

Due Process in Suspension and Expulsion

In February and March 1971, a total of nine students received ten-day suspensions from the Columbus, Ohio, public school system during a period of citywide unrest. One student, in the presence of his principal, physically attacked a police officer who was trying to remove a disruptive student from a high school auditorium. Four others were suspended for similar conduct. Another student was suspended for his involvement in a lunchroom disturbance that resulted in damage to school property. All nine students were suspended in accordance with Ohio law. Some of the students and their parents were offered the opportunity to attend conferences prior to the start of the suspensions, but none of the nine was given a hearing. Asserting that their constitutional rights had been denied, all nine students brought suit against the school system.

In a sharply divided five-to-four decision, the Supreme Court ruled that the students had a legal right to an education, and that this "property right" could be removed only through the application of procedural due process. The court maintained that suspension is a "serious event" in the life of a suspended child and may not be imposed by the school in an arbitrary manner (*Goss v. Lopez* 1975).

As a result of cases such as *Goss v. Lopez*, every state has outlined procedures for school officials to follow in the suspension and expulsion of students. In cases of short-term suspension (defined by the courts as exclusion from school for ten days or less), the due process steps are somewhat flexible and determined by the nature of the infraction and the length of the suspension. As Figure 4.2 shows, however, long-term suspension (more than ten days) and expulsion require a more extensive due process procedure. The disciplinary transfer of a disruptive student to an alternative school, designed to meet his or her needs, is not considered an expulsion (LaMorte 2002).

In response to an increase of unruly students who disrupt the learning of others, a few districts and states have granted teachers the authority to suspend students for up to ten days. Teachers in Cincinnati and Dade County, Florida, for example, have negotiated contracts that give them authority to remove disruptive students from their classrooms; however, district administrators decide how the students will be disciplined. In 1995, Indiana became the first state to grant teachers the power to suspend students, and the following year New York's governor proposed legislation to allow teachers to remove students from their classrooms for

Figure 4.2 Due process in suspension and expulsion.

At minimum, students should be provided with:

Suspension for 10 days or fewer

- Oral or written notification of the nature of the violation and the intended punishment.
- An opportunity to refute the charges before an objective decisionmaker (such a discussion may immediately follow the alleged rule infraction).
- An explanation of the evidence on which the disciplinarian is relying.

Long-term suspension and expulsion

- Written notice of the charges, the intention to expel, and the place, time, and circumstances of the hearing, with sufficient time for a defense to be prepared.
- A full and fair hearing before an impartial adjudicator.
- The right to legal counsel or some other adult representation.
- The right to be fully apprised of the proof or evidence.
- The opportunity to present witnesses or evidence.
- The opportunity to cross-examine opposing witnesses.
- Some type of written record demonstrating that the decision was based on the evidence presented at the hearing.

Source: Adapted from Martha M. McCarthy, Nelda H. Cambron-McCabe, and Stephen B. Thomas, *Public School Law: Teachers' and Students' Rights,* 4th ed. Boston: Allyn and Bacon, 1998, pp. 205, 301.

up to ten days for "committing an act of violence against a student, teacher, or school district employee; possessing or threatening to use a gun, knife, or other dangerous weapon; damaging or destroying school district property; damaging the personal property of teachers or other employees; or defying an order from a teacher or administrator to stop disruptive behavior" (Lindsay 1996, 24).

Reasonable Search and Seizure

You have reason to believe that a student has drugs and possibly a dangerous weapon in his locker. Do you, as a teacher, have the right to search the student's locker and seize any illegal or dangerous items? According to the Fourth Amendment, citizens are protected from **search and seizure** conducted without a search warrant. With the escalation of drug use in schools and school-related violence, however, cases involving the legality of search and seizure in schools have increased. These cases suggest guidelines that you can follow if confronted with a situation such as that described here.

The case of *New Jersey v. T.L.O.* (1985) involved a fourteen-year-old student (T.L.O.) whom a teacher found smoking a cigarette in a rest room. The teacher took the student to the principal's office, whereupon the principal asked to see the contents of her purse. On opening the purse, the principal found a pack of cigarettes and what appeared to be drug paraphernalia and a list titled "People who owe me money." T.L.O. was arrested and later found guilty of delinquency charges.

After being sentenced to one year's probation, T.L.O. appealed, claiming that the evidence found in her purse was obtained in violation of the Fourth Amendment and that her confession to selling marijuana was tainted by an illegal search. The U.S. Supreme Court found that the search had been reasonable. The Court also developed a two-pronged test of "reasonableness" for searches: (1) A school official must have a reasonable suspicion that a student has violated a law or school policy, and (2) the search must be conducted using methods that are reasonable in scope.

Another case focused on the use of trained dogs to conduct searches of 2,780 junior and senior high school students in Highland, Indiana. During a two-and-a-half- to three-hour period, six teams with trained German shepherds sniffed the students. The dogs alerted their handlers a total of fifty times. Seventeen of the searches initiated by the dogs turned up beer, drug paraphernalia, or marijuana. Another eleven students singled out by the dogs, including thirteen-year-old Diane Doe, were strip searched in the nurse's office. It turned out that Diane had played with her dog, who was in heat, that morning and that the police dog had responded to the smell of the other dog on Diane's clothing.

Diane's parents later filed suit, charging that their daughter was searched illegally. The court ruled that the use of dogs did not constitute an unreasonable search, nor did holding students in their homerooms constitute a mass detention in violation of the Fourth Amendment. The court did, however, hold that the strip searches of the students were unreasonable. The court pointed out that the school personnel did not have any evidence to suggest that Diane possessed contraband because, prior to the strip search, she had emptied her pockets as requested. Diane was awarded $7,500 in damages (*Doe v. Renfrow* 1980, 1981).

Court cases involving search and seizure in school settings have maintained that school lockers are the property of the schools, not students, and may be searched by school authorities if reasonable cause exists. In addition, students may be sniffed by police dogs if school authorities have a reasonable suspicion that illegal or dangerous items may be found. Lastly, courts have tended not to allow strip searches; however, as *Cornfield v. Consolidated High School District No. 230* (1993) illustrates, strip searches may be constitutional depending upon the circumstances giving rise to the search, the age of the student, and the severity of the suspected infraction. In *Cornfield*, the court allowed a strip search of a sixteen-year-old student suspected of "crotching" drugs. The court's decision was influenced by "allegations of several recent prior incidents such as dealing in drugs, testing positive for marijuana, possession of drugs, having 'crotched' drugs during a police raid

What are students' rights with regard to their persons, lockers, personal property, and records in school and on school grounds? How are school districts' rights of search and seizure decided? In what ways have students' rights to privacy been upheld?

at his mother's house, failing a urine analysis for cocaine, unsuccessful completion of a drug rehabilitation program, and a report by a bus driver that there was a smell of marijuana where the student sat on the bus" (LaMorte 2002, 153).

In general, the courts have tried to balance the school's need to obtain information and the student's right to privacy. To protect themselves from legal challenges related to searches, educators should follow guidelines that have been suggested by school law experts:

- Inform students and parents at the start of the school year of the procedures for conducting locker and personal searches.
- Base any search on "reasonable suspicion."
- Conduct any search with another staff member present.
- Avoid strip searches or mass searches of groups of students.
- Require that police obtain a search warrant before conducting a search in the school.

Some schools use drug testing as a requirement for either attendance or interscholastic participation, including sports competition, or as a means of discipline. A 1988 court case upheld a urinalysis drug test for randomly selected student athletes because those who tested positively were suspended only from participating in sports for a period of time and no disciplinary or academic penalties were imposed (*Schaill v. Tippecanoe School Corp.* 1988). Similarly, the U.S. Supreme Court reversed a lower court's ruling and stated that a school district's desire to reduce drug use justified the degree of intrusion required by random tests of student athletes' urine (*Acton v. Vernonia School District* 1995). A few school districts have attempted to implement mandatory drug testing of teachers. So far, the courts have upheld the decision rendered in *Patchogue-Medford Congress of Teachers v. Board of Education of Patchogue-Medford Union Free School District* (1987) that drug testing of teachers violates the Fourth Amendment's prohibition of unreasonable searches.

Privacy

Prior to 1974, students and parents were not allowed to examine school records. On November 19, 1974, Congress passed the Family Educational Rights and Privacy Act (FERPA), which gave parents of students under eighteen and students eighteen and older the right to examine their school records. Every public or private educational institution must adhere to the law, known as the **Buckley Amendment**, or lose federal money.

Under the Buckley Amendment, schools must do the following:

- Inform parents and students of their rights.
- Provide information to parents and students about the type of educational records available and how to obtain access to them.
- Allow parents or students to review records, request changes, request a hearing if changes are not allowed, and, if necessary, add their own explanation about the records.
- Not give out personally identifiable information without prior written, informed consent of a parent or students.
- Allow parents and students to see the school's record of disclosures.

The Buckley Amendment actually sets forth the minimum requirements that schools must adhere to, and many states and school districts have gone beyond these minimum guidelines in granting students access to their records. Most high schools, for example, now grant students under eighteen access to their educational records, and all students in Virginia, elementary through secondary, are guaranteed access to their records.

A number of exceptions are allowed by the Buckley Amendment. The teacher's gradebook, psychiatric or treatment records, notes or records written by the teacher for his or her exclusive use or to be shared with a substitute teacher, or the private notes of school law enforcement units, for example, are not normally subject to examination.

The provisions of FERPA came to the nation's attention in 2000 when Kristja Falvo challenged the practice of having students grade one another's papers (peer grading) on the grounds that it was embarrassing to her three children and resulted in grading errors. A district court disagreed and ruled in favor of the school district, maintaining that peer grading is a common school practice. However, the Tenth Circuit Court of Appeals reversed that decision and ruled that the practice of peer grading violated students' privacy since grades are entered into teachers' gradebooks and thus fit the definition of "educational records" (*Falvo v. Owasso Independent School District* 2000). Eventually, however, the case reached the Supreme Court, which ruled nine to zero that the privacy law was not intended to protect grades on day-to-day classroom assignments and that students could grade one another's work (*Owasso Independent School District v. Falvo* 2002).

Cameras in Classrooms An additional privacy-related issue emerged in 2003 when schools in Biloxi, Mississippi, became the first in the nation to use cameras to monitor activities in classrooms. Previously, some schools used cameras to monitor hallways, cafeterias, auditoriums, and parking lots.

Some observers worry that cameras in classrooms will interfere with learning activities and could be misused. Others contend that teachers' and students' privacy is violated by the use of cameras. Nevertheless, regarding the presence of five hundred cameras in classrooms at the start of the school year, a Biloxi School District official pointed out that "Students, parents and teachers don't mind them at all" (Lewis 2003).

Students' Rights to Nondiscrimination

Schools are legally bound to avoid discriminating against students on the basis of race, sex, religion, disability, marital status, or infection with a disease such as HIV/AIDS that poses no threat to students. One trend that has confronted schools with the need to develop more thoughtful and fair policies has been the epidemic in teenage pregnancies.

In regard to students who are married, pregnant, or parents, the courts have been quite clear: Students in these categories may not be treated differently. A 1966 case in Texas involving a sixteen-year-old mother established that schools may provide separate classes or alternative schools on a *voluntary* basis for married and/or pregnant students. However, the district may not *require* such students to attend separate schools, nor may they be made to attend adult or evening schools (*Alvin Independent School District v. Cooper* 1966).

The courts have made an about-face in their positions on whether students who are married, pregnant, or parents can participate in extracurricular activities. Prior to 1972, participation in these activities was considered a privilege rather than a right, and restrictions on those who could participate were upheld. In 1972, however, cases in Montana, Ohio, Tennessee, and Texas established the right of married students (and, in one case, a divorced student) to participate (*Moran v. School District No. 7* 1972; *Davis v. Meek* 1972; *Holt v. Sheldon* 1972; *Romans v. Crenshaw* 1972). Since then, restrictions applicable to extracurricular activities have been universally struck down.

During the 1980s, many school districts became embroiled in controversy over the issue of how to provide for the schooling of young people with HIV/AIDS and whether school employees with HIV/AIDS should be allowed to continue working. In rulings on HIV/AIDS-related cases since then, the courts have sided with the overwhelming medical evidence that students with AIDS pose no "significant risk" of spreading the disease. "To date, courts have revealed a high degree of sensitivity to students with HIV or AIDS and to their being included in the public school mainstream" (LaMorte 2002, 335). In 1987, for example, a judge prevented a Florida school district from requiring that three hemophiliac brothers who were exposed to HIV/AIDS through transfusions be restricted to homebound instruction (*Ray v. School District of DeSoto County* 1987).

To stem the spread of HIV/AIDS, school systems in many large cities—New York, Los Angeles, San Francisco, and Seattle, to name a few—have initiated programs to distribute condoms to high school students. New York's condom-distribution program, which initially did not require parental consent, was challenged in 1993 (*Alfonso v. Fernandez*). The court ruled that the program was a "health issue" and that the district could not dispense condoms without prior parental approval. The court maintained that the program violated parents' due process rights under the Fourteenth Amendment to raise their children as they see fit; however, the program did not violate parents' or students' freedom of religion. Three years later, however, the U.S. Supreme Court declined to review a Massachusetts high court ruling that upheld a school board's decision to place condom machines in high school rest rooms and allow junior- and senior-level students to request condoms from the school nurse (*Curtis v. School Committee of Falmouth* 1995, 1996).

What Are Some Issues in the Legal Rights of School Districts?

Clearly, the law touches just about every aspect of education in the United States today. Daily, the media remind us that ours is an age of litigation; no longer are school districts as protected as they once were from legal problems. Corporal punishment, sexual harassment, religious expression, and home schooling are among the issues in the legal rights of school districts.

Corporal Punishment

The practice of **corporal punishment** has had a long and controversial history in education in the United States. Currently, policies regarding the use of corporal punishment vary widely from state to state, and even from district to district.

Critics believe that corporal punishment "is neither a necessary nor an effective response to misbehavior in school" (Slavin 2000, 391), and some believe the practice is "archaic, cruel, and inhuman and an unjustifiable act on the part of the state" (LaMorte 2002, 137). In spite of such arguments against its effectiveness, corporal punishment continues to be widespread. Nevertheless, almost half of the states and many school districts currently ban corporal punishment, and many others restrict its use (LaMorte 2002).

The most influential Supreme Court case involving corporal punishment is *Ingraham v. Wright*, decided in 1977. In Dade County, Florida, in October 1970, junior high school students James Ingraham and Roosevelt Andrews were paddled with a wooden paddle. Both students received injuries as a result of the paddlings, with Ingraham's being the most severe. Ingraham, who was being punished for being slow to respond to a teacher's directions, refused to assume the "paddling position" and had to be held over a desk by two assistant principals while the principal administered twenty "licks." As a result, Ingraham "suffered a hematoma requiring medical attention and keeping him out of school for several days."

The court had two significant questions to rule on in *Ingraham:* Does the Eighth Amendment's prohibition of cruel and unusual punishment apply to corporal punishment in the schools? And, if it does not, should the due process clause of the Fourteenth Amendment provide any protection to students before punishment is administered? In regard to the first question, the Court, in a sharply divided five-to-four decision, ruled that the Eighth Amendment was not applicable to students being disciplined in school, only to persons convicted of crimes. On the question of due process, the Court said, "We conclude that the Due Process clause does not require notice and a hearing prior to the imposition of corporal punishment in the public schools, as that practice is authorized and limited by the common law." The Court also commented on the severity of the paddlings in *Ingraham* and said that, in such cases, school personnel "may be held liable in damages to the child and, if malice is shown, they may be subject to criminal penalties."

Though the Supreme Court has upheld the constitutionality of corporal punishment, many districts around the country have instituted policies banning its use. Where corporal punishment is used, school personnel are careful to see that it meets criteria that have emerged from other court cases involving corporal punishment:

- Specific warning is given about what behavior may result in corporal punishment.
- Evidence exists that other measures attempted failed to bring about the desired change in behavior.
- Administration of corporal punishment takes place in the presence of a second school official.
- On request, a written statement is provided to parents explaining the reasons for the punishment and the names of all witnesses.
- [The punishment meets] the reasonableness standard—punishment must be within the bounds of reason and humanity.
- [The punishment meets] the good faith standard—the person administering the punishment is not motivated by malice and does not inflict punishment wantonly or excessively (Dunklee and Shoop 2002, 127).

Sexual Harassment

Though few victims report it, sexual harassment affects about four out of every five teenagers in schools across the nation, according to surveys of eighth- through eleventh-graders conducted by the American Association of University Women (AAUW) in 1993 and 2001. Students' responses were based on the following definition: "Sexual harassment is unwanted and unwelcome sexual behavior which interferes with your life. Sexual harassment is not behaviors that you like or want (for example wanted kissing, touching, or flirting)" (American Association of University Women 1993, 2001).

The 2001 survey revealed that the percentage of boys experiencing harassment "often" or "occasionally" increased from 49 percent in 1993 to 56 percent in 2001. On the other hand, the percentage of students reporting that their school has a policy on **sexual harassment** increased from 26 percent in 1993 to 69 percent in 2001. Although most teens report that they are harassed by their schoolmates, 7 percent of boys and girls experiencing physical or nonphysical harassment report being harassed by a teacher. Table 4.4 highlights the results of the 2001 AAUW survey.

As the discussion of this chapter's opening scenario pointed out, a landmark Supreme Court Case (*Davis v. Monroe County Board of Education* 1999) ruled by a narrow five-to-four margin that educators can be held liable if they fail to take steps to end peer sexual harassment. In their majority opinion, five justices disagreed with the claim by the other four justices that "nothing short of expulsion of every student accused of misconduct involving sexual overtones would protect school systems from liability or damages." Instead, their ruling was intended "only for harassment that is so severe, pervasive, and objectively offensive that it effectively bars the victim's access to an educational opportunity or benefit."

The dissenting justices, however, expressed concern about the "avalanche of liability now set in motion" and the "potentially crushing financial liability" for schools.

> A female plaintiff who pleads only that a boy called her offensive names, that she told a teacher, that the teacher's response was unreasonable, and that her school performance suffered as a result, appears to state a successful claim. . . . After today, Johnny will find that the routine problems of adolescence are to be resolved by invoking a federal right to demand assignment to a desk two rows away.

To highlight their concern about the effects of the ruling, the dissenting justices also noted that shortly after a U.S. Department of Education warning that schools could be liable for peer sexual harassment, a North Carolina school suspended a six-year-old boy who kissed a female classmate on the cheek.

In addition to harassment by the opposite sex, same-sex harassment, usually against gay and lesbian students, is a problem at some schools. Since the mid-1990s, several school districts have faced lawsuits filed by gay and lesbian students who claimed that school officials failed to protect them from verbal and physical antigay harassment.

In 1999, six gay and lesbian teenagers in Morgan Hill, California, filed a complaint in a U.S. district court charging that school officials failed to protect them from years of antigay harassment. One of the complainants alleged that teachers regularly witnessed the harassment but did nothing to stop it: "Most [teachers] just don't want the hassle; others will acknowledge that they are homophobic, that they just don't like gays and lesbians." Moreover, the student found that administrators

> **Table 4.4** **Sexual harassment in the nation's schools (Based on a national survey of 2,064 public school students, eighth through eleventh grades)**
>
> - 83% of girls and 79% of boys report having ever experienced harassment.
>   - The number of boys reporting experiences with harassment often or occasionally has increased since 1993 (56% vs. 49%), although girls are still somewhat more likely to experience it.
>   - For many students sexual harassment is an ongoing experience: over 1 in 4 students experience it "often."
>   - These numbers do not differ by whether the school is urban or suburban or rural.
> - 76% of students have experienced nonphysical harassment while 58% have experienced physical harassment. Nonphysical harassment includes taunting, rumors, graffiti, jokes or gestures. One-third of all students report experiencing physical harassment "often or occasionally."
> - There has been a sea change in awareness of school policies about harassment since 1993. Seven in 10 students (69%) say that their school has a policy on sexual harassment, compared to only 26% of students in 1993.
> - Substantial numbers of students fear being sexually harassed or hurt in school.
>   - A substantial number of students—both boys and girls—fear being hurt by someone in their school life. 18% are afraid some or most of the time, and less than half (46%) are "never" afraid in school.
>   - One-third of students fear being sexually harassed in school. Hispanic boys and girls are more likely than African American students to feel afraid.
> - According to the new report, harassment has many facets:
>   - Peer-on-peer harassment is most common for both boys and girls, although 7% of boys and girls experiencing physical or nonphysical harassment report being harassed by a teacher.
>   - Boys are more likely than girls to report nonphysical harassment in locker rooms (28% v. 15%) or restrooms (15% to 9%).
>   - Half of boys reporting harassment have been nonphysically harassed by a girl or woman, and 39% by a group of girls or women. In contrast, girls are most likely to report harassment by one boy or man (73% in nonphysical harassment; 84% in physical harassment).
>   - Over one-third (35%) of students who have been harassed report that they first experienced it in elementary school.
>   - Most harassment occurs under teachers' noses in the classroom (61% for physical harassment and 56% for nonphysical) and in the halls (71% for physical harassment and 64% for nonphysical).
>   - Students are perpetrators, too. Slightly more than half of students (54%) say that they have sexually harassed someone during their school life. This represents a decrease from 1993, when 59% admitted as much. In particular, boys are less likely than in 1993 to report being a "perpetrator" (57% to 66%).
>
> *Source:* Excerpted from American Association of University Women Educational Foundation, *Hostile Hallways: Bullying, Teasing, and Sexual Harassment in School.* New York: Harris Interactive, 2001.

also refused to get involved: "Taking these things [i.e., complaints about antigay harassment] to the administrators and having them, my protectors, say 'Go back to class and stop talking about it' affected me more than anything. I learned that teachers won't do anything for you if they don't get any backup from the administration" (Ruenzel 1999).

A 1996 verdict awarding almost $1 million to a gay student by a U.S. district court was the first time a federal jury found school officials responsible for antigay harassment committed by students (Jacobson 1996). Currently, at least five states and several school districts have education policies that prohibit discrimination based on sexual orientation.

Increased reports of sexual harassment of students by educators and a Supreme Court ruling in 1992 (*Franklin v. Gwinnett County Public Schools*) that students could sue and collect damages for harassment under Title IX of the Education Act of 1972 are causing some teachers to be apprehensive about working closely with students, and a small number of teachers even report that they fear being falsely accused by angry, disgruntled students. As a school superintendent puts it, "There's no question but that the attitudes of personnel in schools are changing because of the many cases [of sexual harassment] that have come up across the country. I think all of us are being extremely cautious in how we handle students and in what we say and do with students and employees" (*Spokesman Review* 1993, 1A). To address the problem, many school districts have suggested guidelines that teachers can follow to show concern for students, offer them encouragement, and congratulate them for their successes.

Religious Expression

Conflicts over the proper role of religion in schools are among the most heated in the continuing debate about the character and purposes of education in the United States. Numerous school districts have found themselves embroiled in legal issues related to school prayer, Bible reading, textbooks, creationism, singing of Christmas carols, distribution of religious literature, New Age beliefs, secular humanism, religious holidays, use of school buildings for religious meetings, and the role of religion in moral education, to name a few. On the one hand, conservative religious groups wish to restore prayer and Christian religious practices to the public schools; on the other, secular liberals see religion as irrelevant to school curricula and maintain that public schools should not promote religion. In addition, somewhere between these two positions are those who believe that, while schools should not be involved in the *teaching of* religion, they should *teach about* religion.

During the last fifty years, scores of court cases have addressed school activities related to the First Amendment principle of separation of church and state. As Michael Imber and Tyll van Geel put it: "By far the most common constitutional objection raised against a school program is that it fails to respect the wall of separation between church and state" (2001, 21). In one of these landmark cases (*Engel v. Vitale* 1962), the U.S. Supreme Court ruled that recitation of a prayer said in the presence of a teacher at the beginning of each school day was unconstitutional and violated the First Amendment, which states: "Congress shall make no law respecting an establishment of religion, or prohibiting the free exercise thereof." Justice Hugo Black, who delivered the opinion of the Court, stated "it is no part of the business of government to compose official prayers for any group of the American people to recite as a part of a religious program carried on by government."

What are the rights of schools with regard to religious expression? What are the rights of students? What kinds of challenges do schools whose students come from mixed religious backgrounds face?

The following year, the U.S. Supreme Court ruled that Bible reading and reciting the Lord's Prayer in school were unconstitutional (*School District of Abington Township v. Schempp* 1963). In response to the district's claim that unless these religious activities were permitted a "religion of secularism" would be established, the Court stated that "we agree of course that the State may not establish a 'religion of secularism' in the sense of affirmatively opposing or showing hostility to religion, thus 'preferring those who believe in no religion over those who do believe.' We do not agree, however, that this decision in any sense has that effect."

To determine whether a state has violated the separation of church and state principle, the courts refer to the decision rendered in *Lemon v. Kurtzman* (1971). In this instance, the U.S. Supreme Court struck down an attempt by the Rhode Island legislature to provide a 15 percent salary supplement to teachers of secular subjects in nonpublic schools and Pennsylvania legislation to provide financial supplements to nonpublic schools through reimbursement for teachers' salaries, texts, and instructional materials in certain secular subjects. According to the three-part test enunciated in *Lemon v. Kurtzman*, governmental practices "must first, have a secular legislative purpose; second, its principal or primary effect must be one that neither advances nor inhibits religion; and, third, it must not foster an excessive government entanglement with religion" (LaMorte 2002, 377). Though criticized vigorously by several Supreme Court justices since 1971, the so-called **Lemon test** has not been overruled.

Since the mid-1990s, the courts heard several cases addressing the question of whether parents' right to direct their children's upbringing meant they could demand curricula and learning activities that were compatible with their religious beliefs. Without exception, the courts have rejected "parent rights" cases against the schools; those rights, according to a U.S. court of appeals ruling in support of a schoolwide assembly on HIV/AIDS, "do not encompass a broad-based right to restrict the flow of information in the public schools" (*Brown v. Hot, Sexy and Safer Productions, Inc.* 1995, 1996). In a similar case, parents objected to a Massachusetts school district's policy of distributing condoms to junior and senior high school students who requested them. The Massachusetts Supreme Judicial Court rejected the parental rights argument and their argument that the program infringed on their First Amendment right to free exercise of religion: "Parents have no right to tailor public school programs to meet their individual religious or moral preferences" (*Curtis v. School Committee of Falmouth* 1995, 1996).

Guidelines for Religious Activities in Schools   In 2003, the U.S. Department of Education issued federal guidelines requiring school districts to allow students and teachers to engage in religious activities at school, including prayer. Districts that violate the rules—or fail to promise in writing that they will comply with the guidelines—risk the loss of federal education funds. The following points are included in the guidelines:

- Students may "read their Bibles or other scriptures, say grace before meals, and pray or study religious materials with fellow students during recess, the lunch hour or other non-instructional time. . . ."
- Teachers should not discriminate against students who "express their beliefs about religion in homework, artwork, and other written and oral assignments."
- In certain circumstances, schools may have to grant parental requests to "excus[e] students from class" for religious reasons.
- Teachers and other school employees, "when acting in their official capacities as representatives of the state," cannot encourage or participate in prayer activities with students. Before school or during lunch, however, school employees are free to meet with other employees for prayer or Bible study (*NEA Today* 2003b, 13).

Home Schooling

One spinoff of the public's heightened awareness of the problems that schools face has been the decision by some parents to educate their children in the home. While most home-schoolers view home schooling as an opportunity to provide their children with a curriculum based on religious values, many home-schoolers are motivated not by religious doctrine but by concern about issues such as school violence, poor academic quality, or peer pressure. The U.S. Department of Education reported in 2001 that there were 850,000 home-schooled children nationwide. Many observers of home schooling estimate the number to be at least one million and definitely growing. In addition, it is estimated that home-schooling parents spend about $700 million a year on instructional materials (Walsh 2002).

Home schooling is legal in all the states and the District of Columbia; however, how it is regulated, and whether resources are allocated, vary greatly. In 1999, the National Home Education Research Institute (NHERI) reported that forty-one states had no minimum academic requirements for parents who decided to home-school their children. More than 60 percent of the states have home-schooling statutes or regulations, and half of the states require that home-schooled students participate in standardized testing (LaMorte 2002). In most states, home-schoolers must demonstrate that their instruction is "equivalent" to that offered in the public schools, a standard set in *New Jersey v. Massa* (1967).

Legal support for home schools has been mixed. In 1998, a Massachusetts court ruled that home visits by a local superintendent were not a valid requirement for approval by school officials of a home-school program (*Brunelle v. Lynn Public Schools* 1998). In 1993 and 1994, legislation to require home-school teachers to be state certified were defeated in South Dakota and Kansas, and similar laws were overturned in Iowa and North Dakota. However, a federal district court upheld a West Virginia statute making children ineligible for home schooling if their standardized test scores fell below the 40th percentile (*Null v. Board of Education* 1993). In Iowa, mandatory home-schooling reports to the state were upheld in *State v. Rivera* (1993); home-schoolers in that state must submit course outlines, weekly lesson plans, and provide the amount of time spent on areas of the curriculum. A Maryland law requiring the state's monitoring of home schooling was upheld despite a parent's claim that the state's curriculum promoted atheism, paganism, and evolution (*Battles v. Anne Arundel County Board of Education* 1995, 1996). And courts have not been sympathetic to home-schoolers who would like to have their children participate in extracurricular activities or other after-school activities (for example, *Swanson v. Guthrie Independent School District No. 1-L* 1998).

Table 4.5 lists chronologically and summarizes the key legislation and court decisions that underlie the legal issues affecting educators that are discussed in this chapter.

As the preceding cases related to home schooling show, school law is not static—instead, it is continually evolving and changing. In addition, laws pertaining to education vary from state to state. Therefore, it is important for the beginning teacher to become familiar with current publications on school law in his or her state.

Table 4.5 Educator's rights and responsibilities

Legislation or Court Ruling	How It Affects Educators
Application of Bay v. State Board of Education, 1963	A past criminal conviction is grounds for being denied a teaching certificate.
Title VII of the Civil Rights Act of 1964	Educators are guaranteed nondiscrimination in hiring situations.
Morrison v. State Board of Education, 1969	An educator's conduct in his/her personal life is not an impairment to professional performance or grounds for revoking a teaching certificate.
Mailloux v. Kiley, 1971	School authorities are free to suspend teachers who use teaching methods of which they disapprove.
Station v. Travelers Insurance Co., 1974	Teachers must provide adequate supervision while students are exposed to dangerous conditions.
Burton v. Cascade School District Union High School No. 5, 1975	A tenured teacher cannot be dismissed unless the employer shows "good and just cause."
Hortonville Joint School District No. 1 v. Hortonville Education Association, 1976	Teachers working under collective bargaining agreements may be dismissed for striking.
Peter Doe v. San Francisco Unified School District, 1976	A school cannot be held responsible for a student's lack of achievement.
Copyright Act of 1980	The fair use doctrine applies to software as well as print materials.
Marcus v. Rowley, 1983	Teachers can make "fair use" of copyrighted material.
Unified School District No. 241 v. Swanson, 1986	Schools cannot assign duties to teachers that are not reasonably related to their teaching.
Edwards v. Aguillard, 1987	"Balanced treatment" laws that mandate curricula that advance particular religious beliefs are unconstitutional.
Mozert v. Hawkins County Board of Education, 1987, 1988, and *Smith v. Board of School Commissioners of Mobile County*, 1987	A school may establish a curriculum despite parental disapproval.
Krizek v. Cicero-Stickney Township High School District No. 201, 1989	Teachers must notify students' parents before using materials that might be found objectionable in the classroom.
Murray v. Pittsburgh Board of Public Education, 1996	Teachers may not have the right to use teaching methods and materials to which school officials object.
Davis v. Monroe County Board of Education, 1999	School districts can be sued in cases involving student-on-student sexual harassment, if the district acts with "deliberate indifference."

Summary

Why Do You Need a Professional Code of Ethics?

- A professional code of ethics guides teachers' actions and enables them to build relationships with students based on trust and respect.

- A code of ethics helps teachers see beyond the short-range consequences of their actions to long-range consequences, and it helps them respond appropriately to ethical dilemmas in the classroom.

What Are Your Legal Rights as a Teacher?

- The right to due process protects teachers from arbitrary treatment by school districts and education officials regarding certification, nondiscrimination, contracts, tenure, dismissal, and academic freedom.

- Several court rulings have illustrated how the constitutional rights of teachers must be balanced against a school's need to promote its educational goals.

Do Student Teachers Have the Same Rights?

- Many states have not clarified the legal status of student teachers to teach. However, student teachers should be aware that a potential for liability exists for them just as it does with certified teachers, and they should clarify their rights and responsibilities prior to beginning student teaching.

- Depending on state statutes, a student teacher may substitute under certain conditions for a cooperating teacher.

What Are Your Legal Responsibilities as a Teacher?

- Teachers are responsible for meeting the terms of their teaching contracts, including providing for their students' safety and well-being.

- Three legal responsibilities that concern teachers are avoiding tort liability (specifically, negligence and educational malpractice); recognizing the physical and behavioral indicators of child abuse and then reporting suspected instances of such abuse; and observing copyright laws as they apply to photocopies, videotapes,

computer software, and materials published on the Internet.

What Are the Legal Rights of Students and Parents?

- Students' rights related to freedom of expression, suspension and expulsion, search and seizure, privacy, and nondiscrimination are based on several landmark legal decisions.

- Generally, students' freedom of expression can be limited if it is disruptive of the educational process or incongruent with the school's mission.

- Students can be neither suspended nor expelled without due process.

- Courts have developed a two-pronged test for search and seizure actions involving students: (1) School officials must have "reasonable" suspicion that a student has violated a law or school policy, and (2) the search must be done using methods that are reasonable and appropriate, given the nature of the infraction.

- Under the Buckley Amendment, students have the right to examine their school records, and schools may not give out information on students without their prior written consent.

- Schools may not discriminate against students on the basis of race, sex, religion, disability, marital status, or infection with a noncommunicable disease such as HIV/AIDS.

What Are Some Issues in the Legal Rights of School Districts?

- In spite of its proven ineffectiveness, corporal punishment has been upheld by the Supreme Court; however, almost half of the states and many school districts ban it, and many others restrict its use.

- About four out of five teenagers are affected by sexual harassment. According to a landmark Supreme Court decision in 1999, school officials can be held responsible if they fail to act on reports of sexual harassment of students by their peers. Schools can also be held responsible for the sexual harassment of students by professional staff, according to a 1992 Supreme Court decision.

- Courts have ruled that school officials can be held responsible if they fail to take steps to protect gay and lesbian students from antigay harassment.

- The First Amendment principle of separation of church and state has been applied to numerous court cases involving religious expression in the public schools. Court rulings banning school prayer, Bible reading, and other religious activities are often based on the three-

part test developed in *Lemon v. Kurtzman* (1971). The courts have ruled consistently against parents who demand curricula and learning activities that are compatible with their religious beliefs.

- Home schooling is legal in all states, though most require home-schoolers to demonstrate that their instruction is "equivalent" to that in public schools.

- The U.S. Department of Education issued guidelines in 2003 allowing students and teachers to engage in certain religious activities at school.

Key Terms and Concepts

academic freedom, 110
Buckley Amendment, 135
censorship, 128
code of ethics, 104
collective bargaining, 110
copyright laws, 123
corporal punishment, 137
Digital Millennium Copyright Act
    (DMCA), 123

dismissal, 109
due process, 105
educational malpractice, 120
ethical dilemmas, 104
fair use, 123
freedom of expression, 128
grievance, 110
Lemon test, 143

negligence, 118
nondiscrimination, 107
search and seizure, 132
sexual harassment, 139
teaching contract, 107
tenure, 108
tort liability, 117

Reflective Application Activities

Discussion Questions

1. A California school district suspended a fourteen-year-old student for writing two essays with violent content for an English assignment. In one essay titled "Goin' Postal" a boy goes to school with a gun and shoots the principal seven times (Walsh 1999a). How should teachers respond to student work—essays, creative writing, videos, and so forth—that has violent content?

2. What is your position regarding corporal punishment? Are there circumstances under which its use is justified?

Professional Journal

1. Read the NEA Code of Ethics for Teachers in Appendix 4.1. Record in your journal examples of situations you observed or experienced in which you feel a teacher may have violated NEA principles. Include one example involving Principle I, a teacher's commitment to students, and one example involving Principle II, a teacher's commitment to the profession. Conclude your analysis of these cases with a personal statement about your goals for ethical conduct as a teacher.

2. What limits do you believe should be placed on *what* teachers teach? On *how* they teach? Which of the legal cases on academic freedom discussed in this chapter support your views?

Online Assignments

1. Conduct an Internet search on one or more of the topics listed below or on another topic from Chapter 4. Narrow your search to issues and information relating to school law and the legal rights and responsibilities of school districts and schools, teachers and administrators, and students and parents. Include a search of news sources, such as *Education Week on the Web*, for summaries of recent court rulings pertaining to education and school law. The texts of many policies, laws, and U.S. Supreme Court decisions are also available online. You may wish to select a particular court case from Chapter 4 to investigate.

Topics on legal issues to search from Chapter 4:

academic freedom	home schooling
censorship	nondiscrimination
collective bargaining	privacy
copyright law	professional ethics
corporal punishment	school prayer
creation science	school uniforms
dress codes	search and seizure
due process	sexual harassment
expulsion	suspension
free speech	teacher dismissal
gay and lesbian rights	teacher tenure

2. Using a keyword search engine, locate and visit the websites of three or more of the following educational journals and publications. At each site, download or record information related to one or more of the education law issues discussed in Chapter 4.

American Educator	*Elementary School*
American School Board	*Journal*
Journal	*High School Journal*
Childhood Education	*Instructor*
Educational Leadership	*Kappa Delta Phi Record*

Phi Delta Kappan	*Teacher Magazine*
PTA Today	*Young Children*

Observations and Interviews

1. Interview several students at a middle school or high school to get their views regarding the legal rights of students. You may wish to develop a questionnaire that explores students' opinions in depth on a particular issue, such as freedom of expression or religion in the schools. Or you might get students' reactions to one of the legal cases summarized in this chapter. Present the results of your interview or survey to your classmates.

2. Interview a school superintendent or principal to find out about any instances of actual or threatened litigation that occurred in the district during the last year or so. Ask him or her to identify procedures the district has in place to ensure due process for teachers and students. Report your findings.

Professional Portfolio

Survey a group of students, teachers, and/or parents regarding a legal issue in education. Among the legal issues and questions you might address are the following:

- Should tenure for teachers be abolished? Does tenure improve the quality of education students receive?

- Under what circumstances should restrictions be placed on what teachers teach and how they teach?

- Should parents be allowed to provide home schooling for their children?

- Are parents justified in filing educational malpractice suits if their children fail to achieve in school?

- Under what circumstances should restrictions be placed on students' freedom of expression?

- Should schools have the right to implement dress codes? Guidelines for students' hairstyles? School uniforms?

- Should corporal punishment be banned? If not, under what circumstances should it be used?

- How should schools combat the problem of sexual harassment?

- To combat drug abuse, should schools implement mandatory drug testing of students? Of teachers?

- Should students have access to their educational records? Should their parents or guardians?

- As part of an HIV/AIDS prevention program, should condoms be distributed to high school students? Should parental approval be required for participation?

The report summarizing the results of your survey should include demographic information such as the following for your sample of respondents: gender, age, whether they have children in school, level of education, and so on. When you analyze the results, look for differences related to these variables.

Appendix 4.1
NEA Code of Ethics for Teachers

PREAMBLE

The educator, believing in the worth and dignity of each human being, recognizes the supreme importance of the pursuit of truth, devotion to excellence, and the nurture of democratic principles. Essential to these goals is the protection of freedom to learn and to teach and the guarantee of equal educational opportunity for all. The educator accepts the responsibility to adhere to the highest ethical standards.

The educator recognizes the magnitude of the responsibility inherent in the teaching process. The desire for the respect and confidence of one's colleagues, of students, of parents, and of the members of the community provides the incentive to attain and maintain the highest possible degree of ethical conduct. The Code of Ethics of the Education Profession indicates the aspiration of all educators and provides standards by which to judge conduct.

The remedies specified by the NEA and/or its affiliates for the violation of any provision of this code shall be exclusive and no such provision shall be enforceable in any form other than one specifically designated by the NEA or its affiliates.

PRINCIPLE I

Commitment to the Student. The educator strives to help each student realize his or her potential as a worthy and effective member of society. The educator therefore works to stimulate the spirit of inquiry, the acquisition of knowledge and understanding, and the thoughtful formulation of worthy goals.

In fulfillment of the obligation to the student, the educator:

1. Shall not unreasonably restrain the student from independent action in the pursuit of learning
2. Shall not unreasonably deny the student access to varying points of view
3. Shall not deliberately suppress or distort subject matter relevant to the student's progress
4. Shall make reasonable effort to protect the student from conditions harmful to learning or to health and safety
5. Shall not intentionally expose the student to embarrassment or disparagement
6. Shall not on the basis of race, color, creed, sex, national origin, marital status, political or religious beliefs, family, social or cultural background, or sexual orientation unfairly:
   (a) Exclude any student from participation in any program

Source: Code of Ethics of the Education Profession, adopted by the NEA Representative Assembly, 1975. The National Education Association, Washington DC. Used with permission.

(b) Deny benefits to any student

(c) Grant any advantage to any student

7. Shall not use professional relationships with students for private advantage

8. Shall not disclose information about students obtained in the course of professional service, unless disclosure serves a compelling professional purpose or is required by law

PRINCIPLE II

Commitment to the Profession. The education profession is vested by the public with a trust and responsibility requiring the highest ideals of professional service.

In the belief that the quality of the services of the education profession directly influences the nation and its citizens, the educator shall exert every effort to raise professional standards, to promote a climate that encourages the exercise of professional judgment, to achieve conditions that attract persons worthy of the trust to careers in education, and to assist in preventing the practice of the profession by unqualified persons.

In fulfillment of the obligation to the profession, the educator:

1. Shall not in an application for a professional position deliberately make a false statement or fail to disclose a material fact related to competency and qualifications

2. Shall not misrepresent his/her professional qualifications

3. Shall not assist any entry into the profession of a person known to be unqualified in respect to character, education, or other relevant attribute

4. Shall not knowingly make a false statement concerning the qualifications of a candidate for a professional position

5. Shall not assist a noneducator in the unauthorized practice of teaching

6. Shall not disclose information about colleagues obtained in the course of professional service unless disclosure serves a compelling professional purpose or is required by law

7. Shall not knowingly make false or malicious statements about a colleague

8. Shall not accept any gratuity, gift, or favor that might impair or appear to influence professional decisions or actions

Appendix 4.2
NEA Bill of Rights for Student Teachers

As a citizen, a student, and a future member of the teaching profession, the individual student teacher has the right:

1. To freedom from unfair discrimination in admission to student teaching and in all aspects of the field experience. Student teachers shall not be denied or removed from an assignment because of race, color, creed, sex, age, national origin, marital status, political or religious beliefs, social or cultural background, or sexual orientation. Nor shall their application be denied because of physical handicap unless it is clear that such handicap will prevent or seriously inhibit their carrying out the duties of the assignment.

2. To be informed in advance of the standards of eligibility for student teaching and of the criteria and procedures for evaluation of his or her classroom performance.

3. To be consulted in advance and have effective voice in decisions regarding assignment, with respect to subject, grade level, school, and cooperating teacher.

4. To be assigned to a cooperating teacher who volunteers to work with the student-teaching program, who is fully qualified to do so, and is appropriately remunerated for the work and given sufficient time to carry out its responsibilities.

5. To be reimbursed by the college or university for any financial hardship caused by the student teaching assignment; for example, for the costs of traveling excessive distances to the cooperating school district, or for the expenses incurred when the student teacher is assigned to a location so remote from his or her

college/university that it is necessary to establish residence there, in addition to the college or university residence.

6. To be informed, prior to the student-teaching period, of all relevant policies and practices of the cooperating school district, including those regarding personnel, curriculum, student requirements, and student-teaching program.

7. To confidentiality of records. Except with the express permission of the student teacher, the college or university shall transmit to the cooperating school district only those student records that are clearly necessary to protect the health and welfare of the student teacher, the cooperating teacher, the students, and others in the cooperating school. All persons having access to the records of student teachers shall respect the confidentiality of those records, as required by law.

8. To be admitted to student teaching and to remain in the student-teaching assignment in the absence of a showing of just cause for termination or transfer through fair and impartial proceedings.

9. To a student-teaching environment that encourages creativity and initiative. The student teacher should have the opportunity, under the perceptive supervision of the cooperating teacher, to develop his or her own techniques of teaching.

10. To a student-teaching environment that encourages the free exploration of ideas and issues as appropriate to the maturity of the students and the topics being studied.

11. To carry out the student-teaching assignment in an atmosphere conducive to learning and to have authority under supervision of the cooper-

Source: National Education Association, 1201 16th Street NW, Washington, DC, 1977.

ating teacher, to use reasonable means to preserve the learning environment and protect the health and safety of students, the student teacher, and others.

12. To participate, with the cooperating teacher and college/university supervisor, in planning the student-teaching schedule to include in addition to work with the assigned cooperating teacher, observation of other classes, attendance at professional meetings, and involvement, as appropriate, in extracurricular activities that will enrich and broaden the range of the field experience.

13. To be assigned to duties that are relevant to the student teacher's learning experience. Student teachers shall not be required to act as substitute teacher or teacher aide, nor to handle any non-teaching duties that are not part of the cooperating teacher's duties.

14. To request transfer in the event of prolonged illness of, or serious personality conflict with, the cooperating teacher and to have that request given favorable consideration without damage to any party's personal or professional status.

15. To a cessation of student-teaching responsibilities in the event and for the duration of a teacher strike at the cooperating school or school district to which the student teacher is assigned. If the strike is a prolonged one, the college or university has the responsibility to reassign the student teacher to another school district.

16. To the same liability protections as are provided the school district for regularly employed certified teachers.

17. To influence the development and continuing evaluation and improvement of the student teacher program, including the formulation and systematic review of standards of student teacher eligibility, and criteria and procedures of student teacher evaluation. Such influence shall be maintained through representation of stu-

dent teachers and recent graduates of the student-teacher program on committees established to accomplish these purposes.

18. To frequent planning and evaluative discussions with the cooperating teacher.

19. To systematic, effective supervision by the college/ university supervisor. Such supervision shall include (1) regularly scheduled classroom observations of sufficient frequency and length to permit thorough insight into the strengths and weaknesses of the student teacher's performance; (2) conferences with college/university supervisor immediately following observation, or as soon thereafter as possible, to discuss results of observation; and (3) regularly scheduled three-way evaluation conferences among student teacher, college supervisor, and cooperating teacher, to ensure that the student teacher is fully apprised of his or her progress and is given substantive assistance in assessing and remedying the weaknesses and reinforcing the strengths of his or her performance.

20. To see, sign, and affix written responses to evaluations of his or her classroom performance.

21. To an equitable and orderly means of resolving grievances relating to the student-teaching assignment. The college/university grievance procedure shall incorporate due process guarantees, including the right to be informed in writing of the reasons for any adverse action regarding his or her assignment, and to appeal any such action, with the right to have both student and teacher representation on committees formulated to hear and adjudicate student teacher grievances.

22. To be free to join, or not to join, on or off campus organizations, and to enjoy privacy and freedom of lifestyle and conscience in out-of-school activities, unless it is clearly evident that those activities have a harmful effect on the student teacher's classroom performance.

5 Competition for Educational Resources

*A*ll people want to maximize their benefits from education while reducing their personal costs. . . . [T]he ideal situation for an individual would be an educational system that increased the individual's political power and economic benefits at a cost being paid by other people.

—Joel Spring
Conflict of Interest: The Politics of American Education, 3rd ed., 1998, p. 53

You are teaching at a school located in a metropolitan county in the Midwest. In two months, the county school board will consider a proposal to redefine the attendance boundaries for the two districts within the county. The proposed redistricting is being driven by demographic shifts within the county. Many middle- to upper-middle class families in your district are moving to the suburban area within the county.

The proposal to be presented to the school board will result in a smaller tax base for your district. It is clear from the proposed redistricting that the other district would have higher property values than your district. Actually, the degree of inequity between your district and the other would be quite large.

Since you are a lead teacher at your school, your principal has asked your assistance in preparing a report to be presented to the school board. The purpose of the report is to explain to the board how the proposed redistricting would have negative consequences for your district. In addition, the principal wants your assistance in developing and then presenting an alternative proposal that would result in a more equitable distribution of funding among the two districts. The goal of this proposal would be to reduce, not increase, the difference between the ability of the county's two districts to finance education.

You and the principal decide that the first step will be for you to prepare a statistical profile for the county's two school districts as they currently exist. What kinds of data will you include in your profiles? Where will you obtain those data?

Guiding Questions

1. **How are schools financed in the United States?**

2. **What are some trends in funding for equity and excellence?**

3. **What is the condition of U.S. school buildings?**

4. **Do all students have equal access to technology?**

The preceding scenario highlights the need for teachers to understand the connection between the distribution of resources for schools and their capacity to provide quality educational experiences for all students. The United States has set for itself an educational mission of truly ambitious proportions—to provide equal educational opportunity to all students. Today, the nation is still moving toward full realization of that mission. To realize this mission will require equitable distribution of resources among all schools. In little more than 370 years, our educational system has grown from one that provided only a minimal education to an advantaged minority to one that now provides maximal educational opportunity to the majority. In spite of the shortcomings of the U.S. system of education, ours is one of the few countries in the world to offer a free public education to all of its citizens.

A dominant political force in the twenty-first century will be continued demands for equity in all sectors of U.S. life, particularly education. The constitutionality of school funding laws will be challenged where inequities are perceived. Various tax reform measures will be adopted to promote equitable school funding. And, as the epigraph for this chapter suggests, various groups will compete to maximize their benefit from educational resources, while minimizing their own contribution to those resources.

A key feature of our nation's educational system is the continuing quest for equity in distributing resources to schools. This quest is based on the dream of free, public, and locally controlled schools envisioned by the "father" of common schools, Horace Mann (1796–1859). Mann's eloquent appeals for a tax-supported school system stir the conscience even today:

> [A free school system] knows no distinction of rich and poor, of bond and free, or between those, who, in the imperfect light of this world, are seeking, through different avenues, to reach the gate of heaven. Without money and without price, it throws open its doors, and spreads the table of its bounty, for all the children of the State. Like the sun, it shines, not only upon the good, but upon the evil, that they may become good; and, like the rain, its blessings descend, not only upon the just, but upon the unjust, that their injustice may depart from them and be known no more (Mann 1868, 754).

This chapter examines the distribution of resources among U.S. schools and illustrates how "important political conflicts occur . . . over the distribution of education funds" (Spring 1998, 78). Since a combination of revenues from local, state, and federal sources is used to finance schools, the chapter examines funding trends at all three levels. To document the continuing quest to achieve equitable distribution of resources the chapter also examines key court cases initiated during the 1970s and various approaches for achieving educational equity.

How Are Schools Financed in the United States?

To provide free public education to all school-age children in the United States is a costly undertaking. Schools must provide services and facilities to students from a wide range of ethnic, racial, social, cultural, linguistic, and individual backgrounds. In addition, "school districts have become big business operations. The financing of public education and the administration of financial resources are increasingly complex" (Garner 2004, 3).

Expenditures for educational services and facilities have been rising rapidly and are expected to continue rising through 2013 (see Figure 5.1). Total expenditures for public elementary and secondary schools in 2000–01 were $454.1 billion, and the total **expenditure per pupil** was $7,524 (in constant 2001–02 dollars) (National Center for Education Statistics 2003). Figure 5.2 shows how the education dollar for public schools is allocated.

The Challenge of Equitable Funding

Financing an enterprise as vast and ambitious as the United States' system of free public schools has not been easy. It has proved difficult both to devise a system that equitably distributes the tax burden for supporting schools and to provide equal

Figure 5.1   Current expenditures of public schools (in constant 2001–02 dollars), with alternative projections: 1987–88 to 2012–13.

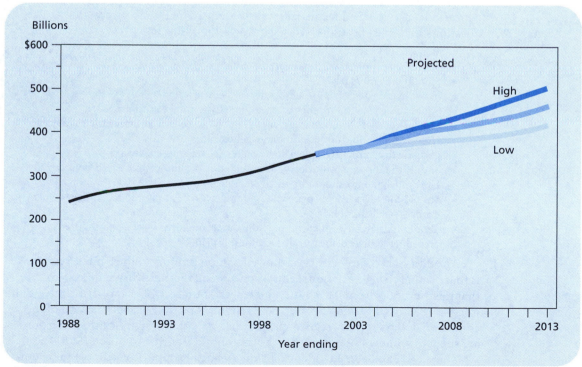

Source: Projection of Education Statistics to 2013, Figure 33. Washington, DC: National Center for Education Statistics, 2003.

Figure 5.2   Average allocation of the 2001–02 school district operating budget.

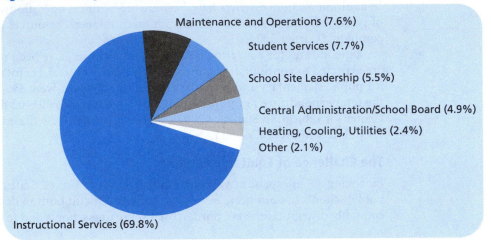

Maintenance and Operations (7.6%)

Student Services (7.7%)

School Site Leadership (5.5%)

Central Administration/School Board (4.9%)

Heating, Cooling, Utilities (2.4%)

Other (2.1%)

Instructional Services (69.8%)

Source: Educational Research Service (ERS) National Survey of School District Budgets, 2001–02. Copyright © by Educational Research Service. Used with permission.

educational services and facilities for all students. The following are among the questions that must be addressed regarding school funding:

- Who should pay?
- Should all people, even those without children, pay for public schools?
- Should only users pay?
- How should education monies be distributed?
- Should all education monies be given directly to public schools?
- Should vouchers be given to parents to purchase an education for their children?
- How should money for education be collected?
- Should educational costs be paid by regressive or progressive taxes?
- Should they be paid by tuition or a combination of tuition and government subsidy?
- How much money should be spent on education?
- Should the government spend enough money on education to maximize the life chances of all children?
- Should the government spend only the money required to educate children according to their demonstrated abilities? (Spring 1998, 55)

An additional complexity regarding education funding in the United States is that, "rather than one national education system, there are fifty state systems that raise revenues from local, state, and federal sources. Dollars are distributed quite unequally across the states, districts, and schools. And only a small fraction of the education dollar supports regular classroom instruction—significant proportions are spent in schools, but outside of the classroom" (Odden and Busch 1998, 4).

There has also been a tendency for the financial support of schools to be outpaced by factors that continually increase the cost of operating schools—inflation, rising enrollments, and the need to update aging facilities, for example. According to the 2003 Gallup Poll of the public's attitudes toward the public schools, "lack of financial support/funding/money" was seen as the number one problem confronting local schools. Moreover, according to the 2001 poll, almost 60 percent of the public believed that the amount of money spent on public schools in their state differs from school district to school district "a great deal" (28 percent) or "quite a lot" (29 percent).

Revenues for education are influenced by many other factors, including the apportionment of taxes among the local, state, and federal levels; the size of the tax base at each level; and competing demands for allocating funds at each level. In addition, funding for education is influenced by the following factors:

- The rate of inflation
- The health of the national economy
- The size of the national budget deficit
- Taxpayer revolts to limit the use of property taxes to raise money, such as Proposition 13 in California and Oregon's property tax limitation
- Changes in the size and distribution of the population
- School-financed lawsuits to equalize funding and ensure educational opportunity

Sources of Funding

A combination of revenues from local, state, and federal sources is used to finance public elementary and secondary schools in the United States. **Local revenues** include revenues from such sources as local property and nonproperty taxes, investments, and revenues from student activities, textbook sales, transportation and tuition fees, and food services. **State revenues** include both direct funds from state governments and revenues in lieu of taxation. Revenues in lieu of taxes are paid to compensate a school district for nontaxable state institutions or facilities within the district's boundary. **Federal revenues** include direct grants-in-aid to schools or agencies, funds distributed through a state or interstate agency, and revenues in lieu of taxes to compensate a school district for nontaxable federal institutions within a district's boundary. In addition, a small percentage of revenues come from the "intermediate" level. **Intermediate revenues** come from sources that are not local or state education agencies, but operate at an intermediate level between local and state education agencies and possess independent fund-raising capability, for example county or municipal agencies.

As Table 5.1 shows, schools received almost half of their 1999–2000 funding from the state, 43.2 percent from local and other sources, and 7.3 percent from the federal government. Since 1980, schools have received almost equal funding from local and state sources; prior to that date, however, schools received most of their revenues from local sources, and early in the twentieth century, nearly all school revenues were generated from local property taxes.

Local Funding   At the local level, most funding for schools comes from **property taxes** that are determined by the value of property in the school district. Property taxes are assessed against real estate and, in some districts, also against personal

Table 5.1	Revenues for public elementary and secondary schools, by source of funds: 1919–20 to 1999–2000

School year	Percentage distribution		
	Federal	State	Local (including intermediate)[1]
1919–20	0.3	16.5	83.2
1929–30	0.4	16.9	82.7
1939–40	1.8	30.3	68.0
1949–50	2.9	39.8	57.3
1959–60	4.4	39.1	56.5
1969–70	8.0	39.9	52.1
1979–80	9.8	46.8	43.4
1989–90	6.1	47.1	46.8
1996–97	6.6	48.0	45.4
1997–98[2]	6.8	48.4	44.8
1998–99	7.1	48.7	44.2
1999–2000	7.3	49.5	43.2

[1]Includes a relatively small amount from nongovernmental private sources (gifts and tuition and transportation fees from patrons). These sources accounted for 2.4 percent of total revenues in 1999–2000.
[2]Revised from previously published figures.
Note: Beginning in 1980–81, revenues for state education agencies are excluded. Beginning in 1988–89, data reflect new survey collection procedures and may not be entirely comparable with figures for earlier years. Details may not sum to totals due to rounding.

Source: Excerpted from U.S. Department of Education, National Center for Education Statistics, *Statistics of State School Systems: Revenues and Expenditures for Public Elementary and Secondary Education*; and Common Core of Data surveys. (This table was prepared May 2002.)

property such as cars, household furniture and appliances, and stocks and bonds. Increasing taxes to meet the rising costs of operating local schools or to fund needed improvements is often a heated issue in many communities.

Although property taxes provide a steady source of revenue for local school districts, there are inequities in the ways in which taxes are determined. By locating in areas where taxes are lowest, for example, businesses and industries often avoid paying higher taxes while continuing to draw on local resources and services. However, the main problem of using property taxes to fund education is that not all districts have the same tax base. A poor district, for example, may have to tax its residents disproportionately compared with residents in a wealthier district.

An additional challenge for local funding is the development of guidelines for assessing the value of property. The fair market value of property is often difficult to assess, and the qualifications and training of assessors vary greatly. Also, groups within a community sometimes pressure assessors to keep taxes on their property as low as possible.

Most states specify by law the minimum property tax rate for local school districts to set. In many districts, an increase in the tax rate must have the approval of voters. Some states place no cap, or upper limit, on tax rates, and other states set a maximum limit.

State Funding   Most state revenues for education come from sales taxes and income taxes. Sales taxes are added to the cost of items such as general goods, gasoline, amusements, alcohol, and insurance. Income taxes are placed on individuals (in many states) and on business and industry.

Some states, such as Florida, set aside for education a percentage of the revenue from state lotteries. However, such schemes may not meet the funding needs of education. In Florida, for example, legislators have used lottery revenues to *replace* rather than augment education dollars that previously came from state taxes. The assumption that high lottery sales would mean less need to raise money for education through taxes proved false.

As mentioned previously, states contribute nearly 50 percent of the resources needed to operate the public schools. The money that a state gives to its cities and towns is known as **state aid**. Table 5.2 compares selected states on the percent of education funds received from federal, state, intermediate, and local sources in relation to total expenditures for 2000–01. Revenues from local sources ranged

Table 5.2   Revenues for public elementary and secondary schools, by source and state: School year 2000–01

State	Revenues	Percent of Total Revenues 2000–01			
		Federal	**State**	**Intermediate**	**Local**
Alaska	$1,370,271	15.8	49.7	0.0	27.1
California	$51,007,510	8.2	61.5	0.0	30.3
District of Columbia	$1,042,711	11.1	–	0.0	88.9
Nevada	$2,393,494	5.1	28.6	0.0	66.3
New Mexico	$2,426,705	13.9	71.1	0.0	15.0
New Jersey	$15,967,075	3.9	41.8	0.0	54.3
New York	$34,266,171	5.7	46.2	0.5	47.6
Oregon	$4,564,408	7.4	56.2	1.4	35.0
Texas	$30,469,570	8.7	42.2	0.2	48.9
Washington	$8,058,875	7.8	62.9	0.0	29.3

Note: Detail may not sum to totals because of rounding.

Source: U.S. Department of Education, National Center for Education Statistics, *The Education Statistics Quarterly*, 5(2), 2003.

from 15.0 percent (New Mexico) to 66.3 percent (Nevada) of total revenues. Revenues from state sources also showed a wide distribution in their share of total revenues. The state revenue share of total revenues was less than 30 percent in Nevada (28.6 percent) and just over 70 percent in New Mexico (71.1 percent). Federal revenues ranged from 3.9 percent in New Jersey to 15.8 percent in Alaska. Federal sources contributed more than 10 percent of the revenues in Alaska, Arizona, the District of Columbia, Louisiana, Mississippi, Montana, New Mexico, North Dakota, Oklahoma, South Dakota, and West Virginia.

Federal Funding The role of the federal government in providing resources for education has been limited. As shown in Table 5.1, the federal share of funding for public elementary and secondary schools peaked in 1979–80 at 9.8 percent and had declined to 6.6 percent by 1996–97. The U.S. Department of Education currently administers a budget of about $63 billion per year that cover all levels of education. The department's elementary and secondary programs annually serve approximately 14,000 school districts and nearly 54 million students attending more than 93,000 public schools and 27,000 private schools (U.S. Department of Education 2004a).

Prior to 1980, the federal government had in effect bypassed the states and provided funding for local programs that were administered through various federal agencies, such as the Office of Economic Opportunity (Head Start, migrant education, and Follow Through) and the Department of Labor (Job Corps and the Comprehensive Employment Training Act [CETA]). Since the Reagan administration (1980–88), federal aid has increasingly been given directly to the states in the form of **block grants**, which a state or local education agency may spend as it wishes with few limitations.

The 1981 **Education Consolidation and Improvement Act (ECIA)** gave the states a broad range of choices in spending federal money. The ECIA significantly reduced federal aid to education, however, thus making state aid to education even more critical.

Though a small proportion of the funds for schools comes from the federal level, the federal government has enacted supplemental programs to help meet the educational needs of special student populations. Such programs are often referred to collectively as **entitlements**.

The most significant entitlement is the Elementary and Secondary Education Act of 1965, which President George W. Bush reauthorized in 2002 as the No Child Left Behind Act (NCLBA). Title I of the act allocates a billion dollars annually to school districts with large numbers of students from low-income families. Among the other funded entitlement programs are the Vocational Education Act (1963), the Manpower Development and Training Act (1963), the Economic Opportunity Act (1964), the Bilingual Education Act (1968), the Indian Education Act (1972), and the Education for All Handicapped Children Act (1975).

The federal government also provides funding for preschool programs such as Project Head Start. Originally started under the Economic Opportunity Act

How does federal funding influence schools at the local level? How does federal funding help to reduce inequities among schools?

of 1964 to provide preschool experiences to poor children, Head Start was later made available to children whose parents were above the poverty level. Funding for Head Start was $4.66 billion in 1999. Reauthorized by Congress in 1998, Head Start served an estimated 830,000 children and their families that year. The Head Start Act Amendments of 1994 also established the Early Head Start program, designed to serve pregnant women and children under three from low-income families.

Support for Education in Other Countries   Compared with other industrialized nations, the United States' expenditures of 3.4 percent of gross domestic product (GDP) is about "average." Figure 5.3 shows the percentage of the 1994 and 1998 education expenditures for the countries known as the G8: the United States, Canada, France, Germany, Italy, Japan, and the United Kingdom. (Data are not included for Russia, since Russia began full participation in the G8 in 1998.) Public expenditures for primary and secondary education as a percent of GDP in the United States were lower than expenditures in Canada and France, and higher than expenditures in Germany and Japan.

Compared to teachers in other countries, U.S. teachers are among the highest paid in the world, in an absolute sense. However, an examination of U.S. teachers' salaries relative to GDP per capita, reveals that what the United States pays its teachers, *relative* to its ability to pay for their professional services, lags behind many industrialized nations. In fact, U.S. spending on teachers is among the lowest in the world (Parkay and Oaks 1998).

Figure 5.3   Total public expenditures for primary and secondary education as a percent of gross domestic product (GDP), by country: 1994 and 1998.

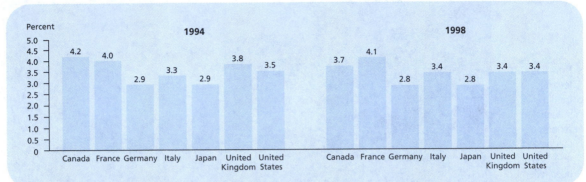

Note. The United Kingdom includes England, Northern Ireland, Scotland, and Wales. Figures for 1998 include postsecondary, nontertiary education in all other countries presented except the United States. Gross domestic product is the producers' value of the gross outputs of resident producers, including distributive trades and transport, less the value of the purchasers' intermediate consumption plus import duties. GDP is expressed in local money (in millions). Prior to 1997, there was no category called "postsecondary, nontertiary" education in the international classification. For 1994, expenditures for this type of education were included in expenditures for secondary education in all other countries presented here except the United States. With the establishment of "postsecondary, nontertiary" education as a separate category in 1997, other countries continued to include expenditures for this category in expenditures for secondary education in data for 1998. Expenditure figures for the United States include expenditures for postsecondary, nontertiary education in expenditures for higher education for 1994 and 1998. Comparisons among countries within a given year are thus more appropriate than comparisons over time.

Sources: Organization for Economic Cooperation and Development, *Education at a Glance*, 2001, Table B2.1b; Organization for Economic Cooperation and Development, *Education at a Glance*, 1996 Table B1.1b. Figure taken from *Comparative Indicators of Education in the United States and Other G8 Countries:* 2002. Washington, DC: National Center for Education Statistics, May 2003, p. 63.

The National Commission on Teaching and America's Future (1996) found that many other countries tend to invest more resources than the United States in hiring teachers. Teachers comprise about 60 to 80 percent of total staff in many other countries; in the United States, teachers comprise slightly more than 40 percent. The Commission (1996, 15) notes that in U.S. schools, "too many people and resources are allocated to activities outside of classrooms, sitting on the sidelines rather than the front lines of teaching and learning." In the Teachers' Voices feature in this chapter, an accomplished educator calls upon the future president of the United States, just prior to the 2004 presidential election, to devote more federal funding to education.

What Are Some Trends in Funding for Equity and Excellence?

The U.S. educational system has made significant progress in its commitment to provide an equal, and excellent, education for all students. And, as the following statement from the beginning of a book on education finance suggests, the distribution of resources to schools will continue to become even more equitable

Teachers' Voices

Why We Stay (A Letter to the Next President)

Jane Butters

Dear Mr./Ms. President,

Our middle school is located in the zip code area that has one of the highest reported crime rates in the city. More than 90 percent of the students live near or below the poverty line, some students have probation officers, and most come from single-parent homes. Ninety-eight percent of our students are Hispanic or African American. Our campus has a high student mobility rate, and approximately 40 percent of our students receive either special education or English as a second language (ESL) services. Our achievement scores fluctuate, but are far from exemplary. Each and every year, our teacher and staff turnover and transfer rate is one of the highest in the district. We have seventy teachers, and there are only seven still at this campus who were here my first year. For many years, we had a crumbling building that required a $10 million renovation to make it a safe and adequate place for students.

Those of us who have stayed experience the honor of working with nine hundred brilliant and capable students who bring beautiful diversity to the school. Despite years of lacking facilities, our students rarely complain about the conditions. In the years before and during our renovation, we often had no gym, no library, no courtyard, and a field covered with work trailers. We had an air conditioning system that usually did not work and often produced hot, uncomfortable classrooms—once during a state test—and still the students rarely complained. They possess a cultivated resistance to these substandard conditions. Our students speak multiple languages and bring an endless flow of creative talents to our campus. Those of us who have stayed do not see deficits in our students; we see deficits in the larger system that repeatedly fails them.

To keep excellent teachers at our most challenging schools across the land, this is what we need from you:

Change the National Tone Toward Public Education and Remove Fear and Humiliation from Models of Judgment. Educators receive painfully mixed mes-

sages. Businesses give us donations and the government gives us funding, but then they both turn around and slap us in the face with fear tactics and systems designed to humiliate us rather than support us. Set high standards for educators, but also set equally high standards for government, businesses, and communities to develop reciprocally supportive and collaborative relationships with schools.

Provide Incentives to Attract and Keep Excellent Teachers at the Neediest Schools. At the heart of all solutions to make our school successful, we simply need the top educators to make long-term commitments to the neediest schools. Most educators do not run to our school beating down the door looking for jobs, especially when they can work at what many call "easier campuses with fewer challenges." If we were able to offer an increased salary for working at a high-needs campus and stipends for multiple-year commitments, we would have a larger and more qualified group of applicants from which to choose. In an ideal world, the very best educators would come to our campus without needing additional financial incentives. We do not live in an ideal world, and the raw fact is that many people choose to work at other campuses.

If you support us, we will not disappoint you. In most schools, there are pictures of presidents on the walls and in textbooks. Most people associate each president with a national priority, a time period, an event, or a persona. We long for the day that we look at a president and think, "Thank you," because we feel your unparalleled support of our schools. We long to stand next to our students in successful, creative, enriching, and democratic classrooms across the United States and pledge allegiance to the flag, to the nation, and to you—a president who upholds and protects the ideals of an education for all.

With faith in your commitment to education in the United States,

Jane Butters

(continued)

Teachers' Voices

Putting Research and Theory into Practice *(Continued)*

Questions

1. At schools with characteristics similar to the one at which Butters works, what are some of the reasons for the high rate of teacher turnovers?
2. "To keep excellent teachers at our most challenging schools across the land," what advice would you give the president?
3. How would you describe the current "national tone toward public education" in the United States?

Jane Butters is an assistant principal and lead mentor teacher at a middle school in Austin, TX. She was voted Teacher of the Year at her school. The preceding is excerpted from her contribution to *Letters to the Next President: What We Can Do About the Real Crisis in Public Education* (Glickman 2004), pp. 127–133, a book that appeared just prior to the 2004 presidential election.

---

during the coming decades: "Educational and financial equity have changed significantly over the years. The window of opportunity to continue improving educational opportunities and performances for the success of all children is likely more open now than ever before" (Garner 2004, 3).

The fact that schools have had to rely heavily on property taxes for support has resulted in the fiscal inequities that continue to be found among schools. Districts with higher property wealth are able to generate more money per pupil than districts with lower property values. The degree of inequity between the wealthiest and the poorest districts, therefore, can be quite large. In some states, for example, the ability of one district to generate local property tax revenues may be several times greater than another district's. Moreover, unequal educational funding in the United States makes it one of the most inequitable countries in the world (Odden and Busch 1998).

In addition, "politics" contribute to funding inequities among schools. The following political factors have made it difficult for school reform efforts to reach students in resource-poor schools, according to the director of the Center on Reinventing Education at the University of Washington:

- Local school boards are political bodies pursuing many agendas, of which educational effectiveness is only one.
- School districts allow money and other resources to follow political influence, so that poor students end up receiving the least money and the worst facilities and equipment.
- Teachers with seniority, superior preparation and other attributes that make them attractive to "nice" schools can usually avoid teaching the most disadvantaged children in a school district (Hill 2003, A11).

As pointed out in Chapter 1, politics play a key role in the struggle to control schools in the United States. In some instances, politics have a positive influence on schools. In others, such as those cited above, they have a negative influence. While our system of schools will never be entirely free of politics, professional educators are committed to ensuring that politics influence the distribution of educational resources in positive ways.

In *Savage Inequalities: Children in America's Schools*, noted educator Jonathan Kozol (1991) presented a compelling analysis of the inequities in school funding. He found that the amount of money spent on each school-age child ranged from $1,500 to $15,000, depending on where the child lived. Disputing those who claim that parental values, not high spending on education, determines how much children learn, Kozol pointed out that high spending on education in affluent districts *does* coincide with high achievement.

Tax Reform and Redistricting

To correct funding inequities, several court suits were initiated during the 1970s. In the 1971 *Serrano v. Priest* case in California, it was successfully argued that the relationship between spending and property wealth violated the state's obligation to provide equal protection and education. The California Supreme Court ruled in a six-to-one decision that the quality of a child's education should not be dependent on the "wealth of his parents and neighbors." The court also recognized that communities with a poor tax base could not be expected to generate the revenues of more affluent districts. Nevertheless, the court did not forbid the use of property taxes to fund education.

How does the system of school funding in the United States contribute to inequities? What are some solutions to the problems of funding inequity?

Case for Reflection

"Rich" and "Poor" School Districts

It is late summer, and today you begin teaching at a school in a major metropolitan area. You live in a new apartment complex located in an affluent suburb adjacent to the city. Across the street from your apartment is an elementary- through secondary-level campus that covers an entire block. The elementary and secondary buildings, each not more than a few years old, sit on well-manicured lawns. Flowers in the beds that line almost the full perimeter of each building are in full bloom. The campus also has a separate building that houses the aquatic center. A huge new sports stadium and track were added to the campus last year.

The homes surrounding the two schools are large and expensive. Many residents of the suburb commute daily into the city. While walking to your car this morning, you see two parents, one driving an expensive imported luxury car and the other a fancy SUV, pull up in front of the school and drop their children off.

After a 45-minute drive, you pull into the faculty parking lot at your school. The school is in a poor, high-crime area of the city. About 90 percent of the school's students are members of minority groups. For the last five years, the area has been severely economically depressed, and unemployment and poverty have touched nearly half the families that have children attending the school. About 70 percent of the students come from families on some form of public assistance, and 85 percent are eligible for the federally funded free lunch program.

During the first two decades following its construction at the end of World War II, the school had a reputation for providing a good education for the children of immigrant, blue-collar families. Since the mid-1960s, however, the area served by the school began to pass through the irreversible stages of urban decline. Today, the school is considered one of the most challenging in the city. The results of annual standardized tests, for example, regularly place the school's students in the lowest percentiles for reading, writing, and mathematics.

The school itself is a dreary looking, three-story yellow brick building that covers half a city block. The building's exterior almost suggests that the school is only marginally successful at providing students with a quality education. Several windows on the first floor have been boarded over. Later, you learn that the school's engineer decided that he could no longer afford to have his crew continue to replace broken panes of glass that appeared almost daily.

The only open area around the school is a gravel lot, once the sight of a warehouse. Later this morning, a teacher tells you that the school has no athletic playing field, and the football team must practice at a city park several blocks away. The battered green doors leading into the school are covered with graffiti that have been spray painted or carved into the wood by anonymous students over the years.

The inside of the school is clean; however, the hallways are dark and dreary. Across from the main office are two large display cases. At most schools such cases would present proud evidence of student accomplishments. At your school, however, they are empty.

As you walk to your classroom, you think about the dramatic contrast between the school campus near your apartment complex and the school at which you will be teaching. Clearly, the vast difference in the assessed value of property in the two districts accounts for the gross funding inequities. Is it possible to achieve equitable funding between a "rich" and a "poor" school district? Is that realistic?

Then, in 1973, the U.S. Supreme Court decided in *San Antonio Independent School District v. Rodriguez* that fiscal inequities stemming from unequal tax bases did not violate the Constitution. That court's decision reversed a lower court's ruling claiming that school financing on the basis of local property taxes was unconstitutional.

Regardless of the mixed outcomes of court challenges, many state legislatures have enacted school finance equity reforms during the last fifteen years. A few states (California, Hawaii, New Mexico, Washington, and West Virginia, for example) have led the way by developing programs to ensure statewide financial equality. These states have **full-funding programs** in which the state sets the same per-pupil expenditure level for all schools and districts.

Recently, the concept of **equitable funding**—providing the same funds for each student regardless of where the student lives or level of family income—is being challenged by the **adequacy of funding** concept. Funding based on the concept of adequacy provides different levels of funding based on a student's educational needs. The public is about evenly divided on whether equal funds should be provided for each student or whether funds should be varied to meet each student's educational needs. The 2003 Phi Delta Kappa/Gallup Poll of the Public's Attitudes Toward the Public Schools showed that 52 percent of the public supported equal funding per student, while 45 percent supported varied funding based on students' needs (Rose and Gallup 2003, 51).

Other states have adopted new funding formulas to try to broaden their revenue base. Among the solutions tried are level funding augmented by sales taxes, cigarette taxes, state lottery revenues, property taxes on second homes, and school choice plans. One of the most dramatic changes in educational funding occurred in Michigan in 1993 with the passage of Proposal A, a plan that greatly reduced school funding from local property taxes and increased funding from the state's sales tax.

Since each state has been free to determine the number of districts within its boundaries, a common approach to achieving equal funding is redistricting, redrawing school district boundaries to reduce the range of variation in the ability of school districts to finance education. (As this chapter's opening scenario indicates, however, redistricting can result in greater inequities among school districts.) Redistricting not only equalizes funding; it can also reduce the cost of maintaining and operating schools if smaller districts are combined. The per-pupil cost of instruction, supplies, and equipment is usually lower in large districts. In addition, greater resources often allow larger districts to offer a broader curriculum and higher salaries to attract more qualified teachers.

Vertical Equity

Other states have developed various mechanisms for providing **vertical equity**, that is, for allocating funds according to legitimate educational needs. Thus, additional support is given to programs that serve students from low-income backgrounds; those with limited English proficiency, or special gifts and talents; and those who need special education or vocational programs.

Additional state-appropriated funds to cover the costs of educating students with special needs are known as **categorical aid**. Funding adjustments are also made to compensate for differences in costs within a state—higher expenses due to rural isolation or the higher cost of living in urban areas, for example. Some states even conduct periodic regional cost-of-living analyses, which are then used to determine adjustments in per-pupil funding.

School Choice

One of the most bitter struggles for control of schools in the United States is centered around **school choice**, the practice of allowing parents to choose the schools their children attend. The issue is especially heated for choice programs that would allow parents to choose a private school to attend at public expense. According to the 2003 Phi Delta Kappa/Gallup Poll of the Public's Attitudes Toward the Public Schools, 60 percent opposed such choice programs, while 38 percent were in favor (Rose and Gallup 2003, 49).

Debate continues about whether school choice programs will, in fact, promote equity and excellence. Advocates of school choice believe that giving parents more options will force public schools to adjust to free-market pressures—low-performing schools would have to improve or shut down. Moreover, they contend that parents whose children must now attend inferior, and sometimes dangerous,

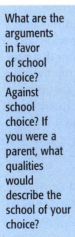

What are the arguments in favor of school choice? Against school choice? If you were a parent, what qualities would describe the school of your choice?

inner-city schools would be able to send their children elsewhere. In addition, some supporters see choice as a way to reduce the influence of top-heavy school bureaucracies and teachers' unions.

On the other hand, opponents believe that school choice would have disastrous consequences for public schools and lead to students being sorted by race, income, and religion. School choice, they argue, would subsidize the wealthy by siphoning money away from the public schools and further widen the gap between rich and poor districts. Moreover, opponents point out that research does not indicate that school choice would improve education (Smith and Meier 1995), nor would it promote educational equity:

> Since poor parents lack the supplemental resources that rich people have for helping their children, some opponents argue that school choice would not help to equalize educational opportunities. For example, rich parents can afford transportation, clothing, and educational supplies to send their children to a private school far away; poor parents may not be able to afford these expenses (Berliner and Biddle 1995).

Other critics contend that school choice could lead to the creation of segregated schools and schools that would be more committed to competing for education dollars and the most able, manageable students. Moreover, a study of the impact of competition on three urban school systems concluded that "competition did not force [the districts] to substantially alter system, governance, management, or operations." And, in the words of an observer at two schools, "teachers have thirty kids in their classroom just like they did last year, just like they did ten years ago. They still teach the same way. [Vouchers] haven't affected what they do" (Hess 2002, 198).

Voucher Systems

One approach to providing educational equity that has generated considerable controversy is the **voucher system** of distributing educational funds. According to voucher plans, parents would be given government funded vouchers to purchase educational services at the schools of their choice.

Voucher systems were first suggested more than fifty years ago by Milton Friedman, a well-known conservative economist and Nobel laureate. Friedman believes that schools would be much better if they were operated by private businesses rather than the government. "If we had a system of free choice we would also have a system of competition, innovation, which would change the character of education. . . . Reform has to come through competition from the outside, and the only way you can get competition is by making it possible for parents to have the ability to choose" (Friedman 2003).

Although various voucher plans have been proposed, one of the most common would give states the freedom to distribute money directly to parents in the form of vouchers. Parents would then use the vouchers to enroll their children in schools of their choice. The most controversial voucher proposals would allow parents to choose from among public as well as private (secular, parochial, for-profit, and charter) schools; others would limit parents' choice to public schools. Voucher programs require that parents and guardians reflect on the kind of educational experiences they want for their children.

Debates about vouchers regularly make the national news. New Mexico's pro-voucher governor clashed with the state's legislature over private school vouchers (*Education Week* 1999a). In 1999, Florida became the first state to offer state-paid tuition to children in failing public schools to attend a public, private, or religious school of choice; however, a Florida judge ruled in 2002 that the program violated the Florida Constitution because it gave tax money to religious schools (*Los Angeles Times* 2002). And, for months, the media covered New York City Schools Chancellor Rudolph Crew's opposition to Mayor Rudolph W. Giuliani's plan to "give poorer parents the same opportunity to make choices about their children's education that the richest and most affluent parents in New York City have" (*Education Week* 1999b).

In 2002, the Supreme Court ruled that a school voucher program in Cleveland did not infringe upon the constitutional separation of church and state (*Zelman v. Simmons-Harris* 2002). In a five-to-four ruling, the Supreme Court said the voucher program did not constitute the establishment of religion. The ruling reversed an appeals court decision, which struck down the program because nearly all the families receiving the tax-supported state tuition scholarships attended Catholic schools in Cleveland. The Supreme Court majority said the parents had a sufficient range of choices among secular and religious schools that the voucher plan does not violate the First Amendment prohibition against the establishment of religion.

Evaluation of Voucher Programs   Currently, there are thirteen different voucher programs in various states. Each program has different rules and regulations controlling its size and scope and the terms of participation. Since "distinguishing those voucher programs that are designed to be large, generous, and inclusive from those that are small, stingy, and restrictive sometimes requires wading through technical legal and regulatory documents" (Enlow 2004, 1–2), the Milton and Rose D. Friedman Foundation released *Grading Vouchers: Ranking America's School Choice Programs* in 2004.

The report evaluates and ranks the nation's thirteen school voucher programs based on three criteria: how many students are eligible to receive a voucher (Student Eligibility); how much money the voucher is worth (Purchasing Power); and how many and what type of private schools parents can choose (School Eligibility). For each category, the program is assigned a letter grade, and the final ranking is based on the average of the three. The criteria reflect Friedman's vision of a voucher system of education in which "all students, regardless of income or any other criteria, are able to use 100 percent of the state and local funds to attend public and private schools that are largely free from government interference" (Enlow 2004, 2).

According to the report, the best voucher program is Florida's McKay Scholarship with a 3.6 GPA or A−, while the lowest scoring voucher program is the Iowa

Personal Tax Credit with a 1.76 GPA or C−. Milwaukee's voucher program, the nation's oldest program for low-income families, receives a grade of C, while Colorado's program, one of the newest, gets a B−. (In 2003, a Denver district court judge struck down Colorado's voucher legislation.)

Another study, the longest voucher study in the country (Metcalf 2003), has evaluated the Cleveland voucher program since 1998. The longitudinal study is following a group of one thousand Cleveland voucher students from the first grade, to determine if they are doing better in private schools compared to their public school peers. The voucher students are being compared with five thousand public school students. The public school students are divided into four groups: (1) those who applied for vouchers but weren't accepted into the program, (2) those who were awarded vouchers but didn't use them, (3) those who used vouchers for one or more years but returned to public school, and (3) those who chose never to apply for the voucher program.

The following are among the findings for the Cleveland voucher program:

- During the first three years of school, public school students, on average, made larger academic gains than students in the voucher program. After the first three years, however, there were no consistent or statistically significant differences in academic achievement as a result of vouchers.
- Many low-income families eligible to participate in the voucher program declined to do so because the cost to attend private school, even with a voucher, was too high. In addition, the limited number and range of participating private schools further discouraged families from using vouchers.
- When low-income families declined to participate, their unused vouchers were likely to be used by students who are not minority, who are more affluent, and who are already enrolled in a private school (Metcalf 2003).

It is clear that the debate over school choice will continue for the foreseeable future. Gradually, support for school choice appears to be increasing—currently, almost half of the states allow some form of "interdistrict" transfer, which would allow students to attend public schools outside of their home district. In fact, Grant and Murray (1999, 235) suggest that "it is conceivable that by 2020 as many as a quarter of all students could be enrolled in some 'school of choice,' whether private or public." While support for vouchers may be increasing slightly, support drops significantly if it means less money for public schools. As Figure 5.4 shows, a 2002 survey indicated that the public favors vouchers by a 51 to 40 percent margin; but when asked if they still support the idea if it means less money for public schools, they oppose vouchers by a 2-to-1 margin.

Corporate-Education Partnerships

To develop additional sources of funding for equity and excellence, many local school districts have established partnerships with the private sector. Businesses may contribute funds or materials needed by a school, sponsor sports teams, award

Figure 5.4 Americans weigh in on school vouchers.

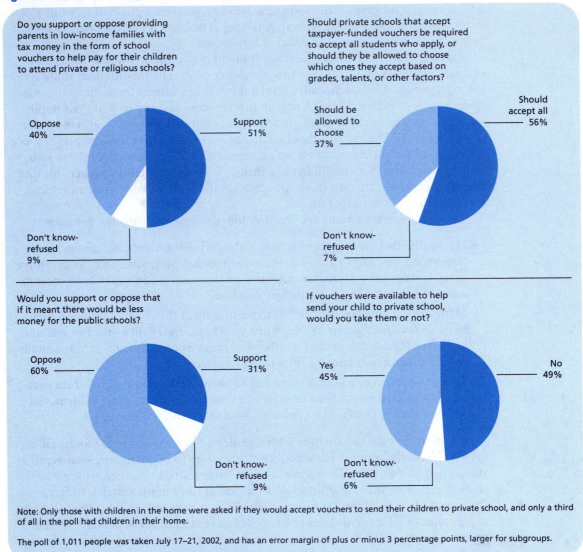

Do you support or oppose providing parents in low-income families with tax money in the form of school vouchers to help pay for their children to attend private or religious schools?

Oppose 40%
Support 51%
Don't know-refused 9%

Should private schools that accept taxpayer-funded vouchers be required to accept all students who apply, or should they be allowed to choose which ones they accept based on grades, talents, or other factors?

Should be allowed to choose 37%
Should accept all 56%
Don't know-refused 7%

Would you support or oppose that if it meant there would be less money for the public schools?

Oppose 60%
Support 31%
Don't know-refused 9%

If vouchers were available to help send your child to private school, would you take them or not?

Yes 45%
No 49%
Don't know-refused 6%

Note: Only those with children in the home were asked if they would accept vouchers to send their children to private school, and only a third of all in the poll had children in their home.

The poll of 1,011 people was taken July 17–21, 2002, and has an error margin of plus or minus 3 percentage points, larger for subgroups.

Source: ICR/International Communications Research for the Associated Press, 2002.

scholarships, provide cash grants for pilot projects and teacher development, and even construct school buildings. One example of a corporate-education partnership is Thomas Jefferson High School for Science and Technology, a college preparatory magnet school in Alexandria, Virginia. Twenty-five local and multinational businesses, including AT&T, Mobil, Boeing, Honeywell, and Exxon, raised almost $1 million for the school. State-of-the-art facilities include a $600,000

Relevant Standards

Obtaining Additional Resources from the Community

As the following standards indicate, professional teachers develop linkages with various community agencies and local businesses to supplement the resources available to the school.

- "[Teacher candidates] are able to foster relationships with school colleagues, parents and families, and agencies in the larger community to support students' learning and well being." (National Council for Accreditation of Teacher Education [NCATE] 2002, 18. Standard 1: Candidate Knowledge, Skills, and Dispositions.)

- "[Teachers] are knowledgeable about specialized school and community resources that can be engaged for their students' benefit, and are skilled at employing such resources as needed." (National Board for Professional Teaching Standards [NBPTS] 2002, 4. Explanation of knowledge, skills, abilities, and commitments essential for Proposition #5: "Teachers are members of learning communities.")

- "The teacher can identify and use community resources to foster student learning." (Interstate New Teacher Assessment and Support Consortium [INTASC] 1992, 34. Performance statement for Principle #10: "The teacher fosters relationships with school colleagues, parents, and agencies in the larger community to support students' learning and well-being.")

- "Teacher is highly proactive in serving students, seeking out resources when necessary." (Praxis Series, distinguished level of performance for Domain 4: Professional Responsibilities, Component 4f: Showing Professionalism.) (From Danielson 1996, 119)

telecommunications lab with a television studio, radio station, weather station, and a satellite earth station. The school has a biotech laboratory for genetic engineering experiments in cloning and cell fission as well as labs for research on energy and computers.

Corporate contributions to education total more than $2 billion annually, with about 9 percent going to elementary and secondary education and the rest to colleges, including grants to improve teacher preparation. A survey of Fortune 500 and Service 500 companies found that 78 percent contributed money to education, 64 percent contributed materials or equipment, 26 percent offered teachers summer employment, and 12 percent provided executives-on-loan to schools (Hopkins and Wendel 1997, 15).

If schools in the United States are to succeed in meeting the challenges of the future, they will need to be funded at a level that provides quality educational experiences to students from a diverse array of backgrounds. Though innovative approaches to school funding have been developed, much remains to be done before both excellence and equity characterize all schools in the United States. This chapter's Relevant Standards feature highlights the professional teacher's ability to identify community resources to enhance the educational experiences of all students.

Community-School Partnerships

To develop additional sources of funding, many local school districts have established partnerships with community groups interested in improving educational opportunities in the schools. Some groups raise money for schools. The American Jewish Committee and the Urban League raised funds for schools in Pittsburgh, for example. Other partners, such as a major airline based in Miami, adopt or sponsor schools and enrich their educational programs by providing funding as well as other resources and services.

Community-school partnerships take many forms. Community groups may contribute funds or materials needed by a school or may visit classrooms. In some dropout prevention programs, community groups adopt individual students, visiting them at school, eating lunch with them once a week, meeting their families, and taking them on personal field trips. Community groups may also provide a variety of special services, such as museum-in-the-schools programs, outdoor education, local history projects, and model government activities. Community-based fraternal, civic, and service organizations also provide valuable support. They may sponsor sports teams, recognize student achievement, or award scholarships.

What Is the Condition of U.S. School Buildings?

The unequal distribution of resources for schools in the United States is perhaps nowhere more evident than in the school buildings themselves. Ideally, as school buildings become outdated and inadequate, they are replaced by new school buildings. However, a weak economy during the first few years of the new century made the public less likely to support the construction of new schools. As a result, some observers contend that many of today's children "are falling behind because they come to learn each day in facilities that are cramped, outdated, inadequate and deteriorating" (Kennedy and Agron 2004).

Deteriorating School Buildings

As mentioned earlier, Jonathan Kozol's *Savage Inequalities: Children in America's Schools* (1991) documented inequities in school funding, especially for schools in inner-city neighborhoods. Kozol also described the grim physical facilities that students and teachers experience daily at many urban schools. Kozol's book awakened the public to how badly many school buildings in the United States had deteriorated.

Recent data suggest that the condition of school buildings has improved little since Kozol's book appeared. Not surprisingly, a poll of 72,000 teenagers reported that the first place they would invest more education dollars would be improved school maintenance and construction (Kennedy & Agron 2004).

The need to improve school buildings goes beyond a desire for more attractive buildings. Inadequate, badly maintained, or poorly designed facilities can hinder students' learning and reduce teachers' effectiveness. Class size, school size, natural light, proper acoustics, and good indoor air quality can affect students' ability to learn (Kennedy and Agron 2004). The American Association of School Administrators (AASA) report, *Schoolhouse in the Red* (1992), found that one in eight public school buildings provided a poor physical environment for learning. Similarly, an analysis of data gathered at Washington, DC, schools revealed that student achievement, as measured by standardized tests, would be 5 to 11 percent higher if physical conditions in the schools improved (Kennedy & Agron, 2004).

Financing School Construction and Renovation

Typically, the burden of paying for school construction and renovation has fallen on local districts and their constituents. But with the needs so large and widespread, it is evident that local communities cannot carry the weight by themselves. One solution would be for the federal government to provide more money to improve schools. By a ratio of 60 to 16 percent, the public would like to see the federal government take a greater role in providing money for school renovations, according to a national survey of 1,005 registered voters conducted in 2004 for the National Education Association.

While the No Child Left Behind (NCLB) Act of 2001 involved the federal government in elementary and secondary education to an unprecedented degree, the act does not include funding to help local school districts build or renovate facilities. Reflecting this lack of federal support, the American Society of Civil Engineers' 2003 *Progress Report on America's Infrastructure* asserts that "the federal government should do more to assist local school districts in maintaining their facilities."

The Society's *Report Card for America's Infrastructure* in 2001 showed that the nation's school infrastructure had improved slightly since the previous *Report Card* in 1998. However, the improvement was only from a grade of F to a grade of D−. And, in its 2003 *Progress Report*, the Society left the D− grade unchanged. The *Progress Report* asserted that "due to either aging, outdated facilities, severe overcrowding, or new mandated class sizes, 75 percent of our nation's school buildings remain inadequate to meet the needs of school children."

According to the Society, the federal government could assist local school districts in maintaining their facilities by enacting the America's Better Classroom Act of 2003, which would help states and localities by using tax credits to pay the interest on school modernization bonds. As of this writing, however, Congress had not enacted this act.

The Need to Improve U.S. School Buildings

At least five factors have contributed to the current need to improve the condition of America's school buildings: (1) gradual deterioration as buildings age, (2) increasing enrollments, (3) mounting evidence that poor facilities diminish student learning, (4) the continuing quest to equalize the distributions of resources for schools, and (5) increased use of technology in schools. If local districts are to respond effectively to these factors, it is clear that they will definitely need more state and/or federal assistance for new school construction.

Building Deterioration   School buildings constructed during the 1950s to cope with the "baby boom" generation are reaching a critical age. Many of those buildings were built quickly and cheaply, and their flaws are becoming more evident as they become older. In addition, years of deferred maintenance have worsened the substandard conditions of many of these buildings.

Increasing Enrollments   As existing facilities became increasingly inadequate, schools across the nation have had to find additional classroom space for increasing student enrollments. Even if there were no problems with existing facilities, districts needed to come up with classrooms for an additional 8.4 million students that accounted for a 19 percent increase in public school enrollment from 1988 to 2001.

Influence of Facilities on Learning   Studies released in the 1990s provided more evidence that improving the condition of a school facility could boost student performance. For example, after studies found a correlation between the amount of daylight in a school building and improved test scores, many school districts sought to upgrade their facilities with windows and skylights.

Other studies made the case that smaller schools and smaller classrooms provided a better learning environment for students. Many districts sought to build smaller schools or construct facilities that could be divided into smaller units to establish a small-school environment. Having smaller class sizes meant districts had to find more classroom space even if their enrollment was static.

In addition, many school districts are mandating a lower student-to-teacher ratio in an effort to improve test scores. For example, Florida has a statewide constitutional amendment limiting class sizes, and the amendment caused the Hillsborough County school district to put a freeze on moving dilapidated portable classrooms from school property.

Quest for Equitable Resources   Court challenges to state education-funding formulas at first dealt only with operating funds, but in the 1990s, reformers began to pursue more equitable facilities funding in their lawsuits. Many states, either because of a judge's order or in an effort to preempt a judicial solution, came up with programs to help pay for school construction and renovation.

Increased Use of Technology   The increased use of technology in teaching has highlighted facility upgrades needed to accommodate the new technologies. In addition, the federal government's E-rate subsidy has made it financially feasible for schools to modernize their buildings. To provide funds to help poor schools connect to the Internet, the federal government launched E-rate in 1998, a controversial program that provides discounts on telecommunications services and wiring to schools and libraries. The increased purchasing power from the **E-rate program** enables schools to direct funds to improving facilities.

The Education rate (E-rate) program distributes about $2.25 billion a year to the schools. Using fees the Federal Communications Commission (FCC) collects from telecommunications companies, the E-rate program provides schools with Internet access at discounted rates based on the income levels of students' families and whether their location is urban or rural (rural communities receive up to a 10 percent discount). Since some companies pass these costs on to consumers, critics claim that the FCC has imposed an illegal tax on telephone users.

The Cost of Improving School Buildings

In its annual report on school construction, *American School & University* found that $26.8 billion was spent on K–12 school construction in 2001. In 2002, this figure declined to $24.3 billion. However, the American Society of Civil Engineers' *Report Card* for 2001 concluded that $3,800 per student would need to be invested in improving U.S. schools. Nationwide, the total amount needed would be $127 billion.

In 2000, the National Education Association prepared its own study ("Modernizing Our Schools: What Will It Cost?") of the nation's school facility needs. The NEA's figure was more than double what the U.S. General Accounting Office estimated in 1995. According to the NEA, modernization needs for the public school infrastructure in the United States totaled more than $268 billion. In addition, the NEA concluded that schools had nearly $54 billion in technology needs, bringing the total figure to modernize the nation's school facilities up to $322 billion to bring the nation's school facilities up to modern standards.

Do All Students Have Equal Access to Technology?

Access to technology is a necessary resource if a school is to provide a quality education for all students. For educational technology to benefit students and teachers, new technologies must be readily available to them. Access to technology involves several elements, including a sufficient number of up-to-date computers and related technological hardware, technical support to maintain the equipment, broadband Internet access, and high-quality software.

Funding for Computers and Technical Support

To enable schools to participate more fully in the computer revolution, some school districts have passed bond measures to fund educational technology, and a few states have adopted long-term budgets for computers and technical support. In Milwaukee, a comprehensive technology plan called for all 156 buildings in the school system to be networked and for a mini-network, a printer, a television, and a multimedia teacher workstation in every classroom. In Cleveland, a state program has provided every primary grade classroom with three multimedia computers and each teacher with a laptop computer (Harrington-Lueker 1999).

As schools continue to work toward the goal of having Internet access in every classroom, about 66 percent of their total technology spending is devoted to purchasing up-to-date hardware, 19 percent to purchasing software, and 15 percent to providing staff development (Market Data Retrieval 2002).

Although schools are getting more computer hardware, most cannot afford to hire sufficient support staff for technology. About 30 percent of schools employ a full-time coordinator of technology, about 40 percent employ a part-time coordinator, and about 30 percent have no onsite technical support personnel (Furger 1999). As a result, most schools rely on central district personnel or computer-savvy teachers for support.

Commercial Computer Labs   Confronted with limited budgets to purchase computers, about two thousand public and private schools during the late 1990s accepted "free" computer labs (complete with software, training, and maintenance) from companies such as California-based ZapMe. In exchange, schools agreed that classes would use the labs at least four hours a day and that students would be exposed to onscreen advertisements that ran continuously in a 2″ × 4″ box in a bottom corner of the screen, changing every fifteen seconds. In addition, schools agreed to allow ZapMe and its for-profit partners to use the labs for computer training and related activities.

However, free, commercially oriented computer labs like ZapMe led critics such as Ralph Nader to compare the labs to the controversial Channel One. Eventually, ZapMe bowed to pressure from critics and ceased providing free labs to schools. On the demise of ZapMe, its founder pointed out that school districts and parents were mostly enthusiastic about the labs and stated that "if you're not going to charge more taxes or bond issues, what options do the schools have?" (Tweney 2000).

Access to Technology for All Students

The nation's schools have made significant strides toward reducing the student–computer ratio. In 1999, a survey by Quality Education Data revealed that only 25 percent of K–12 schools could be characterized as "high-end technology schools" with a student–computer ratio of six to one or less (Anderson and Ronnkvist 1999). By 2002, however, the average ratio was less than four to one per computer used for instruction and less than six to one per multimedia computer, according to a survey of 87,100 schools (Market Data Retrieval 2002).

A "Digital Divide"?   At urban schools, the ability to narrow what has been termed the **digital divide** between poor and more affluent schools is often limited by enormous obstacles, including "limited resources, low expectations, overwhelming poverty, teacher contracts, entrenched bureaucracies, political infighting, and the sheer size of these districts" (Williams 1999). *Barriers and Breakthroughs: Technology in Urban Schools* (Education Writers Association 1999) revealed that, while most urban districts have "lighthouse" schools in which sophisticated technologies are fully integrated into the curriculum, they also have schools with woefully limited technologies. The Technology in Teaching feature on page 183 in this chapter presents criteria for evaluating a school's ability to integrate technology into teaching.

Figure 5.5 shows that Hispanic and African American children—who have lower computer use rates at home—have computer use rates at school that result in their having overall use rates that are comparable to white and Asian American and Pacific Islander children. The overall computer use rate in 2001 for Hispanic children was 84.2 percent; 88.8 percent for African American children; 94 percent for Asian and Pacific Islander children; and 95.4 percent for white children.

Computers and Gender   Discrepancies in access to computers are also related to gender. In *Does Jane Compute? Preserving Our Daughters' Place in the Cyber Revolution*, Roberta Furger (1998), a columnist and contributing editor at *PC World* magazine, estimates that only 16 percent of children and youth online are girls. In a chapter titled "Jane@Home," Furger suggests that boys get the largest share of family computing time. She also cites the lack of software based on girls' interests and even harassment in some male-dominated online forums. In "Jane@School," Furger contends that girls have less access to computers and receive less encouragement to

Figure 5.5   Computer use among ten- to seventeen-year-olds by race and location, 2001.

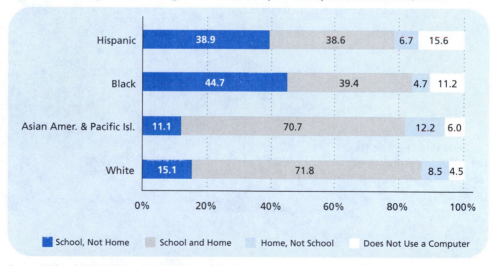

Source: NITA and ESA, U.S. Department of Commerce, using U.S. Census Bureau Current Population Survey Supplements. *A Nation Online: How Americans Are Expanding Their Use of the Internet.* February, 2002, p. 48. Washington, DC: U.S. Department of Commerce.

What steps can teachers take to ensure that students, regardless of gender, acquire essential computer literacy skills?

pursue computer-related careers. Furger also suggests that boys tend to regard the computer as a toy, whereas girls regard it as a tool.

Some schools are taking steps to encourage girls to explore and learn with technology. Schools in Palos Park, Illinois, for example, developed a program called Girls and Technology: Skills, Computers, Awareness, and Peer Empowerment

Technology in Teaching

What are the characteristics of "high-tech" schools?

While schools have reduced the number of students per computer, there is evidence of a "digital divide" if computer use at school and at home is compared to family income and minority-group status. In *A Nation Online: How Americans Are Expanding Their Use of the Internet*, the U.S. Department of Commerce (2002) reported that only 33.1 percent of children (ages ten to seventeen) in the lowest income category use computers at home, compared with 91.7 percent of children in the highest income category. However, schools do help equalize the disparity in computer use among children from various income categories; according to *A Nation Online*, 80.7 percent of children in the lowest income category use computers at school, compared with 88.7 percent of children in the highest income category.

(GATSCAPE). Sixth-, seventh-, and eighth-grade girls at all levels of computer literacy get unrestricted access to technology during classes and after school. As they acquire new skills with technology, the girls are encouraged to pass on these skills to other girls formally and informally (CEO Forum on Education and Technology 1999).

Summary

How Are Schools Financed in the United States?

- Schools are supported with revenues from the local, state, and federal levels, with most funding now coming from the state level.

- Local funding is provided through property taxes, which in many instances result in inequitable funding for schools located in areas with an insufficient tax base.

- One challenge to financing schools has been the development of an equitable means of taxation for the support of education.

- Many other industrialized nations of the world invest more resources in education than the United States.

What Are Some Trends in Funding for Equity and Excellence?

- Inequities among school districts often reflect differences in the value of property that can be taxed for the support of schools.

- Many state legislatures have enacted tax reforms including full-funding programs that set the same per-pupil expenditures for all schools and districts. Some states have achieved greater equity through redistricting—redrawing district boundaries to reduce funding inequities.

- Some states achieve vertical equity by providing additional funding, or categorical aid, to educate students with special needs. Also, many local districts and schools receive additional funding through partnerships with the private sector and/or community groups.

- School choice and voucher programs are two controversial approaches to providing parents the freedom to select the schools their children attend.

What Is the Condition of U.S. School Buildings?

- Many school buildings in the United States are overcrowded, deteriorating, and out-of-date.

- Inadequate, badly maintained, or poorly designed school buildings can hinder students' learning and reduce teachers' effectiveness.

- Since many local communities have insufficient resources, the public favors increased federal support to help local districts build or renovate school facilities.

- Five factors reflect the need to improve America's school buildings: (1) deterioration as buildings age, (2) increasing enrollments, (3) the effect of poor facilities on student learning, (4) the quest to equalize resources among schools, and (5) increased use of educational technology.

Do All Students Have Equal Access to Technology?

- Access to technology for all students is uneven, and many schools report inadequate funding for computers and technical support.

- A "digital divide" is evident when access to computers is compared to minority-group status, family income, and gender.

Key Terms and Concepts

adequacy of funding, 169
block grants, 162
categorical aid, 170
digital divide, 180
Education Consolidation and
   Improvement Act (ECIA), 162
entitlements, 162

equitable funding, 169
E-rate program, 178
expenditure per pupil, 157
federal revenues, 159
full-funding programs, 169
intermediate revenues, 159
local revenues, 159

property taxes, 159
school choice, 170
state aid, 161
state revenues, 159
vertical equity, 169
voucher system, 171

Reflective Application Activities

Discussion Questions

1. With the exception of contributions from the private sector, public schools receive virtually all of their funding from the local, state, and federal levels. What do you think would be an "ideal" formula for funding local schools? The formula should indicate the percentage of revenues that would come from local, state,

federal, and private sources. What criteria would you use for arriving at the various proportions? Finally, compare your formula with information presented in Chapter 5.

2. Should education financing be linked to the performance of schools? Should underperforming schools receive more money or less money?

Professional Journal

1. Imagine that you are given vouchers to send your child to any school in your state. What factors would you consider in making your choice? Compare your results with the following list, most important coming first, from a recent survey of parents:

- Quality of teaching staff
- Maintenance of school discipline
- Courses offered
- Size of classes
- Test scores of students

What are the similarities and differences between the lists? What do the differences reveal about your view of education and schools?

2. What are the challenges of achieving equitable taxation for education and the local and state levels? What barriers might make it difficult to overcome these challenges?

Online Assignments

1. Use the Internet to gather information about school funding in your state. What are the figures for household income and poverty rate? What proportion of school funding in your state is from the local, state, and federal levels? What are the total expenditures and per-pupil expenditures? Begin your data search at the U.S. Department of Education's National Center for Education Statistics (NCES) where you will find NCES data from the *Digest of Education Statistics*, the *Condition of Education, Youth Indicators, Projections of Education Statistics*, the *Directory of Department of Education Publications*, the *Directory of Current OERI-Funded Projects*, and the *Directory of Computer Data Files*.

2. Find information on sources of federal funding for education, education budgets, and issues of education finance. Begin at the U.S. Department of Education and then go to the Budget Office home page of the Department.

Observations and Interviews

1. Interview a school superintendent and ask him or her to comment on how federal, state, and local funding affect education in the district. To what extent does funding from these three different levels help (and/or hinder) the district in accomplishing its goals?

2. Attend a meeting of a local school board and observe the communication and decision-making processes that address the provision of funding and other resources for schools in the district. During your observation, note the following: agenda items that relate to funding and other resources for schools, who set the agenda, who participates in the discussion, who proposes policy related to funding and other resources for schools, and the extent of agreement between superintendent and school board.

Professional Portfolio

Think of businesses and agencies in your community that might be good partners for a school. Select one of them and develop a proposal outlining the nature, activities, and benefits (to both) of the partnership you envision.

6 Standards, Testing, and Accountability in U.S. Schools

Education is controversial. Arguments over the most appropriate aims, the most propitious means, and the most effective control have raged over the centuries.

—James William Noll
Taking Sides: Clashing Views on Controversial Educational Issues, 2004

After a 20-minute drive in light early-morning traffic, you arrive at school for a 7:30 A.M. meeting of your school's Teacher Leadership Team (TLT). At the start of the school year, teachers elected you to serve on the TLT. The TLT works with the principal and her administrative team to develop the school's academic programs.

For the last two months, the TLT has focused on preparing students for the state-mandated Assessment of Student Learning (ASL) given near the end of the school year. Last week, the TLT met with the school's Site-Based Council (SBC) to get the council's input on preparing students for the ASL. The SBC's primary purpose is to provide the principal and her administrative team with advisory input on instructional and curricular issues. SBC members include three teachers, the principal, five community members, and two professors from a nearby university.

Like most schools around the country, the changing demographics of the nation are reflected in the diverse student population at your school. About 15 percent of students are from families who live below the poverty line. One in eight students is identified as limited-English speaking. According to a district survey, students represent eighteen different language groups.

Overall, students at your school score in the lower 25 percent on the ASL. About 30 percent of students go on to college, and 20 percent enroll in other forms of postsecondary programs. After graduation, about half of the students take entry-level jobs at various companies in the city. Or they begin to work in one of the several factories within a two-mile radius of the school.

A few minutes before the meeting begins, you visit the classroom of another TLT member. At the last TLT meeting, you both volunteered to use the Internet to find out what the state teachers' association and teachers at other schools in the state think about the ASL. Also, you were to find out how schools throughout the state are preparing students for the ASL.

"What did you find out on the Internet?" you ask after entering the room. "I was online for about two hours last night. There's a lot of controversy about the ASL."

"I haven't had a chance to do anything yet," your friend says. "I've been pulling together resources for the project-based learning activities my kids start next week."

"I see . . . no problem," you say.

"I promised to give them these handouts today," she continues. "Otherwise, we won't be able to begin next week. The handout has directions for developing an outline and timeline for their projects."

Your friend is seated at her desk, stapling handouts for the project-based learning activities. She takes a handout from a neatly crisscrossed stack on top of her desk and staples it. Instead of placing it on a stack of handouts to her left, she hands it to you.

"This looks great," you say, flipping through the nine-page handout. "A lot of work goes into something like this."

"So, what did you find out about the ASL?" your friend asks.

"Teachers are really concerned about 'teaching to the test,' " you answer.

"Surprise, surprise," your friend says, the sarcasm evident in her voice. "Tell me more."

"The website for the state teachers' association makes a lot of good points. Basically, teachers should focus on *improving student learning*, not *increasing test scores*," you say, your voice emphasizing the two very different views of schooling.

"Yeah, I agree completely," your friend says. "It's like we've lost sight of the fact that the purpose of schooling is to learn, not to get good scores on tests."

"Right . . . Well, I better get out of here and let you finish getting your handouts ready," you say. "We're meeting in about 5 minutes in the third floor conference room."

Walking down the hallway to the conference room, you think about how high-stakes tests are impacting teaching. How much time should teachers spend preparing kids to take high-stakes tests? Does test preparation interfere with teaching?

Guiding Questions

1. What role will standards play in your classroom?
2. What is standards-based education?
3. What controversies surround the effort to raise standards?
4. How are schools and teachers held accountable for student learning?
5. How are high-stakes tests changing education?
6. What does the future hold for you as a teacher?

As the epigraph and the opening scenario for this chapter suggest, today's teachers work in an environment characterized by controversy and change. Education plays an important role in shaping the world of tomorrow. In turn, education is also shaped by current and future political, economic, social, and technological forces. As the mission statement for the International Centre for

Educational Change at the University of Toronto states: "More and more educators are working in a world of intensifying and rapid change. . . . New technologies, greater cultural diversity, the skills called for in a changing economy, restructured approaches to administration and management, and a more sophisticated knowledge-base about teaching and learning, are all pulling students and their teachers in new directions."

The U.S. school system is striving to meet the complex needs of a society undergoing extensive social and economic changes. Indeed, each chapter of this book describes heated controversies and powerful change forces that influence education in the United States. Chapter 1 examines the nature of educational politics in the United States and how they can place teachers "in the line of fire." Chapter 2 reviews how political forces and various interest groups at the local, state, national, and regional levels compete for control of America's schools. Chapter 3 explains how political efforts to influence our nation's schools reflect varied, often conflicting, philosophical beliefs about education. Chapter 4 explains how the law touches almost every aspect of the teacher's professional life and how a steady stream of new court decisions and local, state, and federal laws impact teachers' daily lives. Lastly, Chapter 5 documents the often divisive issues that arise as our nation continues its quest to provide equitable distribution of resources to all schools.

The final chapter of this book also deals with controversy and change in education. The chapter examines three of the "hottest" issues in education today—standards, testing, and accountability for schools and teachers. Heated debates around these issues focus on several questions: What role should standards play in education? What knowledge and skills should students learn? How should student learning be assessed? For *what* outcomes should teachers be held accountable? *How* should they be held accountable?

As the educational reform movement begun in the 1980s continues to be played out during the future, numerous controversies and powerful change forces will generate new challenges, opportunities, and rewards for teachers. As we move into this exciting, unknown educational future, it will be professionals such as you who will use their understanding of these controversies and the change process to provide children and youth with the best education possible.

What Role Will Standards Play in Your Classroom?

As the opening scenario for this chapter—and, indeed, daily newspaper headlines—reminds us, the public is concerned about declining test scores, the performance of U.S. students on international comparisons of achievement, and our nation's standing in a competitive global economy. Pressure to get "back to the basics" and drives by parents, citizen groups, and politicians to hold teachers accountable have led to a nationwide push to raise standards and to develop more effective ways to assess student learning. As a result, state-level standards and large-scale assessment systems will be "facts of life" during your career as a teacher.

Standards and assessments are key elements in the move to hold educators more accountable for student learning. Parents must know that the schools to which they send their children are educating them well. Similarly, the community must know that its investment in school buildings, teachers' salaries, and curricular resources is returning educational "dividends."

Perspectives on Standards

As adults, we are familiar with standards. To obtain a driver's license, we have to demonstrate the knowledge and skills needed to drive a car. At work, we must meet our employer's standards. In these cases, a *standard* refers to a level of knowledge or skill that is generally acknowledged as necessary to perform a specific task or to occupy a particular role in society. In education, however, **standards** represent the criteria students must meet to receive a grade of A, to be promoted to the next grade, or to graduate from elementary or high school.

Educational standards take a variety of different forms. The type of standards most important to the individual often depends on whether one is a school administrator, teacher, or student. Administrators, for example, are primarily concerned about standards related to *students' performance on standardized tests of achievement.* In such instances, the administrator (and his or her school board) might focus on a standard such as the following: "During the next five years, the percentage of students scoring above the norm will increase by at least 2 percent each year."

Teachers, of course, are also concerned about standards related to students' performance on standardized tests. Successful teachers recognize that raising standards

What might be some of the pressures felt by students and teachers as a result of the emphasis on higher academic standards?

Teachers' Voices

Putting Research and Theory into Practice

Rigorous Mondays

Eva Benevento

During September I focus on note-taking. Lots of people think I'm crazy to do this, but I don't think you're going to really think about what's going on in literature until you know the writing on a literal level. Also, I want my students to have a record of their learning. I want them to be able to revisit the works we've read and discussed throughout the year. So on Mondays throughout September I teach them five or six different note-taking techniques. But I don't have to do this alone because September is note-taking month for the whole sixth-grade team. Eventually all the students develop a system that works for them. We don't try to impose one system; we just insist that their notes be accurate, organized, and balanced.

Each month I use my Rigorous Mondays to focus on a different kind of product. In September students work on note-taking. Every Monday night they refine and revise their notes to fit our criteria of accuracy, organization, and balance. In October we focus on retellings. November is our author study month. This year we're doing Chekhov and our theme is "Authors as Teachers," so our Monday night essays have focused on what Chekhov is trying to help us see and understand in each of the four stories I read to them.

Next Monday they'll select their best essay, read it to a peer-editing group, collect feedback, and revise it for Tuesday. It's all *very* regular, and the predictability helps the students. They know what's expected of them each Monday because they produce the same kind of product four times each month. They can see themselves improve, getting better at producing this kind of writing, or at note-taking.

Questions

1. Reflect on your experiences as a K–12 student. Did you have teachers who taught in a very rigorous manner? How did you respond to their teaching?
2. Did you have teachers who taught in a nonrigorous, unchallenging manner? How did you respond to their teaching?
3. What implications do your responses to #1 and #2 above have for you as a teacher?

Eva Benevento teaches sixth grade at a school in Teaneck, New Jersey. Her comments appear in Teaching What Matters Most: Standards and Strategies for Raising Student Achievement, *by Richard W. Strong, Harvey F. Silver, and Matthew J. Perini, published by the Association for Supervision and Curriculum Development, 2001, pp. 25–26.*

involves more than mandating a test for graduation or developing lists of statements that reflect "world-class" standards. They understand that their *expectations for student performance and behavior at the classroom level* are at the heart of higher standards. They demonstrate their commitment to high standards by giving students intellectually demanding reading and writing assignments; providing extensive, thoughtful feedback on their work; and presenting intellectually stimulating lessons.

To illustrate how accomplished teachers convey high standards to students, the Teachers' Voices feature in this chapter describes how one sixth-grade teacher implements "Rigorous Mondays" in her classroom. Each Monday, she begins class by reading aloud one short story by a world renowned author. Students take detailed notes while she reads. After she finishes reading, students break into pairs while one student retells the story and the other "coaches" with prompts, suggestions, and questions.

Students often have yet another perspective on standards. For them, the school curriculum should meet the *standard of being personally relevant, interesting, and meaningful.* The school curriculum should help them meet the developmental challenges of moving from childhood to adulthood. It should help them realize the goals they have set for themselves.

Most teachers and principals believe their school has high academic standards. Figure 6.1, for example, shows that 72 percent of secondary principals and 60 percent of teachers included in the *MetLife Survey of the American Teacher, 2001: Key Elements of Quality Schools* view their schools as having high standards. However, secondary school students have a different perception of academic standards at their schools; only 38 percent of students surveyed believe standards are high. Many high school students, it seems, would agree with an eleventh-grade boy quoted in the MetLife survey: "I can't remember the last time I learned something new. . . . I just get sick of the busy work, and usually just end up throwing it aside and not doing it. I want to be LEARNING things" (Harris Interactive 2001, 44).

Administrators, teachers, students, and parents frequently have different perspectives on standards. However, during the last decade, standards in education (sometimes called *content standards, goals, expectations, learning results,* or *learning outcomes*) are primarily statements that reflect what students should know and be able to do within an academic subject area or at a particular grade level.

What Is Standards-Based Education?

Current efforts at educational reform in the United States emphasize **standards-based education (SBE)**. In other words, curricula, teaching, and the assessment of student learning are based on rigorous, "world-class" standards. SBE is based on the belief that *all* students are capable of meeting high standards. In the past, expectations for students from poor families and students who are members of minority groups were sometimes lower than for other students. Today, SBE is seen as a way of ensuring that excellence and equity become part of our nation's public school system. As President George W. Bush pointed out prior to his election for a second term in 2004: "The educational divide [between African Americans and Hispanic students and white students] is caused by the soft bigotry of low expectations" (Bush 2004, 114).

Developing rigorous academic standards, assessing students' mastery of those standards, and holding students and teachers accountable for meeting those standards are key elements of SBE. Roy Romer, former governor of Colorado and a vocal national advocate for higher standards, explains how higher standards can improve education in the United States:

> Setting standards, raising expectations, and assessing student progress in a meaningful way gives students the tools they need to thrive in the 21st century and the tools parents and teachers need to help them. [Content] standards are a compilation

Figure 6.1 Academic standards: students, teachers, and principals.

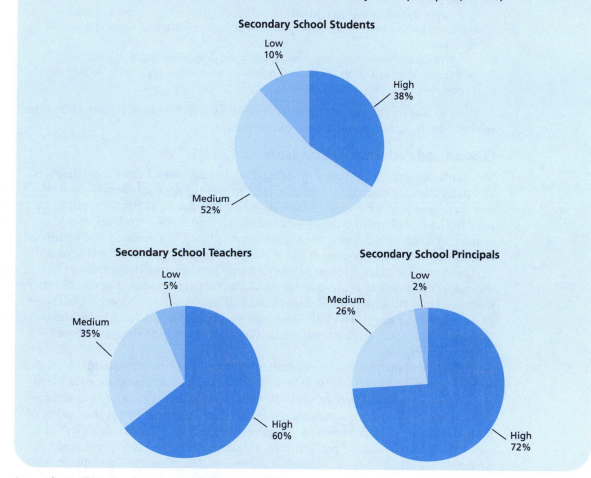

Q240: How would you rate the academic standards at your school?
Base: Secondary school students (N = 2049)

Q305: How would you rate the academic standards at your school?
Base: Secondary school teachers (N = 430)/Secondary school principals (N = 383)

Secondary School Students

Low 10%
High 38%
Medium 52%

Secondary School Teachers

Low 5%
Medium 35%
High 60%

Secondary School Principals

Low 2%
Medium 26%
High 72%

Source: The MetLife Survey of the American Teacher, 2001: Key Elements of Quality Schools. New York: Harris Interactive 2001, p. 46.

of specific statements of what students should know or be able to do. They do not represent the totality of what students should learn at school. They are not curriculum. When standards are well-conceptualized and written, they can focus the education system on common, explicit goals; ensure that rigorous academic content is taught by all teachers in all classrooms and raise expectations for all students (2000, 314–315).

To meet the demand for higher standards, forty-nine states (Iowa is the exception) have adopted state standards for what students should know and be able to do. For example, here are standards in geometry from three states:

Colorado: Students use geometric concepts, properties, and relationships in problem-solving situations and communicate the reasoning used in solving these problems.

North Dakota: Students understand and apply geometric concepts and spatial relationships to represent and solve problems in mathematical and nonmathematical situations.

Wyoming: Students apply geometric concepts, properties, and relationships in problem-solving situations. Students communicate the reasoning used in solving these problems.

As these examples show, state standards are broad statements of learning outcomes against which student achievement can be measured.

Content and Performance Standards

Standards documents prepared by state education agencies, local school districts, and professional associations typically refer to two types of standards—content standards and performance standards. **Content standards**, as the term implies, refer to the agreed-upon content—or knowledge and skills—students should acquire in different academic areas. A common phrase in standards documents is that content standards represent "what students should know and be able to do."

Content standards are often subdivided into benchmarks (frequently called indicators). **Benchmarks** are content standards that are presented as specific statements of what students should understand and be able to do *at specific grade levels or developmental stages*. The following is an example of a benchmark: "At the end of the eighth grade, the student understands basic properties of two- and three-dimensional figures."

In addition, many standards documents refer to performance standards. A performance standard specifies "how good is good enough." **Performance standards** are used to assess the *degree to which* students have attained standards in an academic area. Performance standards require teacher judgment about the quality of performance or level of proficiency required. Performance standards differ from content standards because performance standards reflect levels of proficiency. A performance standard for evaluating students' written essays, for example, might be as follows: 5 = outstanding, 4 = exemplary, 3 = proficient, 2 = progressing, and 1 = standard not met.

Standards Developed by Professional Associations

In addition to national, state, and local efforts to raise standards, professional associations are playing a key role in SBE by developing standards that reflect the knowledge, skills, and attitudes students should acquire in the subject matter disciplines. In many cases, professional associations have developed specific, grade-level performance standards. These standards include statements that reflect desired levels of achievement, quality of performance, or level of proficiency. In addition, professional associations have developed classroom activities related to standards.

Educational stakeholders can use standards developed by professional associations in the following ways:

- State departments of education, school districts, and schools can use the standards as a guide for developing curricula and assessments of student learning.
- Teachers can use standards to (1) develop goals and objectives for units and courses, (2) evaluate their teaching, and (3) develop ideas for instructional activities and classroom assessments.
- Parents and community members can use standards to assess the quality of education in their local schools and to monitor the achievement levels of their children.

Figure 6.2 presents several professional associations that have recommended curriculum standards in various academic disciplines. You can obtain complete sets of standards from the websites these associations maintain.

Figure 6.2 Curriculum standards developed by professional associations.

Language Arts

Standards for the English Language Arts
International Reading Association and the National Council of Teachers of English, 1996

Mathematics

Principles and Standards for School Mathematics
National Council of Teachers of Mathematics, 2000

Science

Atlas of Science Literacy: Mapping K–12 Learning Goals
American Association for the Advancement of Science, 2000

Social Studies

Expectations of Excellence: Curriculum Standards for Social Studies
National Council for the Social Studies, 1994

Standards for Academic Excellence

History

National Standards for History
National Center for History in the Schools, 1996

Foreign Language

Standards for Foreign Language Learning in the 21st Century
American Council on the Teaching of Foreign Languages, 1999

Art Education

National Standards for Art Education: What Every Young American Should Know and Be Able to Do in the Arts
Consortium of National Arts Education Association, 1994

Physical Education

National Standards for Physical Education
National Association for Sport and Physical Education, 1999

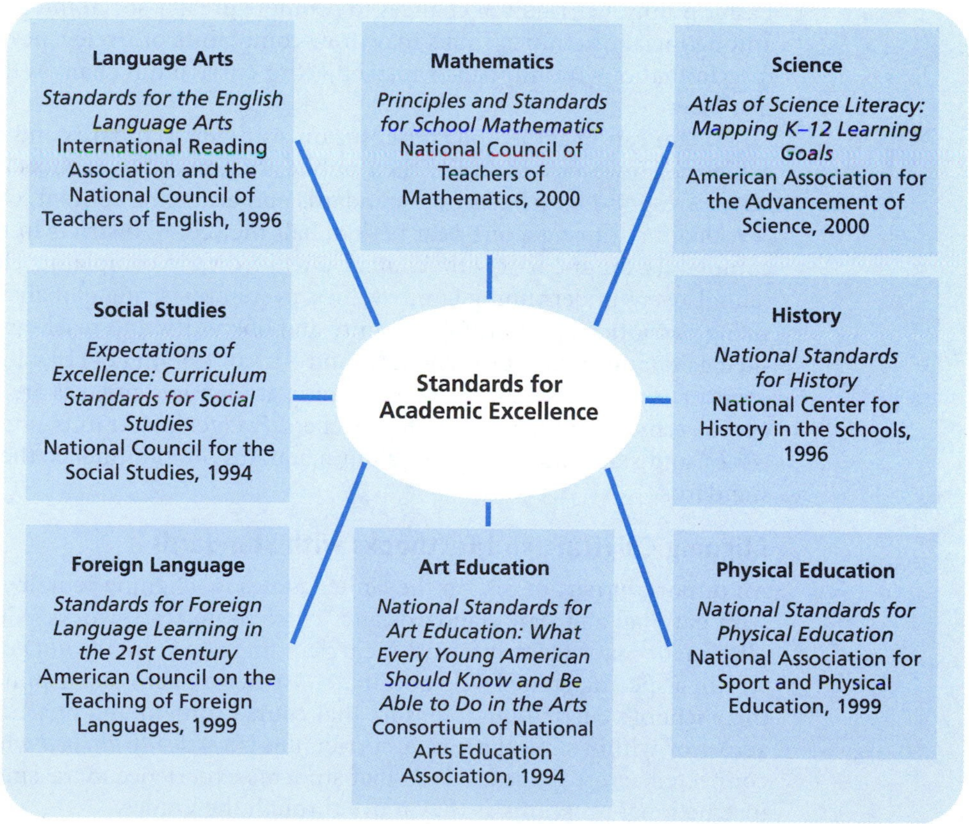

Social Issues and Changing Values

Values that affect the development of educational standards include prevailing educational theories and teachers' educational philosophies. In addition, educators develop standards in response to social issues and changing values in the wider society. As a result, current social concerns find their way into standards, textbooks, teaching aids, and lesson plans. Often curriculum changes are made in the hope that changing what students learn will help solve social problems or achieve local, statewide, or national goals.

Because the United States is so culturally diverse, educational standards can also reflect divergent interests and values. This divergence then leads to controversies over curriculum content and conflicting calls for reform. Recall, for example, the discussion in Chapter 4 of legal issues surrounding the demands of some groups that Christian teachings and observances be included in the public school curricula or that materials regarded as objectionable on religious grounds be censored or banned.

Additional curriculum controversies have arisen over calls for the elimination of all activities or symbols that have their origins in organized religion, including even secularized or commercialized ones such as Halloween and the Easter bunny. Curriculum changes to promote greater social integration or equity among racial or ethnic groups may draw complaints of irrelevancy or reverse discrimination. Traditionalists may object to curriculum changes that reflect feminist views.

As you can imagine, full consensus on academic standards and content is never achieved. However, because of their public accountability, schools must consider how to respond to debates over standards and academic content. One survey revealed that during a one-year period, half the school districts in Florida received complaints about curriculum content. Included were complaints claiming that the schools were undermining family values, overemphasizing globalism, underemphasizing patriotism, permitting profanity and obscenity, and teaching taboo subjects such as satanism and sex (Scheuerer and Parkay 1992, 112–118). In the end, the creative and evaluative tasks of developing academic standards are a source of both empowerment and frustration for teachers. Budget constraints, social and legal issues, and state and local curriculum mandates often influence the development of standards.

Aligning Curricula and Textbooks with Standards

An important part of SBE in the United States is "aligning" curricula and textbooks with national and state standards and "curriculum frameworks." **Curriculum alignment** may take two forms. A curriculum is *horizontally aligned* when teachers within a specific grade level coordinate instruction across disciplines and examine their school's curriculum to ensure that course content and instruction dovetail across or within subject areas. A curriculum is *vertically aligned* when subjects are connected across grade levels so that students experience increasingly complex instructional programs as they move through the grades.

Like teachers, textbook publishers and authors have been influenced significantly by the development of academic standards throughout the nation. Since the "bottom line" for publishing companies is making a profit, they pay close attention to the calls of educational policymakers for more rigorous standards in our nation's schools. Many publishers are revising their textbooks so they are in alignment with state standards and curriculum frameworks, particularly in populous states that make statewide adoptions of textbooks, such as California and Texas. In states such as these, school districts can purchase only textbooks that are on state textbook adoption lists. Since highly populated states influence publishers more than less populated states, it has been observed that "as California and Texas go [regarding the development of state-approved textbook adoption lists], so goes the rest of the nation."

Curriculum Frameworks   A **curriculum framework** is a document, usually published by a state education agency, that provides guidelines, recommended instructional and assessment strategies, suggested resources, and models for teachers to use as they develop curricula that are aligned with national and state standards. Curriculum frameworks are usually written by teams of teachers and state agency personnel, and they serve as a bridge between national and state standards and local curriculum and instructional strategies. In Alaska, for example, curriculum frameworks in CD-ROM format and "Frameworks Resource Kits" in specific subjects are given to teachers by the Department of Education & Early Development. The CD-ROM provides state-of-the-art information in different formats, including video-clips of educators explaining standards-based curricula. Figure 6.3 on page 198, taken from the Alaska frameworks, presents English/language arts process skills for writing.

What Controversies Surround the Effort to Raise Standards?

The push to raise standards has resulted in a widespread, often heated national debate about the role of standards in educational reform. Without a doubt, responses to the call for higher standards have been mixed, and many questions remain unanswered. What are minimum acceptable standards? Who should set those standards? How should students' attainment of those standards be assessed? What should schools do about students who fail to meet those standards? Can standards be raised without increasing dropout rates? Are both excellence and equal opportunity possible if standards are raised? Will expanded testing programs based on higher standards discriminate against minority-group students who traditionally score lower on such tests?

The Advocates: Higher Standards *Will* Improve Education

"We are moving in this country from a local to a national view of education and we need better arrangements to guide the way." So observed the late Ernest Boyer, president of the Carnegie Foundation for the Advancement of Teaching. As Boyer

Figure 6.3 English/language arts process skills.

The following figure presents graphic explanations of the processes of writing as they have been developed and/or adapted and used by Alaskan educators for the last decade. This figure is meant to be illustrative rather than prescriptive.

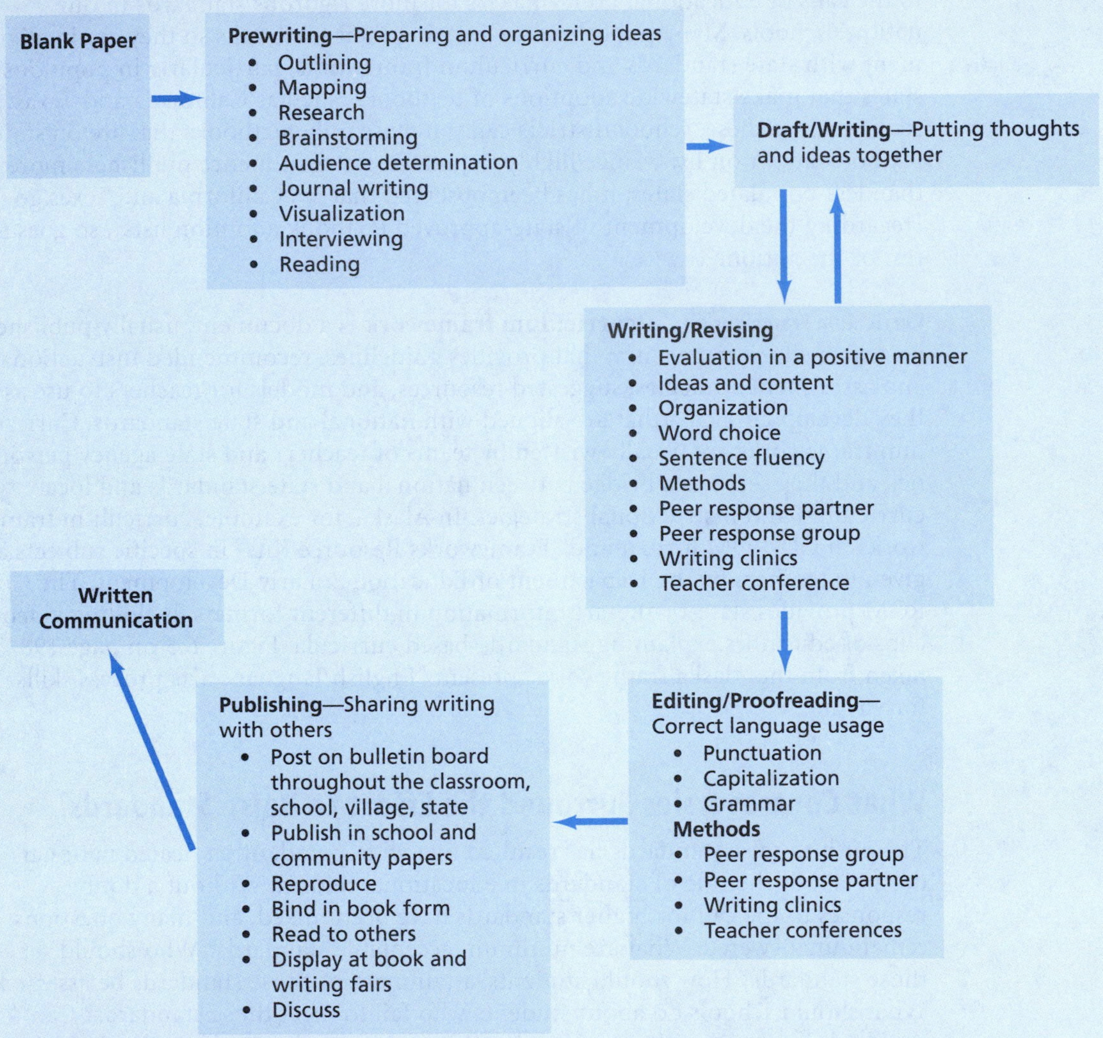

Blank Paper

Prewriting—Preparing and organizing ideas
- Outlining
- Mapping
- Research
- Brainstorming
- Audience determination
- Journal writing
- Visualization
- Interviewing
- Reading

Draft/Writing—Putting thoughts and ideas together

Writing/Revising
- Evaluation in a positive manner
- Ideas and content
- Organization
- Word choice
- Sentence fluency
- Methods
- Peer response partner
- Peer response group
- Writing clinics
- Teacher conference

Written Communication

Publishing—Sharing writing with others
- Post on bulletin board throughout the classroom, school, village, state
- Publish in school and community papers
- Reproduce
- Bind in book form
- Read to others
- Display at book and writing fairs
- Discuss

Editing/Proofreading— Correct language usage
- Punctuation
- Capitalization
- Grammar

Methods
- Peer response group
- Peer response partner
- Writing clinics
- Teacher conferences

The writing process is recursive thinking leading to writing leading to thinking and writing some more. Not every writer will commit every step in the process to paper. Nor will every idea or piece of writing be carried through the entire process. Only pieces that have completed the process—and not all of those— should be assessed.

Source: Used with permission of the Alaska Department of Education & Early Development's Curriculum Frameworks Project. Retrieved from www.educ.state.ak.us/tis/framework/langarts/30content.htm

suggests, the United States, like other nations of the world, needs national goals and standards to motivate its citizens to excel. Without them, people may become complacent and satisfied with mediocrity. Also, like other countries in our increasingly interdependent world, the United States needs to compare the achievement of its students with those of other countries. Just as a runner will run faster when paced by another, the U.S. educational system can become more effective as a result of comparisons with educational systems in other countries.

As an advocate of raising standards and assessing students' attainment of those standards, Diane Ravitch observed that "[a] failing mark on the state test will be only a temporary embarrassment, but a poor education will stigmatize for life" (1997, 106). In *National Standards in American Education: A Citizen's Guide*, Ravitch outlined several additional arguments in support of the effort to raise standards:

- Standards can improve achievement by clearly defining what is to be taught and what kind of performance is expected.
- Standards (national, state, and local) are necessary for equality of opportunity.
- National standards provide a valuable coordinating function.
- Standards and assessments provide consumer protection by supplying accurate information to students and parents.
- Standards and assessments serve as an important signaling device to students, parents, teachers, employers, and colleges (1996, 134–135).

In addition to the arguments outlined above, it is clear that the United States—a country rich in ethnicities, religions, nationalities, and language groups—also needs common, rigorous standards for unity. Immigration continues to bring diverse groups of people to our nation's urban and suburban neighborhoods and rural areas. To meet the educational needs of children and youth from these diverse groups, schools need to provide a common core knowledge about the democratic heritage of our country and a common curriculum based on high academic standards.

As a mobile society, the United States needs common educational standards so that children from one area will not fall behind when they move to another. Children from a farming community in Minnesota should be able to move to the heart of New Orleans without finding themselves behind or ahead of their peers in school. Children from a school in Seattle should be able to transfer to a school in Cincinnati and recognize the curricula studied there.

The Opposition: Higher Standards *Will Not* Improve Education

Opposition to efforts to develop world-class standards that are the centerpiece of educational reform is strong. Critics point to our nation's failure to achieve the national standards that were part of the Goals 2000: Educate American Act. This failure, they believe, is evidence that a new approach to educational reform is needed.

Rather than raising standards, we should become more aware of the lack of uniformity in schools around the country and of the learning needs of the children who attend those schools. As Jonathon Kozol's 1991 book *Savage Inequalities* vividly illustrates, equal education in the United States is an illusion. To compare the

How might national standards help even the playing field for these students? What are some of the arguments against this belief?

performance of a student in a poor Chicago housing project with that of a student in that city's wealthy suburbs is to confront the "savage inequalities" found throughout our educational system.

In addition, critics point out that test score gains attributed to the standards movement do not reflect "real" gains in the knowledge and skills the tests were designed to measure. A phenomenon known as "score inflation" results in students' scores on high-stakes tests rising faster than their scores on other standardized tests given at the same time and measuring the same subjects. Students don't actually know as much as we think they do if we consider only high-stakes test scores. Actually, the standards movement may result in test scores that are less accurate than they were prior to the addition of high-stakes assessments (Stecher and Hamilton 2002).

Also, sanctions imposed on low-performing schools will not ensure that students in those schools are not left behind. The record of success when sanctions such as staff reassignment and school takeover have been imposed is mixed. Students in low-performing schools may not be helped by sanctions, and there is some risk that they will be harmed (Stecher and Hamilton 2002). Thus, higher standards would further bias educational opportunities in favor of students from advantaged backgrounds, intensify the class-based structure of U.S. society, and increase differences between well-funded and poorly funded schools.

Opponents of efforts to develop world-class standards in U.S. schools have raised numerous additional concerns. The following are among their arguments:

- Raising standards might lead to a national curriculum and an expanded role of federal government in education.
- The push to raise standards is fueled by conservative interest groups that wish to undo educational gains made by traditionally underrepresented groups.
- A focus on higher standards diverts attention from more meaningful educational reform.
- Increased emphasis on tested subjects often results in a decrease in emphasis on subjects not tested.
- World-class standards are often vague and not linked to valid assessments and scoring rubrics.
- Standards frequently describe learning activities, not the knowledge and skills students are expected to learn—for example, "Students will experience various forms of literature."
- The scope and sequence of what students should learn with reference to standards and benchmarks has been unclear; in other words, to what degree and in what order should students learn material?
- Grade-level benchmarks have been created that are unrealistic and developmentally inappropriate for some students; often students are hurried through their learning without sufficient time and instruction to acquire underlying concepts and skills.
- SBE and high-stakes tests based on those standards lead to the practice of "teaching-to-the-test," giving priority to academic content covered by the tests and deemphasizing areas of the curriculum not covered. For example, a study of Kentucky's assessment system found that test-related sanctions and rewards influenced teachers to "focus on whatever is thought to raise test scores rather than on instruction aimed at addressing individual student needs" (Jones and Whitford 1997, 277).

As a teacher, you and your colleagues will no doubt participate in an ongoing dialogue about academic standards at your school. Thus, the role that standards will play in your professional life will be significant. Accordingly, the following eight questions may help you decide the nature of SBE in your school:

1. Where will we get our standards?
2. Who will set the standards?

3. What types of standards should we include?
4. In what format will the standards be written?
5. At what levels will benchmarks be written?
6. How should benchmarks and standards be assessed?
7. How will student progress be reported?
8. What will we hold students accountable for? (Marzano 1997, 1–7)

How Are Schools and Teachers Held Accountable for Student Learning?

Controversy also surrounds widespread efforts to hold schools and teachers accountable for students' attainment of state-mandated educational standards. As part of this push for **accountability**, some states—Florida and South Carolina, for example—rank schools on how well their students learn. In Florida, schools are graded from A through F, and those that receive low grades run the risk of being closed. At the end of the 2001–02 academic year, for example, an elementary school in Pensacola was closed by school officials, though it had managed to move from a grade of F to a D (Sandham, 2002).

In South Carolina, schools are graded "good," "average," "below average," or "unsatisfactory." Teachers and principals in high-ranked South Carolina schools receive salary bonuses of up to $1,000 each, while lower-rated schools can face state takeovers or reorganization of their staffs (Richard 2002). This chapter's Relevant Standards feature stresses the need for teachers to accept responsibility for students' learning.

Every state has mandated a standardized test to assess students' mastery of academic standards, and most districts are assisting schools in bringing standards-based reform into classrooms. For example, fourth-, seventh-, and tenth-grade students in Washington State must take the Washington Assessment of Student Learning (WASL) based on the state's Essential Academic Learning Requirements (EALRs) in reading, writing, listening, and mathematics. In Texas, students must take the Texas Assessment of Knowledge and Skills (TAKS) that assesses how well they have mastered the Texas Essential Knowledge and Skills (TEKS) in English language arts, mathematics, science, and social studies. As a result of standards-based reforms at the state level, *how* and *what* teachers teach is changing, and, in many cases, student achievement is increasing. The Technology in Teaching feature on page 204 in this chapter describes how some states are using computer-adaptive online testing systems to deliver statewide assessment tests.

Similarly, at the national level, efforts are being made to hold schools accountable. Since passage of the Goals 2000: Educate America Act in 1994 (subsequently revised as America's Education Goals in 1999), national policymakers have stressed the role that more rigorous standards can play in educational reform. In 2002, the national push for higher standards became even stronger when President George W. Bush, to fulfill his pledge to "leave no child behind," signed into legislation a $26.5 billion comprehensive educational reform bill mandating statewide testing in reading and mathematics each year in grades 3–8. According to the No Child Left

Relevant Standards

Accepting Responsibility for Students' Learning

As the following standards indicate, professional teachers develop linkages with various community agencies and local businesses to supplement the resources available to the school.

- "Teachers and teacher candidates have student learning as the focus of their work." (National Council for Accreditation of Teacher Education [NCATE] 2002, 19. Supporting explanation for Standard 1: Candidate Knowledge, Skills, and Dispositions.)

- Proposition #3: "Teachers are responsible for managing and monitoring student learning. . . . Professional teachers hold high expectations for all students and see themselves as facilitators of student learning." (National Board for Professional Teaching Standards [NBPTS] 2002, 13.)

- "The teacher believes that all children can learn at high levels and persists in helping all children

achieve success." (Interstate New Teacher Assessment and Support Consortium [INTASC] 1992, 18. Disposition statement for Principle #3: "The teacher understands how students differ in their approaches to learning and creates instructional opportunities that are adapted to diverse learners.")

- "Both students and teacher establish and maintain through planning of learning activities, interactions, and the classroom environment high expectations for the learning of all students." (Praxis Series, distinguished level of performance for Domain 2: The Classroom Environment, Component 2b: Establishing a Culture for Learning.) (From Danielson 1996, 82)

Behind Act of 2001 (NCLB), schools whose scores fail to improve over a six-year period could lose staff, and low-income students at those schools could receive federal funds for tutoring or transportation to another public school. Also, NCLB requires that, by the end of the academic year 2013–14, public schools guarantee that all students are prepared to pass state proficiency tests.

Adequate Yearly Progress   A key piece of the No Child Left Behind Act is for schools to provide evidence each year that students are making **adequate yearly progress (AYP)**. Schools that fail to make AYP will be identified as "in need of improvement." The first year a school does not make AYP, it must provide transportation for pupils who want to enroll in another public school. If the school fails to make AYP again, it must pay for "supplemental services," including tutoring.

AYP is determined by students' performance on machine-scored, multiple-choice tests in math and reading. At least 95 percent of students in grades 3–8 at a school must take the tests. However, schools must do more than improve overall average scores. The federal government requires that AYP be made by students in all subgroups according to age, race, ethnicity, and socioeconomic status.

If any one subgroup is not improving, the school will be labeled "in need of improvement." In some areas, especially impoverished urban areas, more than half

Technology in Teaching

How are computer-adaptive online testing systems used to deliver statewide assessment tests?

Some states—Idaho, Oregon, South Dakota, and Virginia, for example—are opting to use online testing systems to deliver their statewide assessments tests. In 2001, South Dakota became the first state to use an online exam linked to state standards of learning.

The online tests used by Idaho and South Dakota differ from paper-and-pencil tests because they are computer-adaptive. The tests "adjust" depending on how well a student is doing. If a student proficient in science keeps getting all the science questions right, the questions become more difficult.

Computer-adaptive testing enables teachers to identify students who are advanced for their grade or below standard grade-level proficiency. Teachers thus get more information about a student's strengths and weaknesses than they receive from paper-and-pencil tests. The South Dakota system uses an artificial intelligence system to determine which grade level a student is testing at in individual units, such as fractions, decimals, and algebraic equations. In one class period, the test can determine exactly where a student is performing at across a twelve-grade range. Test results are then reported, usually within twenty-four hours, with reference to the standards of a specific state or district.

A disadvantage of online testing is that it requires a state-of-the-art technology infrastructure. In South Dakota, for example, every classroom has a T1 line, and the Digital Dakota Network links every school and every K–12 classroom with the state government, technical schools, and higher education institutions. Also, each classroom has broadband access to the Internet, with five or six connection points.

What do you see as some of the advantages and disadvantages of computer-adaptive online testing? Reflect on the standardized tests you have taken. Would you have preferred taking them online?

of all schools are "in need of improvement." At such schools, test preparation is a major part of the curriculum. In fact, many of these schools have suspended instruction in such "nonessential" subjects as art, music, physical education, and foreign language in favor of practicing for the tests.

The concept of AYP has been criticized because schools are judged on one measure only—students' scores on multiple-choice tests in math and language arts. Students' performance on the test becomes the sole measure of student learning.

On the 2003 Phi Delta Kappa/Gallup Poll of the Public's Attitudes Toward the Public Schools, 66 percent of respondents said that a single test does not provide "a fair picture of whether or not a school needs improvement" (Rose and Gallup, 2003, 45). Additionally, 72 percent of respondents reported it is "not possible to accurately judge a student's proficiency in English and math on the basis of a single test" (Rose and Gallup, 2003, 46).

An additional criticism of AYP is that the curriculum often becomes very narrow because teachers tend to teach what's tested. Also, teacher judgments have no role in determining AYP. As one critic commented: "One could argue that AYP tests are designed not to help students, teachers or schools but to catch them. It's a 'gotcha game,' not a process to improve [education]" (Merrow 2003).

Testing for Teachers? A controversial approach to holding teachers accountable for students' learning is to test teachers' knowledge and skills. Increasingly, educational policymakers reason that if teachers do not possess adequate knowledge and skills, they are unable to teach students to reach high academic standards.

Some states and districts have mandated tests to assess teachers' knowledge and skills. For example, in 2002 Pennsylvania began requiring experienced teachers to take the Professional Development Assistance Program (PDAP) tests developed by Educational Testing Service (ETS). The goal was to test 20 percent of the state's teachers in reading and mathematics each year for five years to see what professional development they might need. The PDAP is based on the premise that teachers should at least know the subjects they were teaching, as a vice president at ETS suggested: "You would want your son's fifth-grade teacher to at least know fifth-grade math" (Chute 2003).

Results of the PDAP are given only to the teacher, not the teacher's supervisors. In 2003, the average statewide PDAP scores for teachers ranged from 77 percent in middle school math to 84 percent in high school math. Still, some teachers have complained that the quality of experienced teachers can't be measured by a written test. And some experts acknowledge that a better approach would be evaluating actual classroom performance, like the system developed by the National Board for Professional Teaching Standards (NBPTS). However, NBPTS certification requires that teachers develop portfolios to document their teaching effectiveness, and it typically takes 200 to 400 hours to prepare portfolios. Among the items in the portfolios are specific types of student work as well as videotapes of the teacher in the classroom and written commentaries by the teacher. In addition, the NBPTS assessment is expensive; in 2004, the cost was $2,300 per teacher.

How Are High-Stakes Tests Changing Education?

Testing students to assess their learning is not new. However, state-mandated tests often have high-stakes consequences for students, teachers, and administrators. Performance on **high-stakes tests** may determine whether a student can participate in extracurricular activities or graduate, or whether teachers and administrators are given merit pay increases. Basing such decisions on a single standardized test is acceptable to the public, as revealed by the 2001 Phi Delta Kappa/Gallup Poll: 53 percent approve linking test scores to grade-to-grade promotion, and 57 percent approve linking test scores to determine eligibility for a high school diploma (Rose and Gallup 2001).

Eighteen states require students to pass exit or end-of-course exams (see Figure 6.4) in English and math, and in some cases social studies and science, to receive a high school diploma. By 2008, five additional states will phase in graduation tests, increasing the number of students whose graduation from high school will hinge on an exit exam to seven out of ten students (Feller 2003).

Consequences of High-Stakes Tests

At the conclusion of the 2003–04 school year, several states withheld thousands of diplomas. For example, in Florida about 12,000 seniors failed the Florida Compre-

Figure 6.4 State-level mandatory exit exams for high school graduation.

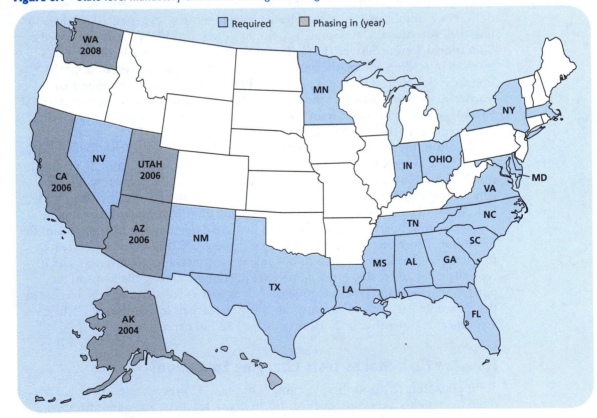

Source: Center on Education Policy.

hensive Assessment Test (FCAT), a requirement for graduation. The Florida seniors had several opportunities to take the test, which is first given in the tenth grade (Associated Press 2004).

In some cases, large numbers of students who failed the exams prompted states to modify their requirements. New York erased the results of a new math test for juniors and seniors after the passing rate fell much lower than the previous year. Local officials got permission to give diplomas to seniors who failed the exam but passed their math courses. California delayed the consequences of its exit exam from 2004 to 2006 after a study projected that about 20 percent of seniors would be denied diplomas (Feller 2003).

In Massachusetts, diplomas were withheld from 4,800 seniors in 2003 who failed to pass the Massachusetts Comprehensive Assessment System (MCAS) exam. That year, some students walked out of class and refused to take the test, often with support from parents. The MCAS exam was implemented in 1998, and 2003 was the first year that a student must pass the exam to graduate. Although 92 percent of seniors statewide passed, some schools graduated a much lower percentage of students. For example, less than 60 percent of the 437 seniors in Lawrence graduated that year (*USA Today* 2003). "Certificates of Attainment" were available for students who didn't pass the exam; however, a high school diploma was still needed for college-bound students and to receive state and federal financial aid for education beyond high school.

High-Stakes Tests and Educator Accountability

For teachers and administrators, test results are frequently linked to merit rewards, increased funding, or sanctions. Some states and large school districts provide additional funds for high-performing schools or bonuses for educators at those schools. For example, California has several merit-based incentive programs for teachers, schools, and administrators, including the "Governor's Performance Awards" that give money to schools based on their "academic performance index." Similarly, in New York City, the school system gives bonuses of up to $15,000 to principals and other administrators whose schools show significant gains on test scores. School system administrators group schools into three performance categories—low, middle, and high—taking into account students' economic circumstances. For high schools, factors such as dropout rates are also used.

On the other hand, schools, and even entire districts, that do poorly on tests can be taken over by the state or, in some cases, closed. Currently, more than twenty states give state boards of education the authority to intervene in academically "bankrupt" schools whose students score too low as a group. Of those states, ten allow students to leave low-performing schools, taking their proportional amount of state funding aid with them. Four of these states directly punish low-performing schools by taking aid away from them. While some states use test scores as one of several accountability indicators, many rely solely on scores.

Testing can also have significant consequences when schools are ranked according to how well they attain a state or district's performance goals. Usually, school rankings are reported in relation to schools of similar size and demographics since test results are closely linked to students' economic backgrounds, with the lowest scores often earned by schools that serve the neediest children (Fetler 2001; Lindjord 2000).

Preparing for High-Stakes Tests

High-stakes testing and the push to hold teachers accountable for student learning has led many districts and schools to place great emphasis on preparing students for the tests. In fact, critics assert that the curricular emphasis in schools is shifting from *academic content* to *test preparation*. In such an environment, many teachers feel compelled to "teach to the test," or to emphasize "item teaching" rather than "curriculum teaching."

> In item teaching, teachers organize their instruction either around the actual items found on a test or around a set of look-alike items. . . . Curriculum teaching, however, requires teachers to direct their instruction toward a specific body of content knowledge or a specific set of cognitive skills represented by a given test. In curriculum teaching, a teacher targets instruction at test-represented content rather than at test items" (Popham 2001, 16–17).

Another controversial approach to preparing students to take high-stakes tests is "test besting." **Test besting** teaches students test-taking skills such as managing time during testing, correctly making responses on answer forms, and clues for making "best guesses" on certain test items. Some districts and schools purchase commercially prepared test besting programs; others develop their own.

Critics of test besting suggest that it "deskills" teachers. In other words, test besting requires that teachers merely present students with tips and strategies for test taking, not intellectually challenging academic content. In addition, test besting adds to the fear students may have about testing, and it may reduce their interest in learning. Lastly, test besting increases, rather than reduces, educational inequities for students whose performance on achievement tests is often below the norm—students of families living in poverty and students whose first language is not English (Firestone, Monfils, & Schorr 2003; McNeil 2000).

> They'd have to be crazy not to want to focus on [test results]. . . . Education's a very large political issue. I mean they're publishing scores in newspapers and they're trying to pass budgets in places where . . . taxes are high and people are reluctant to spend money (Firestone, Monfils, & Schorr 2003, 17).

Some districts and schools are taking a less controversial approach to improving student's scores on high-stakes tests by ensuring that they are well nourished when they are at school. For example, New York City schools offer a free breakfast to every child, rich or poor. School officials believe that a good breakfast each morning will help students concentrate and learn; as the New York City schools chancellor observed: "By ensuring that every student in our schools can enjoy a free, nutritious breakfast, we are supporting teaching and learning in our class-

Case for Reflection

Teaching to the Test

You are teaching at a school located in an urban area on the West Coast. The school has over 1,000 students, 40 percent Anglo European American, 30 percent African American, 20 percent Latino, and 10 percent Asian American. Most families are low-income.

Students at similar schools frequently score below average on state-mandated tests of reading, writing, and mathematics. However, at your school, students score above the state average.

In spite of students' above-average scores, the school experiences intense pressure from parents to increase its ranking among schools in the state. In response, the principal and the school leadership team decided that steps must be taken to increase students' scores.

The principal and the leadership team carefully analyzed last year's test results and identified the skills for which less than 75 percent of students achieved mastery. Based on this analysis, they developed a schoolwide program to focus on preparing students for the state test. To implement the program, they made four decisions. First, teachers' weekly lesson plans would include instruction in the targeted basic skills. Second, teachers would give monthly "practice" tests to prepare students for the state's test in April. Third, the school would launch a schoolwide campaign to stress the importance of increasing test scores. And fourth, two in-service workshops to improve students' test-taking skills would be held before the end of the year.

Today, you and two other teachers, Cynthia and Juan, are meeting with the principal in her office to talk about the schoolwide emphasis on the state test. You have talked with a lot of teachers about preparing students to take the test. About half of the teachers at the school—including you, Cynthia, and Juan—have reservations about "teaching to the test."

"We're not against testing per se," you say, opening the conversation with the principal. "A lot of us, however, think too much emphasis is being placed on the state test."

"That's right," says Cynthia. "The teachers at my grade level agree. Actually, the state test covers only a fraction of our total curriculum. Most of our curriculum is not covered on the test."

"We've all heard the phrase 'What's tested will be taught,' " says Juan, adding to Cynthia's comment. "Because of the emphasis we're placing on the state test, the curriculum we present to kids is very narrow."

"I understand," says the principal. "However, it's important to remember that the standards the test addresses don't include all the thinking skills teachers are supposed to teach.

"Yes," you say, "But some teachers, and most of the students, think *if it's not tested, it's not important.*"

"The test measures bits of information—facts and things like that—not kids' ability to think creatively, to inquire, to analyze. That's what we're really supposed to be teaching kids," says Juan.

As the conversation continues, the principal seems become more open to acknowledging the validity of teachers' reservations about the test preparation program.

"I understand your concerns," the principal says. "However, I still feel a lot of pressure from the community and central administration to increase our performance on the test."

"I've got an idea," the principal continues. "The three of you could form a task force. You could look at innovative approaches other schools have used to ensure that all kids master the basic skills. Then develop a plan that fits our needs here. What do you think about that?"

rooms" (Gootman 2003). The breakfasts are partially paid for by an increase in the price of school lunches for children from families with incomes too high to qualify for government subsidies.

Several urban school districts—Baltimore, Cleveland, and Philadelphia, for example—have begun free breakfast programs, based on the premise that hungry children do not perform well at school. Many believe the increase in breakfast programs stems from increasing pressure to increase students' test scores. As a spokesperson at the Food Research and Action Center in Washington, D.C., said: "It's a growing phenomenon. We find that the general movement towards more academic testing, such as No Child Left Behind, might be one of the reasons that more people have been looking [at breakfast programs]" (Gootman 2003).

Legal Challenges of High-Stakes Tests

Increasingly, the validity of high-stakes tests are being challenged in the courts. For example, to express his belief that his state's high-stakes test unfairly tested students on material that had not been taught, a fourth-grade teacher of the year in Georgia posted six test questions on a parents' website. His school district charged him with violating the state code of ethics for educators. The Georgia Professional Standards Commission (PSC) agreed and voted to suspend his teaching license. The teacher appealed the suspension, and a superior court judge exonerated him of any wrongdoing. The court ruled that the ethics code prohibits teachers only from helping students cheat by providing them with test questions prior to administering the test; however, the teacher didn't do that, according to the court. Subsequently, the Georgia Court of Appeals refused to hear the PSC's case against the teacher (*Gwinnett County Schools v. Hope* 2002).

Nationwide, high-stakes tests are being used increasingly to determine whether a student can participate in extracurricular activities or graduate, or whether teachers and administrators are given merit pay increases. The validity of such tests is often hotly debated, and legal challenges of such tests will no doubt increase. For example, the Chicago public schools fired and then sued a teacher for $1.4 million for publishing parts of the Chicago Academic Standards Examinations (CASE). The teacher had criticized the CASE tests for sloppy wording and inaccurate answers. A federal district court ruled that the teacher violated the copyrighted school district materials. The teacher countersued the board under the First Amendment. Eventually, after additional teacher and student criticisms of the CASE test emerged, the Chicago Board of Education withdrew its lawsuit and eliminated the test (*NEA Today* 2003a).

In Minnesota, National Computer Systems agreed to pay up to $12 million to settle a class action lawsuit alleging that it wrongly scored thousands of the Minnesota Basic Skills Tests in 2000. The company falsely notified eight thousand students that they had failed the high-stakes test. According to the settlement, students denied the opportunity to participate in graduation ceremonies because of the company's error received $16,000, while students who had to attend summer school received up to $1,000.

Finally, in Massachusetts, advocates filed a class action lawsuit claiming that the state's mandatory graduation exam discriminates against black and Hispanic students, as well as students with disabilities and limited English proficiency (*NEA Today*, May 2003a).

Debate over High-Stakes Tests

High-stakes testing is a hotly debated topic among educators, students, and parents. Many observers worry that "when high-stakes consequences are attached to tests, they hold the potential for great harm" (Falk 2002, 614). Tenth-grade students in Massachusetts expressed their concern by creating SCAM (Student Coalition for Alternatives to the Massachusetts Comprehensive Assessment System [MCAS]). The MCAS stipulates that students must pass the tenth-grade MCAS exams to graduate from high school. Reacting to what she calls "MCAS mania," the headmaster of the Boston Arts Academy worries that high-stakes testing will lead to "[more] money spent on test-prep workbooks and Princeton Review-type courses, but not on lowering class size, providing professional development, or helping students learn the skills necessary to complete complex, long-term goals" (Nathan 2002, 600).

The debate is also heating up at the national level. As part of its effort to educate the public on what it perceives as the abuses, misuses, and flaws of national standardized testing, for example, the National Center for Fair & Open Testing (FairTest) contends that the "leave-no-child-behind" education legislation of 2002 should be called the "Leave No Child Untested Act" because the legislation requires national testing. The Center also maintains that national testing will divert funding from programs not covered on the tests (Toppo 2001).

Clearly, the debate over the effectiveness of testing programs based on state-mandated standards will continue for some time. In the meantime, testing programs will no doubt increase, and diverse groups will strive to work together more effectively to improve the quality of schools in the United States. Though teachers, administrators, politicians, parents, and concerned citizens are often in conflict about how schools should operate, they agree more than disagree about the school's primary mission—to provide students with the knowledge and skills needed to live satisfying, productive lives in the future.

What Does the Future Hold for You as a Teacher?

How will education change in the future, and how will those changes impact you as a teacher? How will the current push to raise standards and hold teachers accountable for student learning impact your future? What new school-community linkages will help you meet the needs of all learners? In what ways will your professional life become more collaborative and oriented toward systemwide reform?

Though no one has an educational crystal ball that can give a totally accurate glimpse of how teaching will change and how students will be taught, it is clear that powerful forces are impacting the schools and will continue to do so.

The conditions under which you will teach will provide a dramatic contrast to those that teachers experienced during our nation's past. Instead of isolation, lack of autonomy and self-governance, and few chances for professional growth, you will experience collaboration, empowerment, stronger professionalism, and opportunities to provide leadership for educational change. You and thousands of other teachers will collaborate and play key leadership roles in shaping the future of education.

However, you should remember that the *preferred* image of teaching described in the previous paragraph will not become a reality without hard work and dedication. The positive changes all educators desire will require the dedicated effort of professional teachers such as yourself.

Perhaps teachers of the past let the future happen and merely reacted to emerging conditions. No longer can teachers do that; instead, they must work toward the future they desire. In short, as Alvin Toffler pointed out decades ago in his classic book *Future Shock*, teachers must choose wisely from among several courses of action: "Every society faces not merely a succession of *probable* futures, but an array of *possible* futures, and a conflict over *preferable* futures. The management of change is the effort to convert certain possibles into probables, in pursuit of agreed-on preferables (Toffler 1971, 460).

A *Preferred* Future for Education

Of course, no one really knows how education will change in the future. In spite of the impossibility of foretelling the future, it will be important for you to think carefully about a *preferred* future for education. In that way, the actions you take today will increase the likelihood that tomorrow's future will be the one you prefer. In short, you should recognize the importance of planning for the future and trying to create the future you want. The alternative is to react with neither purpose nor direction to the forces that shape education and the teaching profession.

To think about your future as a teacher, you can use basic concepts from *futures planning*. **Futures planning** involves thinking about the future as a set of possibilities and then taking steps to create a preferred future. To use futures planning, you and other educators can work with students, parents, and other members of the community to identify current educational issues and trends, and then forecast (or project) the effects of those issues and trends. In that way, you can develop different scenarios for the future. Then, you can take concrete steps to "change" the future (or, create a desired future). The alternative, of course, is to do nothing about "changing" the future and merely react as the future unfolds.

Learning to look ahead—to monitor local, state, and national educational politics—is how you can create a desired future. To provide a "compass" for developing that preferred future, this book concludes with a brief hypothetical glimpse into what your future in teaching may be like.

Last year, your school was designated by the state as a Blue Ribbon school. The Blue Ribbon designation was made, in large measure, because you and several other teachers were part of a nationwide network of teachers who field tested an interactive computer simulation developed by an instructional technology laboratory at a major university.

As a follow-up to last year's work, you just received beta-test (trial) software you helped develop, field-test guidelines, and registration materials for a four-day preparatory workshop to be held in two months at the university. The university will pay for your travel and expenses, as well as provide a stipend.

Prior to the workshop, you are to use the software every day for three weeks. You will collect student performance data on a regular basis and samples of students' work. Also, your students will complete a survey at the beginning and at the end of the field test. Lastly, you will interview a randomly selected group of students, using a set of constructivist-oriented questions. The questions are designed to develop an understanding of how students "construct" meaning as they use the interactive software. You are working with university researchers to develop a picture of students' problem-solving strategies as they work through the simulations. In April, you and two other teachers, along with a team of university researchers, will present a paper describing your work at a national conference for educational researchers.

Teachers at your school are hard-working and share a strong commitment to good teaching and to building a collegial professional community. Ample leadership opportunities, common planning periods, stimulating colleagues who are professionally involved, and solid support from the district and community are just a few of the factors that make working conditions at your school very positive.

When you think about your future as a teacher, that future may seem exciting and frightening, attractive and threatening. How will you deal with the political forces and trends that influence teaching? How will you meet continuing calls for accountability in an era of high-stakes testing?

Though the author is unable to hand you a crystal ball to foretell your future as a teacher, this book provides an understanding of how educational politics are shaping that future. In addition to acquiring that understanding, creating a preferred future will require a strong, clear vision of that future and an unwavering dedication to the profession of teaching. Thus, *Political Foundations for Becoming a Teacher* ends by challenging you to become a teacher whose actions demonstrate that vision and dedication.

Summary

What Role Will Standards Play in Your Classroom?

- Standards at the state and national levels are part of the movement to hold educators and schools more accountable for student learning.

- School administrators, teachers, and students have different perspectives on standards. Administrators are pri-

marily concerned with students' performance on standardized tests of achievement; teachers are primarily concerned with student performance and behavior at the classroom level; and students are primarily concerned with the standard of being personally relevant, interesting, and meaningful.

What Is Standards-Based Education?

- Developing rigorous academic standards, assessing students' mastery of those standards, and holding students and teachers accountable for meeting those standards are key elements of SBE.

- Content standards refer to the content—or knowledge and skills—students should acquire in various academic disciplines.

- Performance standards are used to assess how well students have attained standards.

- Benchmarks specify what students should understand and be able to do at specific grade levels or developmental stages.

- Professional associations have developed standards that reflect the knowledge, skills, and attitudes students should develop in the subject matter disciplines.

- Values that affect the development of educational standards include prevailing educational theories and teachers' educational philosophies.

- School curricula and textbooks are horizontally aligned with standards when teachers within a specific grade level coordinate instruction across disciplines and examine their school's curriculum to ensure that course content and instruction dovetail across or within subject areas.

- Vertical alignment with standards occurs when subjects are connected across grade levels so that students experience increasingly complex instructional programs as they move through the grades.

- Curriculum frameworks provide guidelines, recommended instructional and assessment strategies, suggested resources, and models for teachers to use as they develop curricula that are aligned with national and state standards.

What Controversies Surround the Effort to Raise Standards?

- Proponents of higher standards advance several arguments in favor of higher standards, including the

role that standards can play in increasing student achievement.

- Opponents of standards-based education advance several arguments against higher standards, including evidence that indicates that higher standards may result in decreased emphasis on subjects not tested.

How Are Schools and Teachers Held Accountable for Student Learning?

- To hold educators and schools accountable for student learning, some states rank schools on how well their students learn.

- Some states are using computer-adaptive testing systems to deliver statewide assessment tests.

- As part of the No Child Left Behind Act, schools are to provide evidence each year that students are making adequate yearly progress (AYP). Schools that fail to make AYP will be identified as "in need of improvement."

How Are High-Stakes Tests Changing Education?

- State-mandated tests often have high-stakes consequences for students, such as determining eligibility to participate in extracurricular activities or to graduate from elementary or high school.

- For teachers, administrators, and schools, test results can be linked to merit rewards, increased funding, or sanctions.

- A controversial approach to holding teachers accountable for students' learning is to test teachers' knowledge and skills.

- High-stakes testing and the push to hold teachers accountable for student learning has led many districts and schools to place great emphasis on preparing students for the tests.

What Does the Future Hold for You as a Teacher?

- To shape the future, teachers can use futures planning—thinking about the future as a set of possibilities and then taking steps to create the desired future.

Key Terms and Concepts

accountability, 202
adequate yearly progress (AYP), 203
benchmarks, 194
content standards, 194

curriculum alignment, 196
curriculum framework, 197
futures planning, 212
high-stakes tests, 205
performance standards, 194

standards, 190
standards-based education (SBE), 192
test besting, 208

Reflective Application Activities

Discussion Questions

1. Testing is obviously an important part of teaching. To what extent do you think the current emphasis on standardized tests encourages teachers to "teach to the test"?

2. If teachers "teach to the test," is this an effective or ineffective way to promote student learning?

Professional Journal

1. Reflect on your experiences taking standardized tests. What factors increased your anxiety about taking such tests? What factors reduced that anxiety? Based on your own experiences, how might you help your students reduce their anxiety about taking tests?

2. Is it fair to hold teachers accountable for student learning? Should teachers of students whose home backgrounds are less supportive of education be held as accountable as teachers of students whose backgrounds are highly supportive?

Online Assignments

1. Go online to your state's department of education home page and find the link to the state's standards. Then compare your state's standards with the standards from another state. How are the two sets of standards similar? Different? Is one set of standards clearer than the other?

2. Visit the website for a professional association in the subject area for which you are preparing to teach (see

list of professional associations presented in Figure 6.2 on page 195). Locate the curriculum standards developed by the association and compare them with the curriculum standards developed by your state. How are the two sets of standards similar? Different? Is one set of standards clearer than the other?

Observations and Interviews

1. Interview at least one teacher (at the grade level and in the subject area for which you are preparing to teach) for his or her views about standards-based education. Does the teacher believe the effort to raise standards has helped or hurt education?

2. Observe in a classroom at the level you plan to teach. How does the teacher convey to students his or her standards (or expectations) for student learning?

Professional Portfolio

Prepare a set of guidelines or strategies for students to follow when they take a standardized test. The strategies might include items such as the following:

- Survey the test, checking for missing pages.
- Read directions carefully.
- Notice use of double negatives.
- Note use of terms such as *always*, *never*, *best*, etc.
- Read all choices for multiple-choice test items.
- Check answers.

Glossary

A

Academic freedom (p. 110): the right of teachers to teach, free from external constraint, censorship, or interference.

Accountability (p. 12, 202): the practice of holding teachers responsible for adhering to high professional and moral standards and creating effective learning environments for all students.

Adequacy of funding (p. 169): funding for schools that is based on the concept of providing different levels of funding based on students' educational needs.

Adequate yearly progress (AYP) (p. 203): a provision of the No Child Left Behind Act of 2001 requiring that schools provide evidence each year that students are making "adequate yearly progress."

Aesthetics (p. 72): the branch of axiology concerned with values related to beauty and art.

Axiology (p. 71): the study of values, including the identification of criteria for determining what is valuable.

B

Back-to-basics movement (p. 78): a movement begun in the mid-1970s to establish the "basic skills" of reading, writing, speaking, and computation as the core of the school curriculum.

Behaviorism (p. 88): based on behavioristic psychology, this philosophical orientation maintains that environmental factors shape people's behavior.

Benchmarks (p. 194): statements of what students should understand and be able to do at specific grade levels or developmental stages.

Block grants (p. 162): a form of federal aid given directly to the states, which a state or local education agency may spend as it wishes with few limitations.

Buckley Amendment (p. 135): a 1974 law, the Family Educational Rights and Privacy Act, granting parents of students under eighteen and students over eighteen the right to examine their school records.

C

Categorical aid (p. 170): state-appropriated funds to cover the costs of educating students with special needs.

Censorship (p. 128): the act of removing from circulation printed material judged to be libelous, vulgar, or obscene.

Charter (p. 23): an agreement between a charter school's founders and its sponsors specifying how the school will operate and what learning outcomes students will master.

Charter schools (p. 23): independent schools, often founded by teachers, that are given a charter to operate by a school district or a state or national government with the provision that students must demonstrate mastery of predetermined outcomes.

Chicago School Reform Act (p. 21): a comprehensive set of reform measures, including the creation of local school councils, to improve Chicago's public schools.

Chief state school officer (p. 49): the chief administrator of a state department of education and head of the state board of education, often called the *commissioner of education* or *superintendent of public instruction*.

Code of ethics (p. 104): a set of guidelines that defines appropriate behavior for professionals.

Cognitive science (p. 90): the study of the learning process that focuses on how individuals manipulate symbols and process information.

Collective bargaining (p. 110): a process followed by employers and employees in negotiating salaries, hours, and working conditions; in most states, school boards must negotiate contracts with teacher organizations.

Constructivism (p. 90): a psychological orientation that views learning as an active process in which learners construct understanding of the material they learn—in contrast to the view that teachers transmit academic content to students in small segments.

Content standards (p. 194): the content—or knowledge and skills—students should acquire in various academic disciplines.

Copyright laws (p. 123): laws limiting the use of photocopies, videotapes, and computer software programs.

Corporal punishment (p. 137): physical punishment applied to a student by a school employee as a disciplinary measure.

Curriculum alignment (p. 196): the process of ensuring that the content of curricula and textbooks reflects desired learning outcomes, or academic standards, for students.

Curriculum framework (p. 198): a document that provides guidelines, instructional and assessment strategies, resources, and models for teachers to use as they develop curricula aligned with academic standards.

D

Digital divide (p. 180): inequities in access to computer technology that are related to minority-group status, family income, and gender.

Digital Millennium Copyright Act (DMCA) (p. 123): an amendment to the Copyright Act of 1998, making it illegal to reproduce copyrighted works in digital format.

Dismissal (p. 109): the involuntary termination of a teacher's employment; termination must be made for a legally defensible reason with the protection of due process.

Due process (p. 105): a set of specific guidelines that must be followed to protect individuals from arbitrary, capricious treatment by those in authority.

E

Education Consolidation and Improvement Act (ECIA) (p. 162): a 1981 federal law giving the states a broad range of choices for spending federal aid to education.

Educational malpractice (p. 120): liability for injury that results from the failure of a teacher, school, or school district to provide a student with adequate instruction, guidance, counseling, and/or supervision.

Educational philosophy (p. 64): a set of ideas and beliefs about education that guide the professional behavior of educators.

Entitlements (p. 162): federal programs to meet the educational needs of special populations.

Epistemology (p. 70): a branch of philosophy concerned with the nature of knowledge and what it means to know something.

Equitable funding (p. 169): providing the same funds for each student regardless of where the student lives or level of family income.

E-rate program (p. 178): a controversial program that uses fees from telecommunications companies to provide discounts on telecommunications services and wiring to schools and libraries.

Essentialism (p. 77): formulated in part as a response to progressivism, this philosophical orientation holds that a core of common knowledge about the real world should be transmitted to students in a systematic, disciplined way.

Ethical dilemmas (p. 104): problem situations in which an ethical response is difficult to determine; that is, no single response can be called "right" or "wrong."

Ethics (p. 72): a branch of philosophy concerned with principles of conduct and determining what is good and evil, right and wrong, in human behavior.

Existentialism (p. 82): a philosophical orientation that emphasizes the individual's experiences and maintains that each individual must determine his or her own meaning of existence.

Expenditure per pupil (p. 157): the amount of money spent on each pupil in a school, school district, state, or nation; usually computed according to average daily attendance.

F

Fair use (p. 123): the right of an individual to use copyrighted material in a reasonable manner without the copyright holder's consent, provided that use meets certain criteria.

Federal revenues (p. 159): federal funds for the operation of schools, including direct grants-in-aid to schools and funds distributed through the states.

For-profit schools (p. 26): schools that are operated, for profit, by private educational corporations.

Freedom of expression (p. 128): freedom, granted by the First Amendment to the Constitution, to express one's beliefs.

Full-funding programs (p. 169): state programs to ensure statewide financial equity by setting the same per-pupil expenditure level for all schools and districts.

Futures planning (p. 212): the process of planning for the future by making forecasts about the future based on analyses of current social, economic, and technological trends.

G

G.I. Bill of Rights (p. 51): a 1944 federal law that provides veterans with payments for tuition and room and board at colleges and universities and special schools, formally known as the Servicemen's Readjustment Act.

Grievance (p. 110): a formal complaint filed by an employee against his or her employer or supervisor.

H

High-stakes tests (p. 205): achievement tests that have "high-stakes" consequences for students, teachers, and administrators—for example, a test that determines if a student is eligible to graduate or whether educators receive merit pay increases.

Humanism (p. 86): a philosophy based on the belief that individuals control their own destinies through the application of their intelligence and learning.

Humanistic psychology (p. 86): an orientation to human behavior that emphasizes personal freedom, choice, awareness, and personal responsibility.

I

Intermediate revenues (p. 159): funds for the operation of schools that come from sources that are at an "intermediate" level between local and state education agencies, for example, county or municipal agencies.

Interstate New Teacher Assessment and Support Consortium (INTASC) (p. 9): an organization of states established in 1987 to develop performance-based standards for what beginning teachers should know and be able to do.

K

Kentucky Education Reform Act (KERA) (p. 46): comprehensive school-reform legislation requiring all Kentucky schools to form school-based management councils with authority to set policies in eight areas.

L

Lemon test (p. 143): a three-part test, based on *Lemon v. Kurtzman*, to determine whether a state has violated the separation of church and state principle.

Local revenues (p. 159): funds for the operation of schools that come from local sources, such as local property and nonproperty taxes.

Local school council (p. 21): a group of community members that is empowered to develop policies for the operation of local schools.

Local school district (p. 34): an agency at the local level that has the authority to operate schools in the district.

Logic (p. 74): a branch of philosophy concerned with the processes of reasoning and the identification of rules that will enable thinkers to reach valid conclusions.

M

Metaphysics (p. 70): a branch of philosophy concerned with the nature of reality.

N

National Board for Professional Teaching Standards (NBPTS) (p. 9): a board established in 1987 that began issuing professional certificates in 1994–95 to teachers who possess extensive professional knowledge and the ability to perform at a high level.

National Council for Accreditation of Teacher Education (NCATE) (p. 9): an agency that accredits, on a voluntary basis, almost half of the nation's teacher education programs.

National Governor's Association (NGA) (p. 47): an association of state governors that influences

policies in several areas, including teacher education and school reform.

Negligence (p. 118): failure to exercise reasonable, prudent care in providing for the safety of others.

Nondiscrimination (p. 107): conditions characterized by the absence of discrimination; for example, employees receive compensation, privileges, and opportunities for advancement without regard for race, color, religion, sex, or national origin.

P

Perennialism (p. 75): a philosophical orientation that emphasizes the ideas contained in the Great Books and maintain that the true purpose of education is the discovery of universal, or perennial, truths of life.

Performance standards (p. 194): academic standards that reflect levels of proficiency— for example, 1 = outstanding, 2 = exemplary, 3 = proficient, 4 = progressing, and 5 = standard not met.

Philosophy (p. 63): the use of logical reasoning to inquire into the basic truths about being, knowledge, and conduct.

Political foundations of education (p. 4): the political trends, issues, and forces that shape public and private education in the United States.

Praxis Series: Professional Assessments for Beginning Teachers (p. 9): a battery of tests available to states for the initial certification of teachers. Consists of assessments in three areas: academic skills, knowledge of subject, and classroom performance.

Privatization movement (p. 23): Umbrella term for reform initiatives that seek to run public schools as private enterprises.

Progressivism (p. 79): a philosophical orientation based on the belief that life is evolving in a positive direction, that people may be trusted to act in their own best interests, and that education should focus on the needs and interests of students.

Property taxes (p. 159): local taxes assessed against real estate and, in some areas, against personal property in the form of cars, household furniture and appliances, and stocks and bonds.

R

Regional Educational Service Agency (RESA) (p. 50): a state educational agency that provides supportive services to two or more school districts; known in some states as education service centers, intermediate school districts, multi-county education service units, board of cooperative educational services, or educational service regions.

Restructuring (p. 17): reorganizing how schools are controlled at the local level so that teachers, principals, parents, and community members have greater authority.

S

School-based management (p. 18): various approaches to school improvement in which teachers, principals, students, parents, and community members manage individual schools and share in the decision-making processes.

School board (p. 36): the primary governing body of a local school district.

School choice (p. 170): various proposals that would allow parents to choose the schools their children attend.

Search and seizure (p. 132): the process of searching an individual and/or his or her property if that person is suspected of an illegal act; reasonable or probable cause to suspect the individual must be present.

Sexual harassment (p. 139): unwanted and unwelcome sexual behavior directed toward another person, whether of the same or opposite sex.

Social reconstructionism (p. 84): a philosophical orientation based on the belief that social problems can be solved by changing, or reconstructing, society.

Socratic questioning (p. 74): a method of questioning designed to lead students to see errors and inconsistencies in their thinking, based on questioning strategies used by Socrates.

Standards (p. 190): statements that reflect what students should know and be able to do within a particular discipline or at a particular grade level.

Standards-based education (SBE) (p. 192): basing curricula, teaching, and assessment of student learning on rigorous academic standards.

State aid (p. 161): money given by a state to its cities and towns to provide essential services, including the operation of public schools.

State board of education (p. 47): the highest educational agency in a state, charged with regulating the state's system of education.

State department of education (p. 49): the branch of state government, headed by the chief state school officer, charged with implementing the state's educational policies.

State revenues (p. 159): funds for the operation of schools that originate at the state level.

Superintendent (p. 38): the chief administrator of a school district.

T

Teaching contract (p. 107): an agreement between a teacher and a board of education that the teacher will provide specific services in return for a certain salary, benefits, and privileges.

Tenure (p. 108): an employment policy in which teachers, after serving a probationary period, retain their positions indefinitely and can be dismissed only on legally defensible grounds.

Test besting (p. 208): the practice of preparing students to take tests by teaching specific test-taking skills.

Tort liability (p. 117): conditions that would permit the filing of legal charges against a professional for breach of duty and/or behaving in a negligent manner.

U

U.S. Department of Education (p. 54): a department of the federal government that advises the president on education, supports educational research, disseminates the results of research, and administers federal grants for education.

V

Vertical equity (p. 169): an effort to provide equal educational opportunity within a state by providing different levels of funding based on economic needs within school districts.

Voucher system (p. 171): funds allocated to parents that they may use to purchase education for their children from public or private schools in the area.

W

Within-school politics (p. 9): how people use power, influence, and authority to affect instructional and curricular practices within a school or school system.

References

Acton v. Vernonia School District, 66 F.3d 217 (9th Cir.), *vacated*, 515 U.S. 646 (1995).

Alfonso v. Fernandez, 606 N.Y.S.2d 259 (App. Div. 1993).

Alvin Independent School District v. Cooper, 404 S.W.2d 76 (Tex. Civ. App. 1966).

American Association of School Administrators. (1992). *Schoolhouse in the red*. Arlington, VA: Author.

American Association of School Administrators. (1999). *Preparing schools and school systems for the 21st cen-tury*. Arlington, VA: Author.

American Association of University Women (AAUW). (1993). *Hostile hallways: The AAUW survey on sexual harassment in America's schools*. New York: Louis Harris.

American Association of University Women Educational Foundation. (2001). *Hostile hallways: Bullying, teasing, and sexual harassment in school*. New York: Harris Interactive.

American Federation of Teachers. (1998). *Student achievement in Edison schools: Mixed results in an ongoing experiment*. Washington, DC: Author.

American Federation of Teachers. (2002). *Do charter schools measure up? The charter school experiment after 10 years*. Washington, DC: Author.

American Federation of Teachers. (2003). *Update on student achievement for Edison Schools, Inc.* Washington, DC: Author.

American School Board Journal. (2001). Education vital signs. *American School Board Journal*, 188(12).

American School & University. (May 2004). 30th annual official education construction report. Retrieved from www.asumag.com/mag/university_growth_spurt/.

American Society of Civil Engineers. (2001). *Report Card for 2001*. Retrieved from www.asce.org/reportcard/2001/index.cfm

Anderson, R. E., and Ronnkvist, A. (1999). *The presence of computers in American schools*. Irvine, CA: Center for Research on Information Technology and Organizations.

Associated Press (2004, June 10). Study: High school exit tests flimsy. Retrieved from www.cnn.com/2004/EDUCATION/06/10/graduation.tests.ap/

Ayers, W. C., and Miller, J. L. (1998). (Eds). *A light in dark times: Maxine Greene and the unfinished conversation*. New York: Teachers College Press.

Bagley, W. C. (1934). *Education and emergent man*. New York: Ronald.

Battles v. Anne Arundel County Board of Education, 904 F. Supp. 471 (D. Md. 1995), *aff'd*, 95 F.3d 41 (4th Cir. 1996).

Bell, T. (1986, March). Education policy development in the Reagan administration. *Phi Delta Kappan*, 492.

Berliner, D. C., and Biddle, B. J. (1995). *The manufactured crisis: Myths, fraud, and the attack on America's public schools*. Reading, MA: Addison Wesley.

Black, M. (1956). A note on "philosophy of education." *Harvard Educational Review, 26*.

Bracey, G. W. (2002). *The war against America's public schools: Privatizing schools, commercializing education*. Boston: Allyn and Bacon.

Bracey, G. W. (2004). *Setting the record straight: Responses to misconceptions about public education in the U.S.* Portsmouth, NH: Heinemann.

Brameld, T. (1956). *Toward a reconstructed philosophy of education.* New York: Holt, Rinehart, and Winston.

Brameld, T. (1959). Imperatives for a reconstructed philosophy of education. *School and Society, 87.*

Brown v. Hot, Sexy and Safer Productions, Inc., 68 F.3d 525 (1st Cir. 1995), *cert. denied,* 516 U.S. 1159 (1996).

Broudy, H. S. (1979). Arts education: Necessary or just nice? *Phi Delta Kappan 60,* 347–350.

Brunelle v. Lynn Public Schools, 702 N.E.2d 1182 (Mass. 1998).

Buckney, C. (2004). A final word: Ten questions for Paul Vallas' right-hand woman. In A. Russo (Ed.), *School reform in Chicago: Lessons in policy and practice* (pp. 159–162). Cambridge, MA: Harvard Education Press.

Burch v. Barker, 651 F. Supp. 1149 (W.D. Wash. 1987), *rev'd,* 861 F.2d 1149 (9th Cir. 1988).

Burton v. Cascade School District Union High School No. 5, 512 F.2d 850 (9th Cir. 1975).

Bush, G. W. (2004, October). The essential work of democracy. *Phi Delta Kappan, 86*(2), 114, 118–121.

CEO Forum on Education and Technology. (1999). *School technology and readiness report.* Washington, DC: Author.

CEO Forum on Education and Technology (2001). *The CEO forum school technology and readiness report: Key building blocks for student achievement in the 21st century.* Washington, DC: Author.

Chubb, J. E., and Moe, T. (1990). *Politics, markets & America's schools.* Washington, DC: Brookings Institution.

Chute, E. (2003, February 3). Controversial tests' future uncertain. *Pittsburgh Post-Gazette.* Retrieved from http://www.post-gazette.com/localnews/20030203pdap0203p7.asp

Cibulka, J. (1996). The reform and survival of American public schools: An institutional perspective. In R. L. Crowson, W. Boyd, and H. B. Mawhinney (Eds.), *The politics of education and the new institutionalism: Reinventing the American school* Washington, DC: Falmer.

Compayre, G. (1888). *History of pedagogy* (W. H. Payne, Trans.). Boston: Heath.

Cornfield v. Consolidated High School District No. 230, 991 F.2d 1316 (7th Cir. 1993).

Cosby, B. (2004). Where do we start to sweep? In C. Glickman (Ed.), *Letters to the next president: What we can do about the real crisis in public education* (pp. xi–xiv). New York: Teachers College Press.

Counts, G. (1932). *Dare the school build a new social order?* New York: John Day.

Cuban, L. (1985, September). Conflict and leadership in the superintendency. *Phi Delta Kappan,* 28–30.

Cuban, L. (2003). *Why is it so hard to get good schools?* New York: Teachers College Press.

Curtis v. School Committee of Falmouth, 652 N.E.2d 580 (Mass. 1995), *cert. denied,* 516 U.S. 1067 (1996).

Danielson, C. (1996). *Enhancing professional practice: A framework for teaching.* Alexandria, VA: Association for Supervision and Curriculum Development.

Danzberger, J. P. (1994, January). Governing the nation's schools: The case for restructuring local school boards. *Phi Delta Kappan,* 367–373.

Davis v. Meek, 344 F. Supp. 298 (N.D. Ohio 1972).

Davis v. Monroe County Board of Education, 526 U.S. 629 (1999).

Dewey, J. (1916). *Democracy and education: An introduction to the philosophy of education.* New York: Macmillan.

Doe v. Renfrow, 475 F. Supp. 1012 (N.D. Ind. 1979), *modified,* 631 F.2d 91, *reh'g denied,* 635 F.2d 582 (7th Cir. 1980), *cert denied,* 451 U.S. 1022 (1981).

Dubuclet v. Home Insurance Co., 660 So. 2d 67 (La. Ct. App. 1995).

Dunklee, D. R., and Shoop, R. J. (2002). *The principal's quick-reference guide to school law: Reducing liability, litigation, and other potential legal tangles.* Thousand Oaks, CA: Corwin.

Edison Schools, Inc. (2004). Retrieved from http://www.edisonschools.com/home/home.cfm

Education Week. (1996, April 24). Virginia governor victorious in rejecting Goals 2000.

Education Week. (1999a, March 31). N.M. governor digs in his heels on vouchers.

Education Week. (1999b, June 2). Substituting the privilege of choice for the right to equality.

Education Week. (1999c, July 28). *Issue paper: Privatization and public education.*

Education Writers Association. (1999). *Barriers and breakthroughs: Technology in urban schools.* Washington, DC: Author.

Eduventures. (2003, August). Learning markets & opportunities 2003: New models for delivering education and services drive pre-K and postsecondary sector growth. Boston: Author.

Edwards v. Aguillard, 482 U.S. 578 (1987).

Engel v. Vitale, 370 U.S. 421 (1962).

Enlow, R. (2004). Grading vouchers: Ranking America's school choice programs. Indianapolis: Milton and Rose D. Friedman Foundation.

Essex, N. L. (1999). *School law and the public schools: A practical guide for educational leaders.* Boston: Allyn and Bacon.

Fagen v. Summers, 498 P.2d 1227 (Wyo. 1972).

Falk, B. (2002, April). Standards-based reforms: Problems and possibilities. *Phi Delta Kappan*, 612–620.

Falvo v. Owasso Independent School District, 233 F.3d 1203 (10 Cir. 2000).

Feller, B. (2003, August 14). High school exit exams are here to stay. *The Detroit News.* Retrieved from http://www.detnews.com/2003/schools/0308/14/a02-244824.htm

Feller, B. (2004, December 16). Study reveals mixed view of charter schools. *Spokesman Review*, p. 10A.

Fetler, M. (2001). Student mathematics achievement test scores, dropout rates, and teacher characteristics. *Teacher Education Quarterly, 28*(1), 151–168.

Firestone, W. A., Monfils, L., & Schorr, R. Y. (2003, May). Test preparation in New Jersey: Inquiry-oriented and didactic responses. *Assessment in Education.*

Franklin v. Gwinnett County Public Schools, 503 U.S. 60 (1992).

Friedman, M. (2003, March 24). Milton Friedman interview on CNBC: Friedman on school vouchers.

Furger, R. (1998). *Does Jane compute? Preserving our daughters' place in the cyber revolution.* New York: Warner.

Furger, R. (1999, September). Are wired schools failing our kids? *PC World.*

Gaddy, B. B., Hall, W. W., and Marzano, R. J. (1996). *School wars: Resolving our conflicts over religion and values.* San Francisco: Jossey-Bass.

Garan, E. M. (2004). *In defense of our children: When politics, profit, and education collide.* Portsmouth, NH: Heinemann.

Garner, C. W. (2004). *Education finance for school leaders: Strategic planning and administration.* Upper Saddle River, NJ: Pearson.

Gaylord v. Tacoma School District No. 10, 599 P.2d 1340 (Wash. 1977).

Giroux, H. A. (1999). Schools for sale: Public education, corporate culture, and the citizen-consumer. *The Educational Forum, 63*(2), 140–149.

Glickman, C. (Ed.). (2004). *Letters to the next president: What we can do about the real crisis in public education.* New York: Teachers College Press.

Gootman, E. (2003, September 13). To help learning, city offers free breakfast to all pupils. *New York Times*, late ed., p. A1.

Goss v. Lopez, 419 U.S. 565 (1975).

Grant, G., and Murray, C. E. (1999). *Teaching in America: The slow revolution.* Cambridge, MA: Harvard University Press.

Greene, M. (1995a). *Releasing the imagination.* San Francisco: Jossey-Bass.

Greene, M. (1995b). What counts as philosophy of education? In Wendy Kohli (Ed.), *Critical conversations in philosophy of education* New York: Routledge.

Gwinnett County Schools v. Hope (2002). Georgia Court of Appeals.

Harrington-Lueker, D. (Ed.). (1999). *Barriers and breakthroughs: Technology in urban schools.* Washington, DC: Education Writers Association.

Harris Interactive, Inc. (2001). *The MetLife survey of the American teacher, 2001: Key elements of quality schools.* New York: Author.

Hazelwood School District v. Kuhlmeier, 484 U.S. 260 (1988).

Hendrie, C. (1999, May 5). Battle over principals in Chicago: Administration vs. local councils. *Education Week on the Web.*

Hess, F. M. (2002). *Revolution at the margins: The impact of competition on urban school systems.* Washington, DC: Brookings Institution.

Hess, F. M. (2004, March). The political challenge of charter school regulation. *Phi Delta Kappan*, 508–512.

Hess, G. A. (2004). Ending social promotion: A signature reform. In A. Russo (Ed.), *School reform in Chicago: Lessons in policy and practice* (pp. 103–108). Cambridge, MA: Harvard Education Press.

Hill, P. T. (2003, May 12). School reform efforts aren't reaching underserved students. *Spokesman Review*, p. A11.

Holmes, S. (1990, February 1). School reform: Business moves in. *New York Times*, p. D2.

Holt v. Shelton, 341 F. Supp. 821 (M.D. Tenn. 1972).

Hopkins, G. J., and Wendel, F. C. (1997). *Creating school-community-business partnerships.*

Bloomington, IN: Phi Delta Kappa Educational Foundation.

Hortonville Joint School District No. 1 v. Hortonville Education Association, 426 U.S. 482 (1976).

Hoxby, C. M. (2004). *Achievement in charter schools and regular public schools in the United States: Understanding the differences.* Cambridge, MA: Harvard University and National Bureau of Economic Research.

Hoy, W. K., and Miskel, C. G. (2001). *Educational administration: Theory, research, and practice*, 6th ed. Boston: McGraw-Hill.

Hoyt, W. H. (1999). An evaluation of the Kentucky Education Reform Act. In *Kentucky Annual Economic Report 1999* (pp. 21–36). Lexington: University of Kentucky, Center for Business and Economic Research.

Hurwitz, S. (1999, April). New York, New York: Can Rudy Crew hang tough on vouchers and pull off a turnaround in the nation's biggest school system? *The American School Board Journal*, 36–40.

Hutchins, R. M. (1963). *A conversation on education.* Santa Barbara, CA: Fund for the Republic.

Imber, M., and van Geel, T. (1993). *Education law.* New York: McGraw-Hill.

Imber, M., and van Geel, T. (2001). *A teacher's guide to education law*, 2nd ed. Mahwah, NJ: Lawrence Erlbaum.

Immediato v. Rye Neck School District, 73 F.3d 454 (2d Cir. 1996).

Ingraham v. Wright, 430 U.S. 651 (1977).

Interstate New Teacher Assessment and Support Consortium (INTASC). (1992). *Model standards for beginning teacher licensing, assessment, and development: A resource for state dialogue.* Washington, DC: Council of Chief State School Officers.

Jacobson, L. (1996, November 22). Gay student to get nearly $1 million in settlement. *Education Week on the Web.*

Jeglin v. San Jacinto Unified School District, 827 F. Supp. 1459 (C.D. Cal. 1993).

Jones, K., and Whitford, K. (1997, December). Kentucky's conflicting reform principles: High-stakes accountability and student performance assessment. *Phi Delta Kappan*, 276–281.

Joyce, B., and Weil, M. (2004). *Models of Teaching*, 7th ed. Boston: Allyn and Bacon.

Karr v. Schmidt, 401 U.S. 1201 (1972).

Keller, B. (2002, March 27). Unions turn cold shoulder on charter. *Education Week on the Web*.

Kennedy, M., and Agron, J. (2004, March 1). No buildings left behind. *American School & University*. Retrieved from http://asumag.com/issue_20040301/

The Kentucky Institute for Education Research. (2001). *KIER 2000 review of research*. Georgetown, KY: Georgetown College Conference and Training Center.

Kozol, J. (1991). *Savage inequalities: Children in America's schools*. New York: Crown.

Krizek v. Cicero-Stickney Township High School District No. 201, 713 F. Supp. 1131 (N.D. Ill. 1989).

LaMorte, M. W. (2002). *School law: Cases and concepts*, 7th ed. Boston: Allyn and Bacon.

Lemon v. Kurtzman, 403 U.S. 602 (1971).

Lewis, C. (2003, August 13). Is it time for cameras in classrooms? *Philadelphia Inquirer*. Retrieved from http://www.philly.com

Lindjord, D. (2000). Families at the century's turn: The troubling economic trends. *Family Review, 7*(3), 5–6.

Lindsay, D. (1996, March 13). N.Y. bills give teachers power to oust pupils. *Education Week*.

Lipsman v. New York City Board of Education, 1999 WL 498230 (N.Y.).

Los Angeles Times. (2002, August 6). Florida judge overturns state's school voucher program, p. A12.

Mailloux v. Kiley, 323 F. Supp. 1387 (D. Mass.), aff'd, 448 F.2d 1242 (1st Cir. 1971).

Mann, H. (1868). Annual reports on education. In Mary Mann (Ed.), *The life and works of Horace Mann*, vol. 3. Boston: Horace B. Fuller.

Marcus v. Rowley, 695 F.2d 1171 (9th Cir. 1983).

Market Data Retrieval. (2002). *Technology in education 2002*. Shelton, CT: Author.

Marzano, R. J. (1997). *Eight questions you should ask before implementing standards-based education at the local level*. Aurora, CO: Mid-Continent Research for Education and Learning.

Maslow, A. (1954). *Motivation and personality*. New York: Basic.

Maslow, A. (1962). *Toward a psychology of being*. New York: Basic.

Mayer, F. (1973). *A history of educational thought*. Columbus, OH: Merrill.

McCarthy, M. M., Cambron-McCabe, N. H., and Thomas, S. B. (1998). *Public school law: Teachers' and students' rights*, 4th ed. Boston: Allyn and Bacon.

McCarty, D., and Ramsey, C. (1971). *The school managers: Power and conflict in American public education*. Westport, CT: Greenwood.

McNeil, L. M. (2000). *Contradictions of school reform: Educational costs of standardized testing*. New York: Routledge.

Mental Health in Schools Center. (1998). *Restructuring boards of education to enhance effectiveness in addressing barriers to student learning: A Center report*. University of California–Los Angeles: Mental Health in Schools Center. ERIC Document No. ED423-479.

Merrow, J. (2003, May 8). Schools go AYP over test. *Los Angeles Times*, p. B15. Retrieved from http://middleweb.com/MGNEWS1/MGN0514.html

Metcalf, K. K. (2003, March). *Evaluation of the Cleveland scholarship and tutoring program*. Bloomington, IN: Indiana Center for Evaluation.

Miller, S. R., Allensworth, E. M., and Kochanek, J. R. (2002). *Student performance: Course taking, test scores, and outcomes.* Chicago: Consortium on Chicago School Research.

Monsef, P. (2002, July 1). Students find their voices through multimedia. *Edutopia.* San Rafael, CA: The George Lucas Educational Foundation.

Moran v. School District No. 7, 350 F. Supp. 1180 (D. Mont. 1972).

Morris, J. E., and Curtis, K. E. (1983, March/April). Legal issues relating to field-based experiences in teacher education. *Journal of Teacher Education,* 2–6.

Morris, V. C., and Pai, Y. (1976). *Philosophy and the American school: An introduction to the philosophy of education.* Boston: Houghton Mifflin.

Morris, V. C., and Pai, Y. (1994). *Philosophy and the American school: An introduction to the philosophy of education,* 2nd ed. Lanham, MD: University Press of America.

Morrison v. State Board of Education, 82 Cal. Rptr. 175 (Cal. 1969).

Mozert v. Hawkins County Board of Education, 827 F.2d 1058 (6th Cir. 1987), *cert. denied,* 484 U.S. 1066 (1988).

Murname, R. J., and Levy, F. (1996, October). What General Motors can teach U.S. schools about the proper role of markets in education reform. *Phi Delta Kappan,* 108–114.

Murray v. Pittsburgh Board of Public Education, 919 F. Supp. 838 (W.D. Pa. 1996).

Nathan, L. (2002, April). The human face of the high-stakes testing story. *Phi Delta Kappan,* 595–600.

National Board for Professional Teaching Standards (NBPTS). (2002). *What teachers should know and be able to do.* Arlington, VA: Author.

National Center for Education Statistics. (2002). *The condition of education 2002.* Washington, DC: Author.

National Center for Education Statistics. (2003). *Digest of education statistics, 2002.* Washington, DC: Author.

National Commission on Teaching and America's Future. (1996). *What matters most: Teaching for America's future.* New York: Author.

National Council for Accreditation of Teacher Education (NCATE). (2002). *Professional standards for the accreditation of schools, colleges, and departments of education—2002 edition.* Washington, DC: Author.

National Education Association. (May 2003). *Modernizing our schools: What will it cost?* Retrieved at www.nea.org/lac/modern

NEA Today (May 2003a). High-stakes tests spawn high-stakes lawsuits, p. 13.

NEA Today (May 2003b). New federal rule supports school prayer, p. 13.

Nelson, J. L., Carlson, K., and Palonsky, S. B. (2000). *Critical issues in education: A dialectic approach,* 4th ed. New York: McGraw-Hill.

NetDay. (2004). *Insights and ideas of teachers on technol-ogy: National report on NetDay Speak Up Day for Teachers 2004.* Irvine, CA: Author.

New Jersey v. Massa, 231 A.2d 252 (N.J. Sup. Ct. 1967).

New Jersey v. T.L.O. 221 Cal. Rptr. 118 (Cal.), *rev'd,* 469 U.S. 325 (1985).

Newmann, F. M., and Wehlage, G. G. (1995). *Successful school restructuring: A report to the public and educators by the Center on Organization and Restructuring of Schools.* Madison: University of Wisconsin, Center on Organization and Restructuring of Schools.

North Central Regional Educational Laboratory. (1993). *Policy briefs, report 1, 1993.* Elmhurst, IL: Author.

Null v. Board of Education, 815 F. Supp. 937 (D.W. Va. 1993).

Nunnary, M. Y., and Kimbrough, R. B. (1971). *Politics, power, polls, and school elections.* Berkeley, CA: McCutchan.

Odden, A., and Busch, C. (1998). *Financing schools for high performance: Strategies for improving the use of educational resources.* San Francisco: Jossey-Bass.

Ohman v. Board of Education, 93 N.E.2d 927 (N.Y. 1950).

Olson, L. (2002, January 9). Two new projects to examine quality, impact of exit exams. *Education Week on the Web.*

Owasso Independent School District No. 1 v. Falvo, 534 U.S. 426 (2002).

Ozmon, H. A., and Craver, S. M. (1999). *Philosophical foundations of education*, 6th ed. Upper Saddle River, NJ: Merrill.

Ozmon, H. A., and Craver, S. M. (2003). *Philosophical foundations of education*, 7th ed. Upper Saddle River, NJ: Merrill.

Paige, R. (2002, August). All the reforms in the world won't mean a thing if we don't have safe classrooms for students to learn and teachers to teach. Press release from the U.S. Department of Education. Retrieved from www.ed.gov/PressReleases/08-2002/08052002 .html

Parkay, F. W., and Oaks, M. (1998, April). *Promoting the professional development of teachers: What the U.S. can learn from other countries.* Paper presented at the Annual Meeting of the American Educational Research Association, San Diego.

Patchogue-Medford Congress of Teachers v. Board of Education of Patchogue-Medford Union Free School District, 510 N.E.2d 325 (N.Y. 1987).

Peter Doe v. San Francisco Unified School District, 131 Cal. Rptr. 854 (Cal. Ct. App. 1976).

Picarella v. Terrizzi, 893 F. Supp. 1292 (M.D. Pa. 1995).

Popham, J. (2001, March). Teaching to the test? *Educational Leadership*, 16–17.

Portner, J. (1999, May 12). Schools ratchet up the rules on student clothing, threats. *Education Week on the Web.*

Power, E. J. (1982). *Philosophy of education: Studies in philosophies, schooling, and educational policies.* Englewood Cliffs, NJ: Prentice Hall.

Power, E. J. (1996). *Education philosophy: A history from the ancient world to modern America.* New York: Garland.

RAND Corporation. (2004). RAND evaluation of Edison Schools: RAND education statement to appear in Edison Schools annual report. Retrieved at www.rand.org/education/projects /edison.html

Ravitch, D. (1996). *National standards in American education: A citizen's guide.* Washington, DC: Brookings Institution.

Ravitch, D. (1997, December 15). *The fight for standards. Forbes*, 106.

Ray v. School District of DeSoto County, 666 F. Supp. 1524 (M.D. Fla. 1987).

Richard, A. (2002, May 15). Memphis school board wants uniforms for all. *Education Week on the Web.*

Rogers, C. (1961). *On becoming a person.* Boston: Houghton Mifflin.

Rogers, C. (1982). *Freedom to learn in the eighties.* Columbus, OH: Merrill.

Romans v. Crenshaw, 354 F. Supp. 868 (S.D. Tex. 1972).

Romer, R. (2000). Today standards—tomorrow success. In F. W. Parkay and G. Hass (Eds.), *Curriculum planning: A contemporary approach* (pp. 314–317). Boston: Allyn and Bacon.

Rose, L. C., and Gallup, A. M. (2001, September). The 33rd annual Phi Delta Kappa/Gallup poll of the public's attitudes toward the public schools. *Phi Delta Kappan*, 41–58.

Rose, L. C., and Gallup, A. M. (2003, September). The 35th annual Phi Delta Kappa/Gallup poll of the public's attitudes toward the public schools. *Phi Delta Kappan*, 41–56.

Rosenkranz, T. (2002). *2001 CPS test trend review: Iowa Tests of Basic Skills.* Chicago: Consortium on Chicago School Research.

Ruenzel, D. (1999, April). Pride and prejudice. *Teacher Magazine on the Web*.

Russo, A. (Ed.). (2004). *School reform in Chicago: Lessons in policy and practice*. Cambridge, MA: Harvard Education Press.

San Antonio Independent School District v. Rodriguez, 411 U.S. 1 (1973).

Sandham, J. L. (2002, February 6). Board to close Fla. "voucher" school. *Education Week on the Web*.

Sandholtz, J. J., Ringstaff, C., and Dwyer, D.C. (1997). *Teaching with technology: Creating student-centered classrooms*. New York: Teachers College Press.

Sarason, S. (1997). *How schools might be governed and why*. New York: Teachers College Press.

Sartre, J. P. (1972). Existentialism. In John Martin Rich (Ed.), *Readings in the philosophy of education*. Belmont, CA: Wadsworth.

Schaill v. Tippecanoe School Corp., 864 F.2d 1309 (7th Cir. 1988).

Scheuerer, D., and Parkay, F. W. (1992). The new Christian right and the public school curriculum: A Florida report. In J. B. Smith and J. G. Colman, Jr. (Eds.), *School library media annual: 1992*, vol. 10, pp. 112–118. Englewood, CO: Libraries Unlimited.

School Board News: Conference Daily. (2002, April 8). Paige urges school boards to play large roles in implementing new education law.

School District of Abington Township v. Schempp, 374 U.S. 203 (1963).

Schwartz, J. E., and Beichner, R. J. (1999). *Essentials of educational technology*. Boston: Allyn and Bacon.

Scopes, J. (1966). *Center of the storm*. New York: Holt, Rinehart, and Winston.

Scoville v. Board of Education of Joliet Township High School District 204, 425 F.2d 10 (7th Cir.) *cert. denied*, 400 U.S. 826 (1970).

Serrano v. Priest, 961 Cal. Rptr. 601 (Cal. 1971).

Shanley v. Northeast Independent School District, 462 F.2d 960 (5th Cir. 1972).

Simonetti v. School District of Philadelphia, 454 A.2d 1038 (Pa. Super. 1982).

Skinner, B. F. (1972). Utopia through the control of human behavior. In John Martin Rich (Ed.), *Readings in the philosophy of education*. Belmont, CA: Wadsworth.

Slavin, R. E. (2000). *Educational psychology: Theory and practice*, 6th ed. Boston: Allyn and Bacon.

Smith, K. B., and Meier, K. K. J. (1995). *The case against school choice: Politics, markets, and fools*. Armonk, NY: M. E. Sharpe.

Smith v. Board of School Commissioners of Mobile County, 655 F. Supp. 939 (S.D. Ala.), *rev'd*, 827 F.2d 684 (11th Cir. 1987).

Spokesman Review. (1993, June 4). Harassment claims vex teachers.

Spring, J. (1998). *Conflict of interests: The politics of American education*, 3rd ed. Boston: McGraw-Hill.

State v. Rivera, 497 N.W.2d 878 (Iowa 1993).

Station v. Travelers Insurance Co., 292 So. 2d 289 (La. Ct. App. 1974).

Stecher, B., and Hamilton, L. (2002, February 20). Test-based accountability: Making it work better. *Education Week on the Web*.

Strike, K. A., and Soltis, J. F. (1985). *The ethics of teaching*. New York: Teachers College Press.

Sullivan v. Houston Independent School District, 475 F.2d 1071 (5th Cir.), *cert. denied*, 414 U.S. 1032 (1969).

Swanson v. Guthrie Independent School District No. 1-L, 135 F.3d 694 (10th Cir. 1998).

Tinker v. Des Moines Independent Community School District, 393 U.S. 503 (1969).

Toffler, A. (1971). *Future shock*. New York: Bantam.

Toppo, G. (2001, December 19). New law requires standardized school tests. *Spokesman Review*, p. A10.

Tweney, D. (2000, December 7). No more free ride. Tampa, FL: Business 2.0 Media.

Ulich, R. (1950). *History of educational thought.* New York: American Book Company.

USA Today (June 17, 2003). Teens flunk Mass. exam, won't graduate.

Unified School District No. 241 v. Swanson, 717 P.2d 526 (Kan. App. 1986).

U.S. Department of Commerce. (2002). *A nation online: How Americans are expanding their use of the Internet.* Washington, DC: Author.

U.S. Department of Education. (2002a, March 7). Secretary Paige sets the direction of the U.S. Department of Education with his five-year strategic plan. Washington, DC: Author.

U.S. Department of Education. (2002b, July 28). Paige announces new "No Child Left Behind—Blue Ribbon Schools" program. Washington, DC: Author.

U.S. Department of Education. (2004a). Overview: Budget Office—U.S. Department of Education. Washington, DC: Author. Retrieved from www.ed.gov/about/overview/budget/index.html?src=gu

U.S. Department of Education. (2004b, June 1). *The achiever.* Washington, DC: Author.

U.S. Department of Education. Institute for Education Sciences. National Center for Education Statistics. (2004). *The Nation's Report Card: America's Charter School Report,* NCES 2005-456. Washington, DC: National Center for Education Statistics.

Vedder, R. K. (2003). *Can teachers own their own schools? New strategies for educational excellence.* Chicago: Paul.

Walsh, M. (1999a, May 5). Shootings raise host of legal questions. *Education Week on the Web.*

Walsh, M. (1999b, May 19). Two reports offer bright outlook for education industry. *Education Week on the Web.*

Walsh, M. (2002, June 5). Home school enrollment surge fuels "cottage" industry. *Education Week on the Web.*

Watson, J. B. (1925). *Behaviorism,* 2nd ed. New York: People's Institute.

Weisman, J. (1991, July 31). Educators watch with a wary eye as business gains policy muscle. *Education Week,* 1.

Wentz, P. J. (2001). *The student teaching experience: Cases from the classroom,* 2nd ed. Upper Saddle River, NJ: Merrill.

West v. Board of Education of City of New York, 187 N.Y.S.2d 88 (App. Div. 1959).

Williams, J. (1999, April 18). Urban schools' obstacles hindering technology. *Milwaukee Journal Sentinal.*

Wirt, F. M., and Kirst, M. W. (1997). *The political dynamics of American education.* Berkeley: McCutchan.

Wirt, F. M., and Kirst, M. W. (1982). *Schools in conflict: The politics of education.* Berkeley: McCutchan.

Wohlstetter, P., and Anderson, L. (1994, February). What can U.S. charter schools learn from England's grant-maintained schools? *Phi Delta Kappan,* 486–491.

Woolfolk, A. E. (1998). *Educational psychology,* 7th ed. Boston: Allyn and Bacon.

Zelman v. Simmons-Harris, 536 U.S. 639 (2002).

Zucker v. Panitz, 299 F. Supp. 102 (S.D.N.Y. 1969).

Index

Giuliani, Rudolph, 172
Glickman, Carl, 32
Glossary of terms, 216–220
Goals. *See* Standards
Goals 2000: Educate America Act, 56, 199, 202
Goodyear, Marcus, 73
Goss v. Lopez, 131
Governor, educational role of, 46–47
Grading Vouchers: Ranking America's School Choice Programs, 172
Great Books curriculum, 76
Greene, Maxine, 83
Grievance, defined, 110
Gwinnett Cty. Schools v. Hope, 210

H

Hanson, Mary, 116
Harassment, 102
  case study of, 101–102
  defined, 138–139
  incidence of, 138, 140
  policies regarding, 139
Hartford, CT, EAI in, 26
Hawaii
  public schools of, statistics on, 35
  school funding in, 169
Hazelwood S. D. v. Kuhlmeier, 128
Head Start, 162–163
High-stakes tests, 205–206
  consequences of, 206–207
  controversies over, 211
  and educator accountability, 207–208
  legal issues with, 210–211
  pass/fail rates of, 206, 207
  preparation for, 208–210
Hippocratic Oath, 104
History, standards for, 195

HIV/AIDS, discrimination based on, 136
Holt v. Sheldon, 136
Home schooling, 143
  case law regarding, 144
  demographics of, 144
  legality of, 144
Horizontally aligned, defined, 196
Hortonville Joint S. D. No. 1 v. Hortonville Educ. Assn, 110, 145
Houston Independent School District, statistics on, 35
How Gertrude Teaches Her Children, 87
Hufstedler, Shirley, 54
Humanism, 86
Humanistic psychology, 86
  and the classroom, 88
  and self-actualization, 87–88
Hutchins, Robert Maynard, 76
Hyman v. Green, 118

I

Imber, Michael, 141
Immediato v. Rye Neck S. D., 127
In Defense of Our Children, 12
Indian Education Act, 162
Indiana, school discipline in, 131
Inductive thinking, 74
Inert power structure, 36
Influence, 5
Informal authority, 5
Infrastructure
  condition of, 176–177
  cost of improving, 179
  financing construction and renovation, 177
  need for improving, 177–179
Ingraham, James, 138
Ingraham v. Wright, 137–138
Insurance, liability, 119–120
Intermediate revenues, 159

International Reading Association, 195
Internet
  copyright issues, 123, 125–126
  and parental involvement, 43
  publishing on, 125–126
  and study of philosophy of education, 80
  used to influence educational policies, 15
Interstate New Teacher Assessment and Support Consortium (INTASC), teacher standards of, 8, 9
Intuition, knowledge based on, 71
Iowa, voucher program of, 173
Italy, educational expenditures in, 164

J

Japan, educational expenditures in, 164
Jeglin v. San Jacinto Unified S. D., 130
Jonesboro, AR, 130
Joyce, Bruce, 91

K

Karr v. Schmidt, 129
Kentucky Education Reform Act (KERA), 46
Kirst, Michael, 7
Knowledge
  evaluations of, 68–69
  views of, 67–69
  ways of knowing, 70–71
Koerner, James, 77
Kozol, Jonathan, 167, 176, 199
Krizek v. Cicero-Stickney Twp. H. S. Dist. No. 201, 112, 145